CATHY
My Autobiography

CATHY

My Autobiography

CATHY FREEMAN
with SCOTT GULLAN

For children everywhere – Have the courage to follow your dreams

Published in 2004 by Highdown,
an imprint of Raceform Ltd
Compton, Newbury, Berkshire, RG20 6NL
Raceform Ltd is a wholly-owned subsidiary of Trinity Mirror plc

First published in Australia in 2003 by Viking,
an imprint of Penguin Books

A CIP catalogue record for this book is available from the British Library.

ISBN 1-904317-77-4

Designed by Fiona Pike
Printed in Great Britain by William Clowes Ltd, Beccles, Suffolk

ACKNOWLEDGEMENTS

I couldn't have written this book without Scott Gullan. My heartfelt thanks to Scott for helping me to tell my story in my own words, for hanging in there with me, and for making me laugh along the way. My thanks also to Scott's wife, Tess, and son, Noah, for their understanding and support.

Thank you to the team at IMG – Chris Giannopoulos, Michelle Tozer and Joanna Walkley – who convinced me to put pen to paper in the first place, and to my personal assistant, Nicole Keith, for organising everything. Many thanks also to Peter Sinn of Middletons, Alistair Hamblin from the Commercial Advisory Group, and to my sponsors Nike, Channel 7, Qantas, Milo and the *Daily Telegraph*.

I've been lucky enough to know many wonderful people. A number of them gave their time during the writing of this book. In particular, thanks to Alexander Bodecker, Peter Fortune, Nick Bideau, Maurie Plant and Chris Wardlaw. And big hugs to those friends who've been there for me through the good times and the bad – you know who you are!

Thank you to all the guys at Penguin Books, especially to Bob Sessions, Belinda Byrne and Deb Brash. Thanks also to Peter Hanlon, for his help on the first draft.

And, finally, a great big thank you to all of my family, especially my mum, Cecelia; my dad, Norman; Bruce, Anne-Marie, Gavin, Maxine, Gavin Leonard, George, Norman, Michelle, Astrid, Norman Jnr, Brandy, Garth, Lisa, Jackson, Catherine, Jarrod and Daimon. Without their support I'd never have achieved my dream – their love keeps me strong.

CONTENTS

From the moment I enter the stadium it's there, a dull noise
in the back of my head. It's weird. All I can focus on is my lane;
I can't see or hear anything else. I start taking deep breaths
to get as much oxygen into my lungs as possible.
After a couple of run-throughs I discard my tracksuit bottoms
and long-sleeved T-shirt to reveal the swift suit.
I pull and prod at the suit to get comfortable
as I wait behind the blocks.

Just do what you know, Freeman.

My mouth is dry. I take a sip from my water bottle.

Breathe, Freeman. Breathe.

I arch my neck back to get another lungful of oxygen,
lick my lips and wait for the introductions. I pull the hood on,
zip it up and make sure my hair feels comfortable.

Just do what you know.

From somewhere I hear my name read out so I clap a couple of times
above my head. The whistle sounds and we move to the blocks. I get
my legs into position and my fingers perfectly on the line.
I stare down at the track and wait for the gun.
The muffled beating in my head gets louder.

*I'm just a little black girl who can run fast, and here I am in the
Olympic stadium, with one hundred and twelve thousand people
screaming my name.*

How the hell did I get here?

PART ONE: THE EARLY YEARS

CHAPTER 1
GROWING UP BAREFOOT

'What do you want to do when you leave school, Cathy?' the vocational guidance officer kept asking me.

I wasn't sure what a vocational guidance officer actually did, but I knew this was getting me out of class so it couldn't be too bad.

'Now, I know you're only fourteen, Cathy, but you must have thought about what you want to do after you finish high school.'

'Yeah, I want to win a gold medal at the Olympic Games,' I said again.

'OK, but what about after the medals and the Olympics?'

'I don't care.'

I'm not exactly sure when I decided I was going to be an Olympic champion. The dream evolved throughout my childhood and by the time I was at high school I wasn't thinking about anything else. The first thing I remember about running is how happy it made me feel. My first race was an 80m dash for eight-year-olds at St Joseph's Primary School in Mackay, in 1981. I won easily that day, even though I had to run with one eye shut. I'd bumped into a piece of wire sticking out from a steel post on my way to the start. I won again the following week, this time against older kids.

I was soon hooked, especially when I figured out that running came with other benefits. With the help of the school, in particular the sports coordinator, Mrs Bauldry, I found myself on my first plane trip to Brisbane for the state primary school titles. Mrs Bauldry raised the money for the trip and had also bought me a new shirt and blue running spikes. What she forgot to tell me was that you weren't suppose to wear your spikes all the time, especially in a stranger's home – we were all staying with different families – which was predominantly carpeted. I won my first gold medal at those titles and when I got home to Mackay my mum, Cecelia, was waiting on the front porch for me. When she found out I'd won she smothered me with hugs and kisses. I loved how happy I had made her feel. I'd already sensed from Mrs Bauldry the excitement my running generated among adults.

Those were fun times in Mackay. Life was free and easy, the tropical climate was great, and we barefoot kids were allowed to run around everywhere. We did everything together and I think that's the way Mum wanted it. We lived in a small housing-commission bungalow at the bottom of Burston Street. I had to share a bedroom with my two younger brothers, Norman and Garth; my older brother, Gavin, had his own room, as did my parents.

We mainly stayed among our own. On the hill at the top end of our street were some magnificent big brick houses with pools – that was where the white people lived. I thought all white people were rich, and that anyone who owned a car, telephone or even carpet was rich. I often wondered what life was like up there. The other Catherine in our street lived on the hill. She had beautiful blonde hair and blue eyes, just like her mother. I used to watch her walk past to the bus stop and think about how different our lives must be. While I was running around in the dirt with my brothers, she was probably playing with dolls or make-up.

My father, Norman, was a strong man of few words, but we kids knew he adored us. He was a legend around town as a star rugby league player – they called him 'Twinkle Toes' – and every Saturday we'd all go down to watch him play, my brothers decked out in the club's colours. Then something happened. Dad changed. He would stay out drinking and Mum would often pack us all up and take us to Nanna's for the weekend. We couldn't understand why and kept asking Mum where our father was. One day he came home in such a rage he started ripping framed photographs off the wall and smashing them. I hid behind a chair. He walked towards me and knocked my glass of milk off the table. But he never laid a finger on his children or on Mum, instead taking his anger out on furniture or the walls.

Dad left home when I was five and returned to Woorabinda, an Aboriginal mission three hours south-west of Mackay. This was where most of the Freeman clan lived. We blamed Mum when he left; we didn't know what was wrong. She refused to explain it and just went about trying to get our lives back to normal.

Years later, we found out that Dad had become an alcoholic. His problems started after he was diagnosed with severe diabetes, a common illness among Aboriginal people. The diabetes robbed Dad of his great passion – playing rugby. He had always prided himself on his physical fitness. When he no longer had that, the alcohol started to take over his life, until it reached a point where he knew he had to leave for the sake of his children.

With Dad gone, Gavin became the father-figure of the house. He was twelve years older than me. Mum found a job as a cleaner at the local high school to support us. She would be up at 6.30 a.m. to make our lunches, go and clean the school, and then be back in time to wake us up and get us off to school. At the end of the day we'd all go back to the high school with her. I would help her clean while Norman, who was a year younger than me, and Garth, who was three years younger, ran around and played.

Mum was a survivor – tough, very stubborn and never one to burden other people with her problems. She always maintained a quiet dignity, even in the hardest times. She was the eldest of ten children and had grown up on Palm Island, a government-controlled mission. Mum's father, George Sibley, had left the island when she was a baby, and her mother, Alice Mero, had then married Sonny, George's brother. Mum went to a Catholic school run by American nuns but left at fifteen, then taught herself typing and got a job as a switchboard operator for one of the government departments. To go on holidays, visit relatives or even just to leave the island to go shopping in nearby Townsville required a permit. If you failed to return by the nominated time you'd be arrested and taken back to the island by the police. When Mum's stepfather, Sonny Sibley, was moved off the island by the police after he had organised a strike, Mum had to quit her job and follow him and Nanna to Woorabinda.

This was where she met my father, and they struck up a friendship. When Mum was 21 she ran away from Woorabinda to start a new life with an aunt in Innisfail, then moved to Cairns, where Gavin was born in 1961. It was there Mum started to fight for Nanna's freedom. The authorities wouldn't give Nanna, or Mum's brothers and sisters, permits to leave the mission. It was several years before Nanna was allowed to leave Woorabinda. She was definitely the matriarch of the family. Nanna not only raised her own kids but also brought up five of her grandchildren, which is not unusual in the Aboriginal community. Mum would end up doing the same for two of Gavin's sons, Gavin Leonard and George.

We didn't have a car or a telephone but none of us ever complained. I was a happy kid. I just had this temperament where I didn't whinge a lot. The only time I questioned Mum was over the school tuckshop. I wondered why we never got to buy meat pies or iceblocks, like the other kids. I couldn't understand why we were different. Why did we only have Promite sandwiches and maybe a piece of fruit or a muesli bar? Our cause wasn't helped by the fact that Mum was a health freak. We never had lollies or soft drink. Mum's only vice was a craving for cream buns and these would appear on the dinner table every now and again. Even though we'd already been through a lot in our short lives, Mum worked hard to make sure we were one very happy family.

We were strongly influenced by religion while growing up. For most of my childhood I said two prayers every night before I went to sleep. One was a guidance-to-children prayer: 'Oh God, guide me and protect me, illuminate the lamp of my heart and make me a brilliant star...' The second prayer centred around the removal of difficulties in our lives. Mum was always telling me to 'leave it in God's hands'. She had been raised a Catholic but now she practised the Baha'i faith, a religion which focuses on equality of gender and race. Colour doesn't come into it, because everyone is considered equal.

Once a month we went with Mum to prayer meetings called 'Fireside', where we'd all sit around with our legs crossed. Without fail, my brothers and I would crack up when the chanting started. However, we couldn't help but be affected by the warmth and concern people showed each other in these meetings. Black, white, rich or poor, it didn't matter; they all came together and acknowledged each other's problems. We ate in these people's homes and I remember I was so excited when one of the stars from the TV show *The Sullivans* attended a Baha'i barbecue in our backyard.

The prayer groups certainly opened my eyes. Being a young Aborigine in white Australian society meant you experienced a world very different from the one the Baha'i embraced. We were brought up to feel like we didn't belong. There was a saying we often used when we were embarrassed to be Aboriginal – 'Oh, shame!' If there was a room full of white people my brothers and I would avoid going into it. If we had to, we always asked someone to walk with us, and they would say 'Oh, shame!' We never wanted to stand out. This low self-esteem had been passed down from generation to generation. Everyone around us, our family, friends and relatives, behaved this way. Until we experienced the Baha'i faith, all we'd known was that there was a black world and a white world, and we didn't have the right to mix with people in the white world.

Running was my escape. It transported me to another place and another time, away from the black and white world and into one of my own, the world I shared with my older sister, Anne-Marie. She was my inspiration. She gave me an inner strength and determination that set me apart from the rest.

When my mother was eight months pregnant with me she'd been forced to put Anne-Marie, who suffered from cerebral palsy, into a special home in Townsville, and then later one in Rockhampton. It broke Mum's heart to have to let her go. I also carried around some guilt about her. Anne-Marie was so beautiful. Even though she couldn't talk she had charisma, and lit up a room with her big brown eyes and magical smile.

I remember, during our visits when I was young, Anne-Marie used to get annoyed with her little sister and give me this dirty look because I was taking away some of Mum's attention. She simply wanted Mum all to herself.

Despite her muscular deformity, my sister was very alert and knew how to express herself. The sheer excitement Anne-Marie showed when she saw Mum was unbelievable – she'd throw her arms around her wildly. They had a wonderful relationship. We only got to visit her three or four times a year and every time Mum and I would leave in tears. But I would also leave inspired. You couldn't help but think, *Oh my God, I'm so glad I'm not like her*. I was the lucky one. I believed I owed it to Anne-Marie to make the most of my talent for running.

This was rammed home to me by Mum one day when I went through a phase of not wanting to train. I was sick of it, sick of not being able to play with my friends as much as I wanted. I remember Mum hassling me to get ready for training and I was lying on my bed, pretending to be asleep. She barged into my room.

'It's time to go, Catherine. Come on!'

'Mum, I don't want to go. I don't want to do this any more.'

Mum grabbed my arm and glared at me.

'I wish you were Anne-Marie.' I just stared at her in shock, but she continued, 'Look, you know your sister can't walk, can't talk, she can't do all the things that you can. You've got two good arms and two good legs, now go out there and use them.'

I went to training and never missed another session.

CHAPTER 2
LIVING IN A WHITE WORLD

Every time the blue Kingswood pulled up in the drive I ran inside yelling, 'Mum, that white man is here!'

His name was Bruce Barber, and he had begun to show up regularly at our place. He was a Baha'i; that's how he knew Mum and why he had turned up on our doorstep one night looking for somewhere to stay. They say you can go anywhere around the world as a Baha'i and other members of the community will always welcome you into their homes and take care of you. That's what Mum did for Bruce.

Soon the weekend visits turned into a more permanent arrangement, much to the disgust of the rest of the family. It was only just over a year since our father had left and here was this white fella taking his place. How could Mum do this? I hated it. I hated her for it. I decided to write a letter to my father telling him I was still his little girl and would always love him.

When we had to go somewhere in the Kingswood, Mum always sat in the middle of the front seat so she was next to Bruce. It made me angry. Why did she have to sit next to him? To get at her I'd hook my foot under the seat and kick her. 'Who's kicking? Who's doing that?' she would yell. My brothers and I would giggle, as we all felt the same way.

Gavin in particular was furious. One day he came to Norman and me and said he was going to Woorabinda. 'I've got to tell Dad what's going on here.' He returned with Dad, who was wary about the arrival of Bruce but refused to get involved. Not long after this, I went into the kitchen for breakfast one morning to find Bruce at the table with half his face swollen black. 'What happened to you?' I asked. Mum quickly made up some excuse about running into a door or something like that. Years later, I found out that Gavin had punched Bruce.

Our anger towards Bruce remained, even when he told us that he was marrying Mum. We were all in the car one day and he turned to us and said, 'Kids, your mum and I are getting married.' None of us could believe what we'd heard. Surely Mum would have spoken to us about it. Married! What about our Dad? That question was answered soon after when Mum and Bruce packed us up and drove to Woorabinda. When we got there Mum took Dad down to the river-bank where they sat and talked. I'd been playing up at the house and after a while decided to go and look for my parents. When I spotted them I saw something that stopped me in my tracks. They were kissing. It was the only time I'd seen my parents being affectionate; most of my memories involved fights and the furniture getting broken. I felt embarrassed staring, so I ran away.

I learnt later that Mum told Dad that day she wouldn't marry Bruce if he didn't want her to, and that she was prepared to move the family to Woorabinda. Dad knew that the mission was not a good place to raise kids. The use of drugs and alcohol created problems there. He also didn't want his children to see what he was doing to his life, so he told Mum to stay in Mackay. But she always made sure he knew what was happening with his kids and each Christmas we'd visit and go horse riding through the bush with Dad.

Mum and Bruce got married in 1982 at the house of a Baha'i friend. Mum looked pretty in an elegant apricot dress with sheer white stockings and shoes. I was nine and thought I looked pretty good in a red dress with white shoes. The boys had their shirts tucked in and wore shiny shoes. Gavin wasn't there.

The following year Bruce got a job transfer to Hughenden, a dry and dusty coal-mining town five hundred kilometres west of Mackay. None of us wanted to go. I didn't want to leave behind all my friends and cousins; I hated the thought of no more barbecues by the harbour or sleepovers at Nanna's. It sucked. Hughenden was a dot in the desert, a small town that had a feeling of emptiness about it. In a way, that made it safer because everybody knew each other, and we seemed to fit in pretty quickly. We could ride our bikes in the street and play down at the local pool without Mum having to worry.

It was here that I began to realise I might have been wrong about Bruce. This man, who I'd thought was ruining my life, actually ended up changing it for ever. He won me over by showing an interest as I started to make a name for myself at the school athletics carnivals. Our house was near the river so Bruce would try to get us all to do sprints up and down the sand-banks. Naturally I was the only one who did as we were told, and I soon sensed Bruce's genuine enthusiasm about my running. Before long he started training me three times a week at the local high school, where I ran twelve laps of a 400m sawdust track barefoot.

Bruce says it was at Hughenden that he had his first vision of me as an Olympian. He'd been an apprentice jockey and he claimed that the symmetry of my movement reminded him of a champion racehorse. From that moment he was hooked and, at ten years of age, I had my first coach. Bruce wrote to sports associations to get hold of some training programmes, because he didn't really have any idea. I had just qualified for the national age athletics titles. Our routine soon became a four-lap warm-up, followed by exercises, stretches, sprints, starts and a four-lap warm-down.

My success was raising some eyebrows in my new surrounds. I began to notice the dirty looks I was getting from some of the mothers when the new black kid in town kept beating their girls. Bruce was noticing a lot more. As a white man stepping into a black family, he quickly picked up the racial discrimination that came my way in Hughenden. At the country zone titles in Mt Isa, I won four of my five events. When I got home Bruce asked where all my medals were. I'd received certificates, but no medals. A couple of weeks later, Bruce found out that the white girls who'd come second to me had been given the medals. He was furious.

It got worse when a protest was lodged about me competing at the state championships because I was going to a Catholic school, not a public school. It was obvious to Bruce that the jealousy about my performances from the parents of other girls was driving the resentment towards me. He was convinced they were trying to find any excuse to stop me running, without actually coming out and saying the real reason – because I was black. It was only after the public school offered to help raise funds for the trip that my school came around and fought for me. After some heated discussions with the nuns at St Francis's and a visiting priest, Bruce found out that the ruling had been obsolete for the previous five years.

In the end, both schools ended up donating some money, although that wasn't the end of the dramas. When we finally got down to Brisbane for the state championships and I received my uniform, all I got was a pair of shorts and a singlet; all the other girls had tracksuits and tops. Bruce was wild. I overheard him telling Mum that it was blatant racism; we'd paid the same amount of money as the others, yet I was the only one who didn't get the full uniform. Although my parents were rightfully upset about these things, I didn't complain or let them worry me. I was still getting to do what I loved and was getting better and better at it.

After twelve months in Hughenden we were on the move again, this time to Moura, a hundred kilometres west of Rockhampton. It was a lot greener than Hughenden and we lived in a nice house with beautiful golden wattle trees all around it. Mum got a job as a cleaner at the Mitre 10 store and again I had to go along and help her. I'd become Mum's little messenger and her second set of eyes. She liked me to watch over the two boys because they were continually getting into mischief. Norman was really accident-prone. When we were younger and had baths together, he'd always try to climb up on the sink and would regularly slip and crack his head open or suffer some other injury. Garth was a real cutey – I called him 'Bubba' – but he was hyperactive. When my aunty was babysitting she'd have to tie his leg to hers to keep him under control.

A change in Bruce's job saw us packing up and leaving Moura after just nine months. We moved to Coppabella, a tiny railway town. We lived about four hundred metres from the track so during the night I'd lie awake, listening to the sounds of massive coal trains rolling past. It was here that Mum enrolled me and Norman in karate lessons. Our teacher was really strict and if you didn't do it right he'd make you do push-ups or sit-ups. One day we were being tested for our grades and he got Norman and me to spar together. I was still slightly taller than my brother and that caused trouble, as one of my right-foot kicks ended with my big toe in his eye. Norman hit the deck as if he was drunk. He curled up on the ground in agony and some of the parents had to carry him out. I wanted to go with him but the teacher told me to finish my test and replaced Norman with a kid who had a black belt. I was too worried about my little brother to do anything and our days as the 'Karate Kids' came to an end soon after.

I started high school, which was a 45-minute bus ride there and back. We were also on the road every weekend for competitions, most of them back in Mackay at Melaleuca Park. It was a beautiful little oval right next to the ocean on Slade Point. It had a tiny grandstand and was surrounded by huge paperbark and umbrella trees. The track was grass, and the lanes were marked with sump oil. It regularly got scorching in Mackay, but the sea breezes made Melaleuca Park the only place you'd want to be on a Sunday. Norman didn't always feel the same way, and he would often hide behind the trees at the start of the 200m because he didn't want to run. I had started to race against the older girls. At age eleven, I finished third in the Campbell Miles Trophy for the women's open 100m at the north Queensland zone titles. I won my first national titles in 1984 at the Pacific Schools Games in Melbourne, winning the gold medal in the 200m and high jump, and silver in the 100m. Not long after, I suffered my first serious setback – glandular fever. I was forced to miss almost two months of school. On the track I lost all my strength, and even six months later I still wasn't myself. For the first time I wasn't winning; it was all I could do to finish second or third behind girls I'd easily beaten before. Bruce told me to be patient and have faith that my old self would return.

By 1985 we had moved back to Mackay. My health deteriorated again when I contracted shingles, and Mum and Bruce decided to pull me out of the following year's athletics season. By the time I returned to full health and my winning ways, Norman was also dominating the state and zone titles, so Bruce was out there raising funds to get us both to the national titles. He started by selling lamingtons – small, iced sponge cakes – door to door and then progressed to raffling a meat tray outside the butcher's shop every Saturday and Sunday. He also raffled a 44-gallon drum of petrol that had been donated by the local service station. A country and western dance night, which he organised with another family, raised the final few hundred dollars we needed.

The big bonus for us was that Bruce's job on the railways gave us free travel throughout Queensland and one free inter-state trip a year, which we always used to go to the national championships. I loved the long trips on the train to see new places. It was our family's big adventure.

It was on one of these trips, in 1986, that I experienced racism at first hand. I knew there was a difference between the white and black worlds, but we kids had been protected from the actual extent of that divide. Our stepfather was white, we lived quite comfortably in a white neighbourhood, and in Mackay everyone – blacks and whites – seemed to get along with each other. There was still the 'Oh, shame!' mentality, of course, and on our first day at high school in Mackay, Norman and I, both very shy and nervous about going to this new, big school, hid our bikes behind some trees across the road instead of parking them in the racks next to all the others. Generally, though, you felt pretty comfortable, knowing that if you walked into a room there was every chance of another black person being around.

Bruce had already seen many incidents of racism involving me, but it had never registered in my own mind until this day on the platform at Melbourne's Flinders Street station. I was only thirteen. We were waiting to board a train and I was stretched out along one of the benches. I had just started to doze off when a woman's voice woke me. Then she began to shake me.

'Get up! Get off! We need to sit down.'

Bruce leapt up from his seat. 'What do you think you're doing?'

The woman looked at him, confused by the intervention of this white man on behalf of the Aboriginal girl. 'This is no place to be lying down, and it's none of your business anyway,' she said.

I could see the blood rush to Bruce's head. 'Yes, it is my business. I'm her father – so get out of here.'

As the lady left I looked around the station and saw plenty of empty seats. I didn't understand. Did I have no right to lie on the bench because I was black? I was very confused by that experience.

A similar thing happened in Sydney. I was standing in front of a florist's shop while Bruce was buying us some lunch when this lady came out and told me to move. 'Get away from here,' she said. 'I don't want you standing here.'

'What?' I said, before rushing over to Mum and Bruce. He asked me what had happened. 'She told me to get away from her shop,' I said.

Bruce stormed over to speak to the woman.

'How would you like it if I came and stood in front of your place?' she yelled at him.

'You're quite welcome,' he replied. 'I come from a place called Coppabella, and you're welcome to come and stand in front of my place every day.'

It wasn't in my personality to get upset about it, although there was one day in Year 9 when I wished I'd had the courage to stand up for myself. We were doing square dancing. There was this white boy named John and he was partnered with Melinda, the most popular girl in the class. As we rotated around during the dance, I was next in line. He said to Melinda, 'I hate how I have to dance with the boong next.'

It didn't matter to him that I was right next to them and could hear every word. I pretended I hadn't, though. I just accepted it, like my parents and their parents before them.

CHAPTER 3
Hello, Mainstream Australia

'Catherine, I can't coach you any more.'

I was sitting on the ground taking off my running shoes when Bruce dropped his bombshell. I turned around and asked him why.

'I just don't have enough knowledge and there's only so much I can do now. You're going to have to go away to boarding school where you can get some good coaching.'

Boarding school. Sounded interesting. 'OK.'

A few months went by and nothing happened so I didn't give boarding school too much thought. I didn't think about what a massive change to my life it would be or how I would cope leaving behind family and friends. I was too busy growing up. I was fourteen and starting to break out of my tomboy ways. I had been anything but a girly girl. My cousin had about a hundred dolls, whereas I only had one or two, although that was also because we simply couldn't afford them. I had never sought the attention of the opposite sex. I was too shy. I wasn't one of those girls who took time over their appearance and wanted to wear push-up bras at an early age.

A few things started to change once I was in high school. For the first time I wanted to break away from my mother's ultra-protective hold. I loved her and I knew that her determination to watch my every move had a lot to do with Anne-Marie. I could understand that, but I needed to breathe, needed to do things other teenage girls were doing. Mum never let me go anywhere. My friends were allowed to go to the movies or blue-light discos, but I had to stay at home and practise the organ. Mum liked me to play for anyone who visited our house. I hated it. My friends were always laughing at me because when Mum was around I would be practising and playing properly, but when she went out of the room I'd be cursing that organ. Eventually I got up the courage to start sneaking out to meet up with my cousins Tracey, Ralda and Lea, who lived on the other side of Mackay. We weren't bad girls, just a little mischievous. Whenever I was with my cousins I felt braver. Our adventures mostly involved seeing boys and smoking cigarettes. Sometimes for laughs we'd throw rocks at people's roofs, wait for the lights to come on and then bolt.

It was around this time that I had the chat with the vocational guidance officer at my school. My responses obviously set off some alarm bells. He rang Bruce and Mum the next day and questioned them. They totally supported my Olympic dream. By this stage I had won numerous state titles and national titles in the high jump, 100m, 200m and my new event, the 400m. Bruce explained that he'd begun searching for a scholarship at a southern Queensland school, as he thought I needed to be challenged more in my running. His preference was Toowoomba because that was where Paul Faithful was based. Paul had coached one of my idols, Glynis Nunn, to a heptathlon gold medal at the Los Angeles Olympics in 1984.

Money had become an issue. Norman was also winning title after title, and travelling all over the place for our running was using up the family's budget. In desperation, Mum compiled a résumé of our impressive records so far and posted it to several government bodies. It proved a masterstroke. The Aboriginal and Torres Strait Islander Commission eventually agreed – although only after several follow-up calls and a visit to its Canberra offices by Mum – to provide $8,000 each to Norman and me as part of a new pilot programme.

A week after Bruce had spoken with the vocational guidance officer he received a call from the headmaster's office. The headmaster had managed to arrange a scholarship at Fairholme College, the exclusive girls' school in Toowoomba. Bruce was over the moon. I didn't really know what to make of it all as we packed up and piled into the car for the long trip south.

As we drove through the gates of Fairholme, I couldn't believe how big and old the buildings were. We parked our blue Kingswood, which now had one brown door courtesy of a recent run-in with a bull, next to a Mercedes Benz outside the main office. I had never seen anything like this before and was still in a bit of daze when we were called into the headmaster's office. He took one look at me and told me I'd better get my hair cut. I'd just spent a week doing work experience at a hairdresser's where they'd put grey streaks through my hair. Apparently this wasn't acceptable at Fairholme, along with a host of other things. As the headmaster explained everything to Mum and Bruce, I looked around the office. It was so neat, books lined up perfectly along each wall. It all seemed so old. And it was then that it first struck me: what was a little black girl doing in a place like this?

I couldn't stop crying.

'Mum, I want to come home,' I bawled into the telephone. I wasn't even through my first month at Fairholme and I was scared. 'You have to come and get me.'

By the time I got off the phone, Mum was crying as well. I'd never experienced such loneliness. How was I going to live in this place? I was in a dormitory that felt like a prison. It was so dark and I was petrified. I had to bury my face in the pillow so the other girls couldn't hear my sobbing. Night after night it was the same. Once a week I would call home and the phone call always ended with me and Mum in tears.

What I found the hardest about Fairholme – apart from the fact that I was one of only three black students out of six hundred – was its rules and regulations. For a young Aboriginal girl used to the laidback lifestyle of tropical Mackay, it was a major culture shock. We couldn't go to dinner with wet hair, or wear skirts above the knees; we weren't allowed earrings or nail polish and could only have a certain type of bow in our hair. There was no TV. We had to study for at least one hour every night and it was lights out at nine p.m. Church was compulsory every Sunday and we weren't allowed to leave the school grounds. To top it all off, we could be fined if our beds weren't properly made, and we were woken every morning by one of the teachers ringing a cow bell next to our heads. It was like boot camp. Not all the girls lived at the school, but for boarders the only chance to see the outside world was two weekends each term, plus a couple of day passes.

Fairholme was my introduction to mainstream Australia. It was a world I had never experienced before. The place reeked of wealth, with flash cars constantly pulling up at the school. The girls dressed in designer brands and wore leather shoes like loafers, while I had a two-dollar pair of cotton, Asian-style shoes.

I couldn't get over the confidence of these girls. They were always fussing over their appearance, soaping up their faces and applying lotions with fancy brushes. Every one of them had her own beauty routine. They were all so motivated to achieve their ambitions. While I dreamt only of running fast, they were focused on becoming doctors, lawyers and politicians. The pressure to succeed at Fairholme was so great it scared me. Girls would break down in class if they got an A for a test instead of an A+. The head prefect was a girl named Katharine Tonkin. I used to go and watch her in debating competitions. I was amazed by this girl who could stand up in front of all those people and speak so confidently on any subject. She had no fear and could do anything she wanted. I wished I could be the same.

I eventually started to come out of my shell, thanks mainly to falling in with a couple of fellow north Queensland country girls, Tanya Anderson and Lyn West. We mucked around a bit and got up to some mischief, like hiding other girls' mattresses. Some of the girls would sneak out to meet boys, and one painted the headmaster's cat green. Some girls were angry at Fairholme when they left, and, in the past, dead animal carcasses had been found on the veranda of the boarding house. I could understand why.

My nickname at Fairholme was 'Flowers'. For my birthday Mum and Bruce sent me some flowers, but the problem was that Valentine's Day is 14 February and my birthday is 16 February. Some of the girls knew about this boy, Terry, who had a crush on me and they assumed the flowers had come from him. I was too embarrassed to carry them from reception up to the dormitory. From then on at school I was known as 'Flowers'. Whenever I ran at an athletics carnival, that's what the girls would be chanting as I raced. Even the sports master, John Sessarago, called me that.

The onset of winter dampened my spirits. I became more withdrawn and really struggled. I resorted to wearing tracksuit pants under my tartan skirt, pulling them up over my knees so you couldn't see them. We had to get up early for the cross-country runs and it was a farce; we had to wear tracksuits, beanies and scarves because it was bitterly cold. Even though I hated the cross-country, sport was my outlet at Fairholme. Everything else about the place frustrated me.

I didn't do any work in class; I just spent most of my time staring out the window in my own little dream world. I had loved to daydream ever since I was a small girl. Now, I thought about home, about how much I missed my mum and my family, and how I'd taken for granted the joy of coming home from school every day in Mackay. I missed everyone smiling. No one seemed to smile at Fairholme. Back home you'd always find people outside playing the guitar, laughing, dancing and singing, because that was an integral part of Aboriginal and Torres Strait Island cultures. Mackay was obviously a warmer place, but it wasn't just the climate, it was also that people were close to one another. In Toowoomba everyone was a stranger, nobody seemed that happy, and everyone was on their own with no real sense of family. People seemed a lot more guarded and a bit more selfish. It was just so different from what I had grown up with.

Mr Sessarago, or 'Sess' as we all called him, helped me to come to terms with everything. He was my high-jump coach and he was also in charge of the touch-football team. Sometimes, on my weekend leave, I'd go to his house and hang out with his family. Other times I'd stay at Uncle Darby's, the former champion Aboriginal jockey Darby McCarthy. Uncle Darby had two daughters a little younger than me and we liked to sit and watch television and eat chocolate. Running was obviously my focus, but I also made the state team in touch football. Netball was my second love, and I was our school team's gun defender, either goal defence or keeper.

When the 1988 Seoul Olympics were on, Sess let the athletics team sit around and watch it on the television. As we watched Carl Lewis and Florence Griffith-Joyner, my two favourites, win medals, Sess turned around and said to me, 'Flowers, you can be up there with those guys one day.' It stuck in my head. Bruce was the only other person who had ever spoken to me like that. As I saw those athletes on TV and thought more about what Sess had said, a picture started to form in my mind. Later, Sess gave me a framed black and white photograph of me high jumping, with a quote from F.D. Roosevelt written on it: 'The only limit to our realisation of tomorrow will be our doubts of today.'

The picture in my mind became even clearer on a trip to America as part of an International Athletics Exchange tour. A squad of twenty of Australia's leading junior athletes were selected to go to the Mt SAC relays in California, all expenses paid. I was so excited about my first trip overseas but even more excited about the possibility of meeting Carl and Flo-Jo. We'd only been at the track for a few minutes when someone yelled, 'There she is!' Suddenly all these kids sprinted towards Flo-Jo, who was sitting on the ground doing some stretching. I couldn't believe how small she was. When she was signing a piece of paper for me, I couldn't take my eyes off her long fingernails and was shocked to see her write out her full name. I thought she would just do 'Flo-Jo' and be done with it. She told us it had taken her twenty years to win her gold medals so you just had to be patient and work hard. Minutes later, the sprint was on again when Carl was spotted in the warm-up area. The group was mainly made up of girls so we were giggling uncontrollably at the sight of him. I got his autograph as well and decided I'd get them both laminated and put them in a special photo album. Sess's words kept coming back to me. One day I could be like Flo-Jo and Carl. One day it could be me sitting on the track stretching, with giggling teenagers wanting my autograph. I liked that picture.

We were all billeted out to different homes, and I stayed with a white family in Walnut, an outer suburb of Los Angeles. We managed to take in some of the sights, including Disneyland, but the biggest adventure came during a simple stroll down a local street. I was with the daughter of the family. She was a year younger than me but she always wore heaps of make-up and hair spray and seemed determined to grow up fast. This night we were walking along the street when a black guy came up and pulled a knife on us. 'Hey, what are you doing?' the girl said. 'It's me!' She knew him from school so he just took off. It all happened so fast I didn't really have time to panic.

I was intrigued by the way black Americans acted. They were loud, in your face and proud of who they were – the complete opposite to black Australians. At the athletics track you could smell their aggression and strength. They intimidated the white athletes. It was an eye-opening experience.

When I got back to Fairholme, I ran up to Sess and gave him a big hug and yelled, 'I met Carl!' The only thing the other girls wanted to know about was whether I'd touched his big, muscled back.

I soon crashed back to reality when I was told that because of my poor marks I'd be kept down in Year 11 for the 1989 school year. Some of the girls actually thought I was slow. While it was true that my heart wasn't in the classroom, I was disappointed that the teachers didn't support me more. It seemed to me they didn't attempt to understand how it felt to be the only black girl in the class. They were white, and everywhere I looked there were white people. I was too shy and scared to put up my hand and ask a question if I didn't know what was going on. I didn't want to bring any attention to myself; that was the way I had been raised.

Once again it was my love for running that got me through. I was finding out more about myself on the track. Although I wasn't so keen on training, as soon as I got on the start line for the competitions I found my laidback attitude disappearing and being replaced by a win-at-all-costs mentality. Maybe it was about pride, about proving that I was worthy. Being the sports star and the first to be picked in everyone's team did that. One of the sports captains at Fairholme was Vanessa Gray, a girl I'd competed against during my primary school days. We had both represented Queensland in the high jump at the national titles. She always joked about how, back then, if I won the high jump, on the next jump I'd walk up and tip the bar off with my hand. I never liked going for records and always only did enough to win. That was the lazy north Queensland side of me coming out. As long as I won, the rest didn't interest me.

My training with Paul Faithful wasn't working out as I had hoped. Twice a week I'd go into town to his local club for training with a group of other young athletes. I don't think he took me seriously. There was no one-on-one coaching and I was just drifting through the sessions. I was still drifting through school as well.

My brother Norman had won a scholarship to St Joseph's Nudgee College in Brisbane, and Sess offered to take me down there to watch him compete in the private schools carnival. It was a bit of fun checking out all the boys, and while I was there I was introduced to Norman's athletics coach, a man named Mike Danila.

CHAPTER 4
GOLDEN HEARTACHE

'Are there boys there?' I asked Mike Danila.

'Yes,' he said with a laugh.

'OK then, let's go.'

My life had just taken another turn. It was the winter holidays of 1989 and I was back in Mackay at an athletics clinic with Norman, run by his former teacher. Bruce and Mum had just told me that because of a problem with my scholarship at Fairholme they had organised for me to transfer to the Kooralbyn International School, where Danila was now head track and field coach.

The timing was right on a number of fronts. My marks weren't improving at Fairholme, the Paul Faithful situation wasn't working out and my parents had just moved down to Brisbane, which was only an hour's drive from my new school. It was funny, though. When it finally came to leaving Fairholme, I was a bit apprehensive. The place that had given me so much hell had actually grown on me. After eighteen months there, I was much more confident in myself and had learnt a lot about the world from the students and teachers.

But I could tell Kooralbyn was what Mum wanted for her sixteen-year-old daughter, and that was enough for me. So in early August, Danila came with her to pick me up from Fairholme and take me to my new home. The minute I saw the place I knew I was in heaven.

Kooralbyn International School was only ten years old and sat at the foothills of a beautiful mountain range. It looked so peaceful. The school was next door to the Kooralbyn Valley Resort, a fancy new hotel with a golf course and polo fields. The school had its own four-lane running track, which was very similar to the one at Melaleuca Park in Mackay where I'd done my junior racing. There were only 250 students, about 30 per cent of them from overseas. The great thing for me was that there were heaps of black kids from all over the place – Papua New Guinea, some Pacific islands and even Cuba.

I soon learnt that Kooralbyn was a school where you could express yourself. We had a uniform but you could wear whatever shoes you wanted, skirts could be as short as you liked and jewellery was allowed. There was a lot more soul and culture about the place. It was so easy to blend in and make friends. It was on a whole different level to Fairholme. When one of my friends from PNG, named Argo, cut his finger, I cut mine so we could put them together and be blood brother and sister for ever. One day Redman, an American-Cuban guy, came to school with a T-shirt that said 'Get Fucked'. He was one of a group of students who, even though they were in the minority, seemed like the majority because they were larger than life. Often they would have teachers in tears and running out of the classroom. While mischief at Fairholme was hiding mattresses, at Kooralbyn a lot of the students smoked marijuana and regularly rocked up to class stoned, and the boys were always sneaking over to the girls' dormitories.

On the track, Mike Danila was like a man possessed. He was from Romania and had been a handy 400m/800m runner himself before turning to coaching. He'd fled his homeland in 1987 on a trip to Yugoslavia, when he was coach of the Romanian team at the World Student Games. He escaped to Vienna, asked for asylum and then applied for a visa to start a new life in Australia. He brought with him that Eastern Bloc attitude that you have to work incredibly hard to achieve anything worthwhile. He was so passionate, so driven. You couldn't help but get caught up in his energy and ambition. I had become lazy at Fairholme, training two or, at the most, three times a week. Danila had us at the track every day. Although we trained in a group, Danila always spent extra time with me, encouraging and pushing me further. It didn't take long for the results to come. My personal best in the 100m came down by almost a second in the first three months to 11.67s.

At a squad meeting in November, Danila was lecturing the group about the dangers of junk food. He often got us into the resort to use the spa and pool facilities, and that day we were all sitting around the spa.

'You'd better practise your signature,' Danila said to me.

'What for?' I said, laughing at him.

'Soon you will start having to write down hundreds of signatures.'

He was thinking about entering me in the Commonwealth Games trials the following month. This was news to me.

'Do you think I'm good enough?' I quizzed him.

My coach had done his homework and according to him my times had me right in the mix.

The trials were at Randwick in Sydney. Danila was more nervous than I was. I just treated the final of the 100m like any other race and ended up in a dead-heat for third with Kathy Sambell in 11.42s, behind Kerry Johnson and Monique Dunstan. I had made the relay team. While it wasn't official immediately and we were told we'd have to wait until the following week for the team to be announced, everyone around me was so excited. I even had a journalist from the Melbourne *Sun* approach me for an interview. He asked about my motivation.

'I have a sister, Anne-Marie, who has cerebral palsy,' I said. 'My mother told me I have two good arms and two good legs, so use them.'

The journalist's name was Nick Bideau.

I didn't really know what was going on. Here I was, a sixteen-year-old Aboriginal girl sitting in a conference room in Auckland surrounded by all these superstar athletes. Darren Clark and Debbie Flintoff-King were sitting just opposite and Rob de Castella was down in the front row of the team meeting. They were my idols. I had watched Deek and Debbie win gold medals on TV, and here I was next to them wearing the same green and gold tracksuit. I spent the first few days just walking around with my mouth open, staring at everyone and everything. I was so excited. I'd already had my photo taken with Jamaican legend Merlene Ottey and the Nigerian twins Davidson and Osmond Ezinwa, who were both gun sprinters. Another sprinter, Linford Christie, and hurdler Colin Jackson had chatted with me in the dining room. Other athletes were intrigued by Australia having a young black girl on its team. Back at Fairholme, I'd watched with Sess as Clark ran fourth in the 400m at the Seoul Olympics; now he'd come and sit on the end of my bunk, put a stocking over his head and ask me if I knew how to throw a boomerang. It was hilarious. I couldn't believe all this was really happening to me.

The excitement soon switched to boredom as the relay wasn't until the final day of competition. To amuse myself I made up a song about my French boyfriend, Laurent, from Kooralbyn, repeating it over and over, driving my room-mate, Monique, mad. I also became the official nail painter of the team. I played on the computers at the village and attended every function there, which included a meeting with Prince Andrew. However, most of the time all I was doing was eating and sleeping. I couldn't believe you could eat as much chocolate cake, muffins and cheesecake as you liked in the athletes' dining room.

Mike Danila, who had gained accreditation to the Games village, was shocked when he saw me at the end of the first week. He took one look at my legs and said, 'My God, you've put on so much weight.' I had put on three kilos. I wasn't concerned, although that changed the following day while I was hanging out in the unit's lounge room. I could hear a woman's voice getting louder and louder. It was coming from a bedroom down the hall, and when I moved closer to the door I heard my name being called out and I realised it was Kerry Johnson's voice.

Kerry was our number one sprinter and she had been my greatest supporter from day one, helping me at training and generally looking out for the baby of the team.

'No! No way,' Kerry was saying. 'If she doesn't run, I don't run.'

My heart sank. Someone didn't want me in the team.

I bolted into my bedroom. My mind was racing. Kerry and I had been having a few problems during relay practice and had dropped the baton a couple of times, but surely they weren't getting rid of me because of that. Suddenly I had flashbacks of the discrimination from my childhood.

Please don't let it happen again.

After an anxious afternoon, the girls arrived to tell me that team management had considered replacing me with heptathlete Jane Flemming. However, after Kerry had stood up for me, they backed down. It prodded me into action, and I was determined not to disappoint Kerry. She had already won two silver medals at these Games, behind Ottey. She was like a mother figure and called us all together on the morning of the relay for a pep talk.

'Now, it's important to sweat in your warm-up,' she explained, looking at me. The girls talked about how it was the most relaxed competitors who did the best. That sounded good to me. 'I think we'll win this today,' were Kerry's final words.

As I lined up next to powerful women from Canada and England, reality struck.

Oh my God, this is it, Freeman!

I was running the third leg and receiving the baton from Kathy. As she approached I waited until the final second before taking off.

Better to be safe than sorry.

With the baton safely in my hand, I just put my head down and went for it. The exchange to Kerry was perfect and she exploded away. I wasn't sure whether we'd won until I saw Monique and Kerry hugging each other. Then, just as I was about to let out a squeal of joy, an official carrying a red protest flag walked across my lane. Thankfully, he was just crossing the track. We did a victory lap with a boxing kangaroo flag before the girls got out their make-up bags and applied lipstick for the medal ceremony. I felt my emotions start to build when the medal was put around my neck.

I didn't expect to see so many people at the press conference afterwards but apparently someone had written about how I was the first Aboriginal Commonwealth Games track and field gold medallist. So now I was suddenly the flavour of the month. They were firing questions at me about my people and background. I was having trouble concentrating because I was giggling so much. Finally, I managed to thank my greatest fan, Anne-Marie, and in response to a question about my Aboriginality I said, 'Being Aboriginal means everything to me. I feel for my people all the time. A lot of my friends have the talent but lack the opportunity.'

I had seized my opportunity, and now it was time to party. Just as Fairholme had opened my eyes to a world I'd never experienced before, being part of the Australian track and field team had given me insight into a new world, but this time I knew I belonged. The party after the closing ceremony was out of control; people were dancing on tables and I got really, really drunk. I remember a guy I didn't know sticking his tongue in my ear. It was madness. I loved it and didn't want the night to end, although I also couldn't wait to get back home and tell my family and friends all about it.

Monday, 5 February 1990. A day I will never forget. It was a typically hot summer's day in Brisbane and we were all at our next-door neighbour's house, watching a replay of the closing ceremony from the Auckland Commonwealth Games.

'There you are, Catherine!' my mum screamed as a mass of green and gold appeared on the television screen.

I'd only returned to Brisbane from New Zealand that morning, after two of the biggest weeks of my short life. I had made my first Australian senior team, run my first big international race and won my first gold medal. The media frenzy that had followed our victory in the 4 x 100m had shocked me. I hated all the attention and was so relieved to be back in familiar surroundings with Mum and Bruce, who was proudly examining every centimetre of the gold medal. Mum, as usual, had 100 questions about the Games. Who did you meet? What was the village like? What did you eat?

I had begun telling her how I'd nearly fallen over as we were doing a curtsy in front of the Royal Box on our victory lap when I noticed Bruce was at the doorway. There had been a phone call for him. I'd presumed it was from his work, but by the look on his face something was horribly wrong.

'Anne-Marie is dead,' he said.

It took a few seconds to register in my mind. My Mum started squealing hysterically, and then I lost it. I couldn't believe it. I didn't want to believe it. Anne-Marie was only 24 and she was my greatest motivation.

'No, no. She can't be. No!' I yelled at Bruce.

But she was. She had died of an acute asthma attack.

The next few days were a blur. Bruce arranged for us to get the train up to Rockhampton almost immediately. During the trip north I decided I wanted to have my gold medal buried with Anne-Marie.

'Mum, I want Anne-Marie to have it,' I said.

'I don't think you should, Catherine,' she said. 'You've earned that medal, and one day you'll want to show it to your grandchildren. That's what she would have wanted.'

We finally agreed that the flower posy from the medal ceremony was a suitable replacement.

My father had made the trip up from Woorabinda to be at the funeral, and as I scanned the large crowd I thought about how it took the death of a loved one to bring our whole clan together. Why couldn't it be in happier times? I clung to Mum at the cemetery and managed to keep my emotions in check until they started lowering the coffin. My older brother, Gavin, was holding on to the coffin and I could see the pain etched on his face.

'Anne-Marie, Anne-Marie!' he started screaming.

His outburst had a domino effect. Suddenly, everyone's emotions boiled over. I saw the tears streaming down my cousin Tracey's face and then, like a tidal wave, it hit me. I had the gold medal in my hand and I started yelling, 'Anne-Marie, I won this for you. I did it for you.' I could feel my body trembling. 'Every race I run now is for you, Anne-Marie.'

I knew my life had changed for ever. The death of my sister charged me with a sense of purpose. I had this gift, and I was going to do everything in my power to make sure I succeeded.

I would do it for Anne-Marie.

CHAPTER 5
THE FIRST STEP

'I understand your pain, but often the best way to deal with it is to direct your feelings towards something in your own life, remembering the strength of character you saw in your sister. Make the lessons you learnt from Anne-Marie really count for something rather than be lost with her passing.'

The touching note was waiting for me when I returned to Brisbane. It was from Nick Bideau, sending his condolences. He called a few weeks later because he wanted to do a story on Norman and me, the brother–sister team from north Queensland. I found it very easy to talk to him and our paths crossed again the following month when I was in Melbourne for the national championships. After being upset in the U/18 100m and then losing the women's 100m by a whisker to Jane Flemming, I easily won the 200m and became the first Aborigine to win an open Australian track title. My victory meant that I finished on top of the rankings in the 200m for the grand prix series and therefore I had to attend a gala dinner at the Grand Hyatt, where I'd be presented with the prize money of $1,500. Gala dinner meant a fancy dress, and I had nothing to wear. Enter Nick.

Footwear giant Nike had seen the feature article Nick had written and had asked him to invite me round to accept a gift of running gear. He came and picked me up from my motel in Carlton and took me to Nike. I found myself feeling very comfortable in his presence. After we'd finished at Nike we drove to the trendy shopping strip of Chapel Street in Prahran to look for a dress. Nick insisted on paying because he knew my situation: I didn't have anything to wear and I didn't have any money. It was one of the nicest things anyone had ever done for me and I was touched. I had a great night at the dinner, too. Athletics legend Raelene Boyle presented my award, and I was so excited to meet her I kept hugging her and hugging her.

Back at Kooralbyn, things were starting to get out of control. People were constantly ringing up to talk to me, so the school organised a manager, Ian Guiver from Celebrity Sports Marketing, who also looked after some big names, including Test cricketers Craig McDermott and Ian Healy, and Brisbane Bullets basketball player Leroy Loggins.

The Melbourne bid for the 1996 Olympic Games wanted to use me as part of their sales pitch. I was more than willing, especially as the deal included several free trips down south for rehearsals, which meant I could hook up with Nick.

In July 1990 I travelled to Europe to race in preparation for the world junior championships in Bulgaria. I ran in the English AAA championships and bumped into Nick again. He was covering the tour for News Limited. Even though he was nearly thirteen years older than me, I spent all my time with him. By the time we got to Bulgaria, I knew people had started talking about us.

A couple of months later I was back in Melbourne for the Olympic bid and Nick came and picked me up after a function. He was going to a party and asked if I wanted to come. We were there for about ten minutes and I felt really awkward. I was the only black person there, and the only teenager, as all Nick's friends were in their thirties. He realised I was uncomfortable so we left. We just drove around for a while, chatting, and I saw the Westgate Bridge and asked him what was down there. He explained how it went down the coast to Lorne, so I said, 'Let's go.'

'No, I think I'd better take you home,' he said. 'Maybe another time.'

We both knew our relationship was going to another level. I liked the way I could say anything to him and be completely relaxed around him. Maybe that was helped by the fact that he had dark olive skin with strong Mediterranean features. He had even been called an Aborigine at school. Nick was fanatical about athletics and had been a good middle-distance runner in the American college system for a couple of years. He knew everything about the sport and was always giving me snippets of advice. I simply liked the way he had shown an interest in me, that he had gone to the trouble of looking out for me. I felt I could rely on him.

The Olympic decision was to be made in Tokyo in September, and I was very impressed when we were ushered into first class on the plane. I couldn't believe the personal service and how big and roomy the seats were. It was so exciting, and I immediately understood why famous people only flew first class. I was in elite company with Prime Minister Bob Hawke, AOC boss Kevan Gosper, Victorian premier Joan Kirner and Olympic swimming gold medallist Michelle Ford. Brisbane's Lord Mayor, Sallyanne Atkinson, took me under her wing. I had to wear a bright red dress for the presentation and Sallyanne was scared I would forget my lines. I was a little unsure myself. The rehearsals had been fun because they had got me out of school and down to Melbourne to see Nick. Now, though, I had to perform in front of all these strangers.

I walked to the front, took a deep breath and gave a big smile. I said, 'For a young Australian Aboriginal athlete there is an enormous thrill in competing in Europe and America.' *If only the Fairholme girls could see me now!* 'Barcelona would be a great adventure for me. However, Melbourne would be an adventure for the rest of the world.'

I had pulled off my small part, but unfortunately it wasn't enough – Atlanta was awarded the Games. The mayor of Atlanta actually came up to me afterwards and drew me aside before whispering, 'Don't worry – Sydney 2000.'

I just stared at him. How could he know already? Then I started doing some calculations. I would be 27 in 2000, right in the prime of my career. A lot of the foreign delegates came up to congratulate me, believing that I was African-American and part of Atlanta's successful bid. I kept repeating, 'Sorry, I'm Australian.'

New Year's Day, 1991. Kooralbyn was deserted. I was preparing for the start of the grand prix series so I had stayed on to train. I was sitting on the oval stretching my hamstrings. It was a beautiful, sunny afternoon and I was daydreaming, thinking about my friends and family back in Brisbane and Mackay. Then I noticed a shiny red car come through the school gates. Who could this be? I was straining to see when the car pulled up next to the oval, and then I realised. It was Nick Bideau.

'Oh my God!' I yelled, and ran to him. Nick had been out with his mates the previous night, then flown to Queensland on the spur of the moment. He was like my knight in shining armour. We made love on the bonnet of the car, just up the road from the principal's house. It was crazy, passionate, but it felt right. Afterwards we sat on the oval and Nick said, 'There's more to life than this. If you want to be a good athlete, come to Melbourne where there are proper tracks, good facilities and the best runners to train with.'

I just nodded. I knew changes had to be made.

A couple of weeks later, Ian Guiver announced that he'd got me a job at the Kooralbyn Valley Resort. I would be tutored there in hotel management and could still train with coach Danila. But before I could start I had an important appointment at Government House in Kirribilli, where I'd been invited as Young Australian of the Year. Since the Commonwealth Games success, my life had taken off. I had raced overseas, got myself a serious boyfriend and now here I was shaking hands with the Prime Minister. It was all a bit overwhelming, and I felt uncomfortable until I met the Australian of the Year, Professor Fred Hollows, the prominent eye surgeon, and his wife, Gabi. We instantly hit it off; he made me laugh so much. He was a little rough, swore a bit, but he was an amazingly hard worker for his cause and you could tell he had a heart of gold. He was someone I aspired to be like and I asked him if I could go with him into the outback and help at one of his clinics down the track.

Back at Kooralbyn, I became the hotel's recreation officer. Guests could find me behind a little desk at reception. If you wanted to know what was going on at the resort, anything from archery to aquarobics, I was your girl. While the job was boring, the nightlife certainly made up for it. I had an apartment of my own at the resort and there would always be people coming over to party.

One particular night, my friend Christine and I got pretty wasted. I'd forgotten that the next day I was to do an interview with *60 Minutes*. When Jeff McMullen and his crew arrived, I was still stoned. I couldn't believe what I was doing. The director was eyeing me suspiciously and one of the camera guys asked if I felt all right. He told me I looked a bit out of it. If only they knew. Luckily they were around for a week so my performance improved greatly. I don't think Jeff realised. I had done a few crazy things to this point in my life but I knew this one topped them all. Like most teenagers, I had plenty of drinking and smoking stories. We were just kids having a bit of fun.

Nick was in town again but only for a brief stay, and on the way to the airport I got him to drop me and Christine at her sister's place in Brisbane. We were nearly there when Christine pulled out a joint and lit up in the back seat. As she passed it over to me, I saw the look of surprise on Nick's face.

'You don't mind, do you?' I asked.

'It's got nothing to do with me,' he replied, 'but if you ask me, if you want to be a world-class athlete, that's not the way to go.'

I couldn't believe what I was hearing. I was being sacked from the resort. Sacked! Apparently I'd kept a group of guests who wanted to go kite-flying waiting for half an hour. In a way I was glad this had happened. Since Nick had mentioned moving to Melbourne, the idea had been gathering strength in my mind. My coach had been away pursuing his own interests with clinics in Fiji so the timing couldn't have been better.

My relationship with Nick was now well and truly out. I could thank relay coach Nancy Atterton for that. During the recent relays camp I had stayed with Nick at his Brisbane motel. One morning there was a knock on his door. I was in the bathroom when I heard Atterton's voice. 'Melinda, Melinda, get out here. You've got to get to training.' Nick ignored it, but five minutes later she returned with the maid and the key. When she walked in, Nick was sitting on the bed in a running shirt and shorts and I was next to him. Atterton stared at us both and then turned to leave, obviously realising it wasn't Melinda Gainsford's room. She paused at the door, looked back in at me and added, 'And you, you're late for training.' I didn't even know that training was on. Nick ran out after her while I slumped on the bed, laughing.

The 4 x 100m relay team was attempting to qualify for the world championships at the Mt SAC Relays in America in April. I decided that would be a perfect time to make the big move. I would simply replace Brisbane with Melbourne as my return destination. In one way I knew what I was doing could be seen as madness. I had only just turned eighteen and here I was, about to leave my family, my home and everything that was familiar to me, to live in a strange city with a man I'd only known for a year. But it felt right. Packing up and starting again wasn't exactly foreign territory for me anyway. I'd done it many times as a kid. Taking Nick out of the equation and thinking purely from an athletics viewpoint, it was still a good move. I needed to be challenged, I needed to improve, and though Mike Danila had taken me a long way in a short time I could sense he was enjoying seeking other challenges and it was time for me to do the same. There was one major snag in my bold plan – how was I going to tell Mum?

First of all I rang Nick and told him how I'd been sacked and that I was changing my ticket to return to Melbourne. He was happy to hear it and offered to come to Brisbane to get my things before I left. Suddenly, everything was happening so fast. I didn't know anyone else in Melbourne and had no idea what I'd do in terms of a job or money, but my instinct told me it was the right move. I got a lot of confidence from my Nanna. She'd met Nick on a recent trip to Mackay and got on famously with him. I trusted Nanna's judgement. I knew I was comfortable with this guy and for some reason I was sure he would look after me.

My manager had just broken the news to Bruce and Mum about my sacking when I arrived home with Nick. I could tell by the look on Mum's face that she was shattered. It soon got worse.

'Mum, I'm leaving. I'm going to Melbourne,' I said.

She burst into tears, and when Bruce tried to comfort her, she pushed him away.

'Tell her she can't go!' she screamed at Nick, who I could tell was uncomfortable at the sight of my distraught mother.

'I can't tell her,' he said. 'She's eighteen years old. She's got to make up her own mind about what she wants to do.'

I knew I had to be strong. 'No, Mum. No, Mum, I'm going.'

Mum had always been so protective of me, mainly because of what had happened with Anne-Marie. She simply couldn't bear to lose another daughter.

It was all too much, and I grabbed Nick and pushed him out of the door. He was concerned about Mum but we had to get out, and that night we stayed in a motel.

CHAPTER 6
FINDING MYSELF

'You've got a lot of ability,' she said, 'but so what? So did I. Those who win Olympic gold are just as talented as you, but they work hard too. Unless you're prepared to do that, you'll go nowhere.'

An angry Raelene Boyle was staring me in the eye. I was getting the feeling our working relationship was about to end. It had been Nick's idea to get us together after we'd met following my appearance on the *Sportsworld* show with Bruce McAvaney. I'd been selected for the 1991 world championships in Tokyo in August, and Channel 7 wanted me to appear alongside Raelene. I was very excited to have the opportunity to learn from a triple Olympic silver medallist, but the problem was that Raelene couldn't be at every session. Her work and study commitments meant a lot of the responsibility was left with me to follow the training programme she'd mapped out. The trouble with this set-up was the fact that I was becoming bored, with no family or friends in Melbourne. I was actually starting to wonder what I had done moving south. I had left the sun of Queensland for this wet, miserable place. *Smart move, Catherine!*

I had gone into hibernation. Nick would go off to work and I would just lie in bed and watch TV. If I did go for a run, I often had to slosh around through the mud and rain. I had a lot of time to kill and began to amuse myself with shopping or getting my hair done. One night I was late for training because I'd had extensions put in my hair, and when I finally arrived Raelene was at Olympic Park waiting for me.

'One thing in my career – I was never late for training,' she yelled at me.

We'd only been working together for a couple of months when Raelene sat me down for the heart-to-heart chat. While I was taken aback by her initial outburst, I could sense the passion and feeling in her words. Raelene wasn't going to coach me any more, but she really cared and wanted me to understand that I couldn't be casual about my running, and that the accolades I'd received after the Commonwealth Games gold medal meant absolutely nothing in the elite world of athletics. I had a lump in my throat when Raelene finished. I also had the feeling that it was a conversation I'd remember for years to come.

Just as I was coming to grips with the departure of my coach, I became sick. It was horrible. I was in hospital for five days with a pelvic infection. It was a very nasty business and we thought it best to keep it a secret from my parents, as they were upset enough about me in my new environment. I subsequently lost heaps of weight and wasn't fit by the time I left for Tokyo with the Australian team. Although I was termed a 'relay alternative', I had beaten most of the girls in the squad in a time-trial just before we left, so I was convinced I'd be in the team, as in Auckland. But that wasn't the case. Before our scheduled team meeting one of the girls casually let slip that I wasn't running. I was shocked, and refused to believe it until the coaches told me. None of them had bothered to speak to me, and I only found out in the team meeting when my name wasn't read out.

Nick came to the hotel that night and I instantly burst into tears.

'What happened at the team meeting?' he asked.

'I'm not running,' I said. 'Why don't they like me? Don't they realise how good I am? Don't they realise how good I can be?'

He grabbed me and calmly said, 'Forget about it. Just train hard and you'll never have to be in this situation again.'

I pushed him away and yelled, 'This is the last time, the very last time I'm going to be in a team just for the relay. From now on I'll be in for my own event.'

I had met Peter Fortune, the guy Nick wanted to coach me, just before I'd left for Tokyo. He was middle-aged, with grey hair, and seemed pretty calm and low-key, which definitely suited my style. Fort had coached the 1984 Australian 400m champion Gary Minihan, but had given it away to pursue his love of racing touring cars. Chris Wardlaw, the coach of marathon runner Steve Moneghetti, had recommended Fort to Nick, and we sealed the deal with a hug after having dinner together.

The relay snub still hurt. I felt embarrassed around other athletes and basically didn't want anyone from the track and field world to see me. Fort wanted us to meet at Olympic Park for our first training session together in November, but when I arrived there were a lot of other athletes working out. I freaked, and decided not to go in. Eventually, Fort found me jogging around the outside of the grandstand. He understood my concerns, so we went to the park across the road. I wanted to train hard out of the spotlight for a while, and then, when I was ready, come back and prove some people wrong. Fort's first priority was to get me into the gym to build my strength. I had never done anything like that before, but he had me working out at the Wesley College gym several times a week.

Like a number of coaches before him, Fort was convinced that my fluent and smooth running style was ideally suited to the 400m. I had run a few over the years but had never really focused on it. One of the first 400m races I ever ran was in the juniors when I was twelve. I ate a Mars Bar just before the race, and all the way around I could feel it. I collapsed once I crossed the finish line and nearly vomited.

After six months in Melbourne my life had become a lot more settled. Nick and I had moved into a new house in Richmond, which we shared with Fitzroy footballer Brett Stephens. We regularly went to watch Brett play football, and it was through him that I met Peta Powell, my first Melbourne girlfriend. She was this tall, blonde-haired girl whose outgoing personality made her seem larger than life. We started chatting at the football one day and it turned out that she was a professional runner. As we got on famously, I asked her to come and train with Fort. I craved a female companion.

Nick wanted me to do something with my free time to break the boredom. I decided to look for a job and picked out a couple of positions in sandwich bars – I figured I could handle making sandwiches. Nick, however, didn't think that was suitable for an aspiring Olympic athlete so he arranged for me to work at a sports store in Cheltenham owned by former pro runner John Toleman. I'd catch the train down in the morning, work for four hours and then be back for my afternoon training session. Just having a regular routine was good for me, but the major plus about the job was that it forced me to meet people and feel comfortable talking to them. I was still very much a shy Aboriginal girl from north Queensland who much preferred sitting on the couch at home, hiding from the world.

The next big step was university. Nick was always on about self-improvement and I figured I'd missed a lot at secondary school so I enrolled in an Australian history and politics course at Melbourne University. Although I was far from committed – I'd go to a couple of classes and tutorials a week at best – uni proved to be a revelation on a number of fronts. I was initially blown away by the way the students aggressively argued points with the lecturers. I was still in Fairholme mode and instantly loved how people were allowed to express themselves. I quickly fell in with a group of Aborigines and Islanders who had their own student body. We used to hang out in the lounge and talk. Every day someone would come in, throw their bag down and share an issue that was affecting their life. It then became our subject of the day. I was exposed to a lot of different characters, from radical lesbians and drug addicts to people with unwanted pregnancies and depression, and to a whole range of issues.

The most moving topic was the plight of the Aboriginal people. I'd never had the chance to explore the history of my people. I knew my mother and Nanna had been through some tough times, but they never really spoke about it. The more I learnt at uni, the more it made me angry. I became aware of Gary Foley and others like him who were devoted to fighting for Aboriginal rights. Although I'd had a basic understanding of these issues, I'd never realised the full extent of the problem and how much anger it generated in these people who were my new friends.

Early in 1992 I took up a position with Australia Post as part of the Olympic Job Opportunities Program, an AOC initiative. I was assigned to work behind the counter at the GPO in Bourke Street Mall. Being part of the workforce was a lot of fun, and having a normal life really appealed to me. Somehow I knew that if my running took me to where I wanted to go, I wouldn't have a normal life for too much longer. The post office was a very multicultural work environment and I loved the way I could blend in with the surroundings, although there were some exceptions.

One particular lunchtime, a queue was starting to form and we were flat out. 'Next, please,' I said to the middle-aged man at the front of the line. He looked at me, then looked away. 'Excuse me, next, please.' The man didn't move. I couldn't believe it. He didn't want to be served by a black person. As soon as the next teller was ready he went straight to him. Sadly, there were many similar incidents, including people not wanting to get into the same lift as me because I was Aboriginal.

On the track, my new attitude and strength-training seemed to be paying dividends. After upsetting national champion Sharon Stewart with a whopping personal best of 52.06s in the 400m at the Victorian championships, I arrived in Adelaide in March for the Barcelona Olympic trials full of confidence. I think Fort and Nick sensed how fired up I was and tried to calm me down before the race. It didn't work. When the gun sounded in the 400m final I pinged from the blocks. I don't know what the time was, but the first 200 metres felt really fast and I was miles ahead as we hit the top of the straight. Then it happened: I hit the wall. Suddenly my legs became cement and I was helpless as Stewart and then Michelle Lock ran past me. Somehow I managed to hold on for third. Despite the pain I felt as I gasped for air, I knew I'd just learnt a valuable lesson on how to run the 400m, and I logged it in the memory bank. Though the race had been a tactical disaster, it hadn't cost me a spot in the team. Finishing third qualified me for the individual 400m and the relay in Barcelona.

While we were in Adelaide, Nick and I were approached about a sponsorship deal. Balarinji Design Studio, a small clothing company run by Aboriginal John Moriarty and his wife, Ros, offered me $2,000 in exchange for wearing their colourful Aboriginal motifs on my racing body suits. I was so excited that someone was actually paying me money to wear clothes. By the time the Olympics came round I also had small deals with Oakley sunglasses and Nike.

Just before I left for Europe, one of my university friends, Lisa, gave me my first Aboriginal flag. I had always admired its colours – black for the people, red for the earth, yellow for the sun – and I promised her I would take it with me to the Olympics. I really wanted to show it to the rest of the world.

CHAPTER 7
REALITY BITES

'What do you think it'll take to win here?'

'Oh, about forty-eight-something,' Nick said.

'Do you reckon I can run that?'

He paused. 'Well, probably not. It's unlikely this year, but you never know, it might happen.'

I kept at him. 'But what if I try really, really hard?'

I was remarkably calm and confident when we arrived in Barcelona, even though the lead-up had been a little more action-packed than any of us had expected. Although I had also qualified for the 200m at the Olympics, we'd decided to focus on the 400m and the 4 x 400m relay. However, my spot in the 400m at Barcelona wasn't as secure as Nick, Fort and I had thought. It turned out that the British AAA titles in Birmingham would decide whether Michelle Lock or I got the third spot. I won this race in a personal best 51.14s, with Lock a close second. I had kept my promise never to be just a relay runner again.

My first task once I got to the athletes' village was to pin my Aboriginal flag on to the wall of the room I was sharing with walker Kerry Saxby. However, it wasn't long before I ran into my first problem. The enormity of being at the Olympics took hold of me. I was overawed and wasn't thinking about my running, about what I needed in order to do the best I could on the track. Some of the track and field athletes didn't march in the opening ceremony, but I was up there in the front row of the Australian team. The crowd went wild when we entered the stadium and you could feel the electricity in the air. It was an amazing high.

I spent the next couple of days exploring the beauty of Barcelona and learning about the Spanish people. I roamed the streets like a tourist and got excited when I brushed past basketball star Charles Barkley. I'd become close friends with high-jumper Tim Forsyth, who had been part of the world junior team in 1990. We'd hung out together during the European lead-up to the Games and I had been by his side when he got the news that his great-grandfather had died back in Australia. It had helped that I could tell him about my experiences dealing with Anne-Marie's death. I dragged Tim along to a major Nike press conference involving Sergei Bubka and Michael Jordan, because I knew he was a big basketball fan. I just wanted to watch because I loved star spotting. Boris Becker caught me staring at him in the village and he looked straight back at me so I sheepishly turned away and scurried off.

I knew the Frenchwoman Marie-José Pérec was the one to beat in the 400m. She had run 49.13s to win the world championships in Tokyo the previous year. When I saw her for the first time close-up at the Games, I couldn't believe how tall and skinny she was. She saw me checking her out and gave me a strange look. I wondered if she knew who I was.

I struck Pérec in my first heat, but that didn't worry me; I was too busy looking around the crowded stadium and taking in my first race at the Olympic Games. It went smoothly, both of us entering the straight together before I eased down on the line to let Pérec win.

Mum had decided she wanted to be in Barcelona to see her nineteen-year-old daughter make history as the first Aboriginal woman to compete at the Olympics. Somehow she had raised the necessary funds, but she wasn't able to get a flight to Spain until the day after my first round. I was on edge waiting for her, and when the team bus pulled up outside the Olympic stadium, I saw her being interviewed by a television crew. 'Mum, Mum!' I screamed out of the window. I was so happy to see her and was a bit teary as we hugged with the cameras all around us. That night Mum asked Nick if we were going to have a party after I'd won the gold medal. She was used to her daughter triumphing and couldn't understand why the Olympics should be any different.

Again I sensed something missing as I walked out for the second round. I was smiling away and seemingly in control of the normal pre-race nerves, but when the gun sounded I was still in my own dream world and subsequently ran a bad race tactically. I had waited too long out the back and left my run late. Despite closing hard and being full of running I only managed to grab fifth spot, which meant I was out of the semi-finals; the girls in the first four places were in. The result didn't really hit home until I found out that Lock, who had received a last-minute call-up to the team when Sharon Stewart withdrew injured, and Renee Poetschka, Australia's other representative and a semi-finalist at the Tokyo world championships, had both cruised through to the semi-finals. I had beaten both of those girls in lead-up races to the Olympics and had run significantly faster than them in my heat, yet my Games were over.

My mother sat me on her lap, ran her fingers through my hair and nursed me like she had when I was a baby. It was weird, because while I realised that my poor performance was probably due to my mind not being 100 per cent on the job, I still needed my mother's reassurance. It was the perfect tonic.

I watched the 400m final from the stands. Pérec won easily in 48.82s, the fastest in the world for four years. We finished seventh in the final of the 4 x 400m relay, but by then I'd had enough. I was exhausted by the whole Olympic experience, although we still managed to party hard because Tim Forsyth had won a bronze medal in the high jump. That night he was so drunk he needed the help of a tree to walk up a tiny hill, and his room was littered with messages written in shaving cream by the other guys. I was so happy for him. I wondered whether I would be the one celebrating next time.

I learnt a lot from my first Olympic experience. Despite being overawed, I knew I would be back. It was this in-built belief I had – that it was my destiny. Even as a kid at school I knew I had this gift. An incident at the Nike Games hospitality centre, the place where all Nike-sponsored athletes could relax during the Games, reminded me of it. It bubbled to the surface when Nick and I were greeted by one of the senior Nike executives. After a minute or so of small talk, he saw one of America's leading athletes walk in and ditched us cold. I got really pissed off with his attitude. I don't know why, and I certainly had no right to – I mean, who the hell was I? – but I wanted to walk over, tap him on the shoulder and say, 'One of these days, what you're doing with her you will be doing with me. One day I'll warrant the same respect.' I couldn't believe the arrogance that for twenty seconds had invaded my mind.

It was something Bruce had come up with. He used to read lots of books about positive thinking and the subconscious. Back in Moura, when I was eleven and had started dreaming about being an Olympic gold medallist, I wrote on a piece of paper I AM THE WORLD'S GREATEST ATHLETE, and then I stuck it above my bed. Bruce had this theory that if you looked at something for long enough every day, it would sink in.

When I got back from Barcelona I found a label on which I wrote 48.60, ATLANTA; I stuck it on the mirror beside my bed. This, or even better, was the time I thought I'd have to run in the final of the 1996 Olympics. It was the time I thought Pérec had run to win in Barcelona; it was only years later that I realised she had in fact run two-tenths slower. Above the Atlanta message I again wrote the words I AM THE WORLD'S GREATEST ATHLETE. I figured that if it had got me this far, maybe it could work again.

Nick and Fort wanted me to focus on the 200m for the 1993 season, to improve my speed and strength. It meant going head to head with Melinda Gainsford, the young sprinter everyone was talking about. Running against the clock I'm not good at; hunting down other people is what motivates me. Gainsford was my challenge for the season. I started training twice a day, and was doing a hundred sit-ups and push-ups a day because I'd found out that was what Debbie Flintoff-King had done to win her Seoul 400m hurdles gold medal. So when I arrived at the opening grand prix meet of the year in Sydney, I was ready. A personal best of 22.62s left Gainsford five metres in my wake and reminded everyone who was number one.

Our next meeting was in Adelaide. In the 100m there was the added bonus of Jane Flemming in the race. I have a long memory, and with Auckland still in my mind I flew the start and clocked 11.43s to beat Gainsford, with Flemming well back. Instead of resting up for the

200m, I was mistakenly summoned for a drug test, so my preparation wasn't the best; consequently I was slightly off my game and Gainsford shot clear by three metres off the bend. The good thing was I didn't panic. I remembered Nick had reminded me that I would have the superior strength in the last part of the race, and on the line I lunged to dead-heat in 22.73s.

Melbourne in late February was next, and one of the biggest crowds I had seen, some fifteen thousand people, had gathered at Olympic Park to see the showdown between 'Australia's two sprint queens', according to the massive sign out the front. I didn't run the 100m, electing to focus solely on the 200m. I knew I was on this night, and as we came round the bend I already had Melinda covered. I strode away and, in a rare show of emotion, punched the air as I crossed the line in another personal best of 22.54s. Oh, yeah! That felt good. I went up to congratulate Melinda, but she was distraught.

A couple of days before the national championships in Brisbane I went home to Mackay with American long-jumper Mike Powell to do a coaching clinic. It was great catching up with all my family and friends, but it probably wasn't the best preparation. I again stood out of the 100m, which Gainsford won easily. She looked strong. As we entered the straight in the 200m, for the first time for the whole season I didn't know whether I could catch her. With thirty metres to go I knew I was gone. For some reason I had nothing there, and she won easily in a personal best of 22.49s. I was furious. To rub salt into my wounds, Jane Flemming ended up winning the $10,000 Female Athlete of the Year award because of my loss to Gainsford.

The domestic season ended with a trip to Toronto for the world indoor championships in March. I had never raced indoors before and I soon realised it didn't suit my long-striding style. I felt claustrophobic. It was no surprise to me that I was disqualified for running out of my lane in the heat. However, I then had to sit and watch as Gainsford and Damien Marsh won silver medals in the 200m and Darren Clark a bronze in the 400m. I decided never to run indoors again. 'This is a waste of my time,' I told Nick. 'I'm not coming back here.'

My chance for redemption came in August, at the world championships in Stuttgart. I had restored my confidence against Gainsford with two victories over her in lead-up races in the British AAAs and the Welsh Games. The rivalry was obviously good for both of us, but it frustrated me how Melinda seemed to take it personally. I liked to leave everything on the track. I was more than happy to be friends with my rivals, but Melinda was different. In Stuttgart we were on a bus coming back from the warm-up track to the village. There was no one else on the bus but still she couldn't talk to me. I made it through to the semi-finals where I ran into Pérec. Again she kept me out of a final by finishing fourth while I was fifth. I was just four-hundredths off my best and I would have made the final if I had been in the other semi. Melinda ended up pulling out because of a hamstring injury.

In the lead-up to the world championships I'd spent six weeks living in an apartment in London with Nick and Fort. I raced several times in Europe during my first real venture overseas, which had been organised by Maurie Plant, a friend of Nick's who worked as a circuit agent. If you wanted to get into a race on the lucrative European circuit, then Maurie was your man. He wheeled and dealed with the directors of all the big meets to get the athletes he represented into races. Maurie had become an integral part of what people were starting to call 'Team Freeman'. It was very weird to hear that term, embarrassing really, because I never thought of the people around me as my own personal team. However, Nick had set things up so that all areas were covered. Nick was the manager, Fort the coach, Maurie the racing agent, Garry Miritis the masseur I visited twice a week, and Dr Peter Fuller provided the medical back-up.

Maurie was a big man with a booming voice and he loved a laugh. I really enjoyed his company as he always had a joke or said something to liven up the moment. Maurie knew everything there was to know about the track and field world, and was an invaluable source of knowledge for me. Maurie's Anglo-Indian wife, Kate, was dark-skinned like me, which became a bond between us. In this male-dominated environment, she was a welcome female face.

After Stuttgart, Maurie urged us to stay in Europe and get more experience. We flew to Sheffield in England where I finished second to the world 400m champion, American Jearl Miles. While we were there, Maurie got word from Australia that his father, who had been ill for a long time, had died. Maurie had just started a new role with the International Amateur Athletics Federation. Despite hours of trying, he was unable to arrange a flight that would get him back to London in time for the upcoming grand prix, which was critical as part of his new job. Instead we went to his parents-in-law's house near London for our own little wake.

As soon as we'd finished unpacking the car, Nick asked me to come upstairs with him. 'Kate just received a phone call from someone in Queensland,' he said. 'Your dad has died.'

No! Not again! Not another loved one! I burst into tears. Part of me thought it was a relief, because he had been sick; another part of me was angry that I had spent so much time apart from him. Even though my dad hadn't been around much, I had always been his little girl and regularly wrote him letters to say how much I loved him. He told me once that it made him cry. Whenever we got the chance to visit Woorabinda, I'd always get him to take me horse riding. It was so much fun. My dad was one of the funniest people I'd ever met. He would always make me laugh. One of my favourite memories of him was from just a few years earlier, at my brother Norman's Aboriginal debutant ball in Brisbane. Dad had travelled down from Woorabinda. I don't know how it happened, but the three of us ended up on the dance floor. Dad and Norman had taken off their jackets and ties and we began doing the 'Chicken Dance'. It was hilarious, arms and legs flying everywhere and the three of us yelling, 'Quack, quack, quack!' It was one of the happiest moments of my life.

'I have to get home,' I said to Nick. 'I have to be there.'

Nick rang around the airlines but nothing was working out. I got more and more frustrated. I was used to him organising everything. This time, though, I didn't believe he was trying hard enough. I don't think he understood the urgency. It soon became obvious that I wasn't going to make it home in time. Maurie had been great and we shared our grief, but I was devastated about missing Dad's funeral. I felt that

Nick had let me down just when I needed him the most.

Nick and Maurie decided that we should press on with my European racing schedule. I had become withdrawn and, despite winning the 200m in Brussels, my mind was a million miles away. My last race was in a tiny town called Rieti, near Rome. I decided to dedicate the run to my father. I let all my emotions out on the track and ran brilliantly, clocking a new personal best of 22.37s.

The flight home to Australia in September gave me a chance to reflect and take stock of my life, which had changed so dramatically in the past three years. I hadn't prepared myself for the moment when everything became real, for the moment when I became a world-class athlete. The pressure of success was starting to mount and I kept asking myself, 'Catherine, do you really want to go ahead with all this?' I thought about all the training, and the weight of the Aboriginal role-model thing. I considered the financial rewards that were starting to come my way, as I had just recently signed a contract with Nike. Was I capable of making this gig work? Did I want it to be my life? The overriding factor in making the decision was that I loved running. I figured while that was still there, I could handle the other stuff. I just needed to give it everything.

I grabbed a piece of scrap paper from my purse and wrote some objectives for the lead-up to the 1994 Commonwealth Games. *My 400m personal best has to improve. More 300, 400 and 500 sessions have to be done and they have to be of good quality. My training sessions have to be of a higher and better quality.* On the last line, I summed up my feelings: *I DO NOT WANT TO FAIL!*

CHAPTER 8
ARTHUR AND THE FLAG

As I walked towards the departure gate, I stopped and turned for one last wave to my parents. I was about to board a plane for Europe, and then on to Canada for the Commonwealth Games. But instead of waving, I held up two fingers and mouthed the words 'two gold'. I couldn't believe it. I had just predicted to my parents that I was going to win two gold medals at the Commonwealth Games.

Where did that confidence come from? It was so strange, but I knew my time had come. I had decided that the world was going to find out a lot more about Catherine Astrid Salome Freeman in Victoria, Canada. My career so far had been a series of small steps. After winning relay gold at the 1990 Commonwealth Games, I'd been a relay reserve at the world championships the following year, made the second round of the 400m at the 1992 Olympics and improved again to the semi-finals at last year's world championships.

During the summer of 1994 I had set a new personal best for the 100m, 11.24s, as my battles with Gainsford intensified. She'd set a new Australian record in the 200m in Hobart in February, which really got under my skin, and I responded two weeks later by reversing the result at the national championships in Sydney. My days as a uni student were over and my Australia Post appearances were getting fewer and fewer because my training and racing schedule had become so full on. I'd gone over to America for several races against Pérec and claimed one significant milestone. In May I broke 51 seconds for the first time when I finished second to the Olympic champion in San José in 50.82s.

If my confidence could get any higher, it did in Europe. The track and field scene was so different over there. It was all glitz and glamour. The races were held in some of the most beautiful cities in the world – Monte Carlo, Rome and Paris. The prize money was out of this world, and Olympic champions such as Pérec charging appearance fees of up to US$50,000 just to race. The constant travelling from country to country took some getting used to, though. Nick and Maurie were adamant that I had to get used to racing week in, week out, because that's what the elite world of athletics was all about. At just 21, I was on a very steep learning curve.

We travelled to Monte Carlo for my last 400m race before the Games. This was Pérec's first race in Europe that season and there were camera crews and photographers all over the track before the race. I was in lane two and couldn't do my pre-race warm-up because of all the camera leads. For ten minutes we all stood around waiting for Pérec to appear and then for everyone to clear the track. Not surprisingly, I started badly, and running into the straight was placed fourth. Halfway down I started to get moving but, as usual, Pérec had flown earlier and I wasn't able to catch her. I knew it was a fast time and I waited anxiously for it to appear on the big screen. First, Pérec in 49.77s. Second, Freeman in 50.18s.

Yes! I've beaten Renee Poetschka's Australian record by a hundredth of a second!

Instead of going to Canada in time for the Games' opening ceremony, we went to Zurich for the biggest grand prix meet of the season. In pouring rain and a biting cold wind I finished fourth in the 200m, beating Pérec, and just a metre behind Merlene Ottey. Nick told me later that Ottey, the favourite for the 200m in Victoria, wasn't going to the Commonwealth Games, preferring the money meets in Europe. He seemed buoyed by the news but, if anything, I was slightly disappointed. I saw it as a privilege to be racing alongside these phenomenal athletes, even when I lost. I figured that racing the best was the only way I'd learn to become the best.

We slipped into Victoria on the Friday and I stayed with Nick in his hotel. On the Saturday morning I made my first appearance in the athletes' village and word quickly spread through the media that I had arrived. I could sense from everybody in the team that there were high expectations for Cathy Freeman. This was uncharted territory. The pressure was on and Nick knew as much, so he took me shopping. Nick hated shopping but he knew it was a good distraction for me.

My first heat was on the Sunday, and I comfortably took that out. Nick wanted me to finish first or second in the semi-final to ensure a good lane in the final. I went stride for stride with Jamaica's Sandie Richards down the straight before switching off over the final few metres to let her win in 51.23s. I was second in 51.57s.

Before I went down for breakfast on the morning of the final, I pulled out my Aboriginal flag from the bottom of my suitcase. *It's time to show the world.* At the breakfast table I asked Nick to arrange it for me. 'Can someone be near the finish line to wave this flag for me so I'll know where they are?' Nick knew not to question my actions. There was no need for mind games or anything like that for motivation today. I was ready, and he knew it. This was my race, and no one was going to stop me telling the world how proud I was to be Aboriginal.

Somewhere deep inside, I'd absorbed all the pain and suffering my people had endured and turned it into a source of strength. Before I left for the Commonwealth Games, I had my picture taken by the *Herald Sun* in front of an Aboriginal mural on St George's Road, Thornbury, in Melbourne. The mural depicts Aboriginal slavery with two black men chained together around their necks. The images made me sick, but they were a graphic illustration of the atrocities committed against my people.

What sort of human being condones taking little children away from their parents and placing them into a totally different society, hell-bent on changing their heritage? My own grandmother didn't know her mother. She was taken away when she was eight years old. She wasn't allowed to speak her native tribal tongue and spent most of her life in missions that were effectively prisons, where you had to fight for a pass to be allowed to leave.

Can you imagine being eight years old and being taken away from your mother?

Can you imagine walking past your child or your mother in the street and not being allowed to talk to them?

Can you imagine people coming into your home, burning it down and destroying everything?

Can you imagine somebody poisoning the water in your taps to try to kill you?

That is what happened to my people.

All this pain inspires me. I want to be a freedom fighter. I want to break down the stereotype of Aboriginal people as alcoholics and criminals. Alcoholism is something that is close to me, with my father and other relatives affected by the disease. I look at these people and I know they have so much more to offer, but they are a product of what has happened many years before. They are trapped, and their spirits are broken. On my father's mission, it even got to the point where the officials paid people in alcohol instead of money. How could they do that?

Every time I go home or out into the bush, I see the pain everywhere, the low self-esteem. I feel this amazing affinity to my people and I carry around what has happened to them in my heart. I want the kids to look up to me and see that a girl with the same colour skin and background as them can break down all the barriers and make it in the white man's world. I want them to think, 'If she can do it, why can't I do it?' Right then I wanted the elders in the outback to be sitting around their fires and shaking their heads, talking about how they never thought they'd see a black person walking around the Commonwealth Games stadium carrying an Aboriginal flag. Most of all I wanted my family to feel proud. *I hope you can see me up there, Anne-Marie.*

As the starter called us to our blocks I adjusted my lucky charm, a black, red and gold scrunchie I was using as a hair tie. Nick's pre-race advice had been to make sure I ran right through to the line. I had a tendency to coast to the finish because I always only did just enough to win. It had been my style ever since I was a little girl at primary school where, amazingly, I didn't hold one school record.

I was in lane three with my two main threats on my outside: Nigeria's Fatima Yusuf in four and Sandie Richards in five. For the first two hundred metres everything remained in order, then halfway round the home bend I went for it. All the adrenaline that had been building up for the race was suddenly released and I found myself three metres clear at the top of the straight.

I'm going to do it. I'm going to fly my flag.

With thirty metres to go, I felt a change come over me. My body was starting to tire, the early surge beginning to take its toll.

Don't worry. Focus on the finish line, Freeman. Just get past that line.

With a couple of metres left, I still couldn't hear or sense anyone near me. I had done it. Yusuf dived late, but it was my gold medal in a new Games record time of 50.38s. As Renee Poetschka, who had finished fifth, came over to give me a hug, I scanned the crowd. Where was my flag? Then I saw one of Nick's work colleagues sprinting down the stairs with it. I took the flag, draped it over my shoulders like a cape and trotted off. I wanted to shout, 'Look at me, look at my skin! I'm black and I'm the best!' There was no more shame.

The moment was better than I could have ever imagined, even though in my dreams I was doing it at the Olympic Games. That will come in time, I told myself.

I was given an Australian flag by a woman and I placed it around my other shoulder to show that the two belonged side by side. I knew a lot of people would be happy to see me win, black Australians and white Australians, and this way – with both flags – they could all share this great moment with me.

As soon as I saw Nick he congratulated me, but he also reminded me to start focusing on the 200m. Only half the job was done. I stayed in the village that night and shared the victory with Tim Forsyth and a few of the guys. When I woke up the next morning, there was a message on my phone from Nick warning me that a media pack was waiting for me outside. The Australian chef de mission, Arthur Tunstall, had released a statement criticising me for carrying the Aboriginal flag; he had said I wasn't allowed to do it again if I won the 200m. I had about fifty metres to walk to the warm-up track and Nick told me to put my head down and not answer any questions. The only way the issue could be inflamed was if I said anything. I put on a white baseball cap, which I pulled down low over my eyes, grabbed my back pack and headed for the door. Nick was right: there were about fifty journalists with cameras and tape recorders, and as soon as I stepped outside they swarmed.

'Cathy, what about the flag? Are you worried about Arthur Tunstall?'

As I got to the gate, I turned and looked at one particular guy who had just asked, 'If you win the two hundred will you carry the flag again, even though you might be banned?'

I smiled. 'Yeah, I suppose so.'

Of course I'm going to carry my flag.

On the afternoon of the 200m final I was on my way to the dining room in the village when I saw Tunstall walking towards me. *C'mon, Arthur, what have you got to say to me?* I kept my head down and he paused, then wished me good luck. Not a word about the flag.

No one had actually told me I couldn't carry the flag. Apart from Tunstall, everyone seemed to be supportive. What sealed the whole episode for me was a letter of congratulations from the then Prime Minister Paul Keating saying, in part, 'In the circumstances your carrying of both flags was an important reminder of your pride in your heritage as an Aboriginal Australian.'

Nick's pre-race pep talk for the 200m focused on not worrying, even if the favourite, Nigerian Mary Onyali, seemed to be a long way in front of me in the straight.

'No matter if it looks like you're gone,' he said. 'Remember, Onyali gets the staggers all the time at the end of her two-hundred-metre races.'

I was in lane three with Melinda Gainsford on my inside, Pauline Davis from the Bahamas in four and Onyali in five. My starts had always been my problem, and again I was slow out. As we entered the straight Melinda had already caught me, with Onyali at least three metres ahead.

Wake up, Freeman. You've got to go now!

With eighty metres to go I started to get moving. I edged past Gainsford and started out after Onyali. Nick had been right, because with twenty metres to go Onyali started to wobble. She was within reach.

Oh, my God. It feels like I'm running downhill. I'm flying.

With three strides to go I gobbled Onyali up to take the gold medal. It had been the most amazing race of my life. I had never before experienced that feeling of flight, and when I looked at the clock I wasn't surprised to see 22.25s beside my name, which was not only a new personal best but also a new Games and Australian record.

I couldn't believe what I had just done. I couldn't stop laughing. But where were my flags? I remembered that team management had arranged for one of their officials, Geoff Rowe, and my friend Tiffany Cherry to be sitting together with both flags. As I went across to them I was wary about which flag to pick up first, because I didn't want any more controversy. 'Geoff, make sure I've got them both together,' I said. He tied the flag ends together and I set off with both firmly around me. I started laughing again.

Hey, world! If you missed it the first time, here I am again, black and proud of it.

Melinda joined me on the victory lap. She had won the bronze medal by a hundredth of a second and had her own Australian flag draped over her shoulders. I was so excited for her. Despite what we'd been through, I was happy to share this moment with her.

The media horde seemed to have tripled by the time I got to them. Every question was about the flag. I switched off, just answering all the different questions in the same way. This was the part I disliked about these big events – dealing with the media, then having to go through a drug test, and everyone wanting a piece of you along the way. I felt smothered and needed to get out of there, but Nick was adamant I had to wait around at the Channel 10 studios to do an interview.

Just as I was about to do my block after an hour of waiting, in through the doors came Mum and Bruce. It was perfect. Channel 10 had flown them over at the last minute and I couldn't stop yelling with delight as I hugged them. But we kept the celebrations in check because I still had two relays to run. There was talk in the press that I could win four gold medals, but rarely do things go according to plan with Australian relays.

Surprisingly, the team relay coaches had me run the second leg in the 4 x 100m relay, where we could only manage the silver medal behind Nigeria. I did anchor the 4 x 400m relay an hour later, but found myself in a tangle with 150 metres to go. England's Sally Gunnell was leading, Sandie Richards was second on the outside and Fatima Yusuf had moved up on my outside, blocking me in. The 400m relay is so different from the individual event because after the first lap the lane positions no longer apply. I was absolutely jogging and knew I had to get out of this position in a hurry. I angled out of the pocket and in the process accidentally spiked Yusuf's knee. It was a very slight bump but she threw up her arm in dramatic fashion to make sure everyone saw it. By the time I got around her, Gunnell was leading by three metres as we entered the straight. I owned this track so I knew I could get her, and I did, with a metre to spare.

As I crossed the line I threw up my arms in triumph. Three gold medals! I'd been one out with my prediction. The euphoria only lasted a couple of minutes though. Nigeria was quick to protest over my alleged 'push' on Yusuf. I didn't think it was a major deal as it happened all the time in 800m and 1500m races. I felt terrible when the decision to disqualify us was announced. I was also frustrated because none of the coaches had explained the rules and procedures to us. I'd run plenty of 4 x 100m relays, but the 4 x 400m was still a relatively new event for me. If I'd known my actions could have been grounds for protest, I would have been more careful. I simply didn't know that slight contact was grounds for a protest in 400m relays. I felt bad that I already had my gold medals and the other girls on the team might never get another chance to win one. 'We're still the best,' I said to a teary Lee Naylor. 'We just won't get a medal for it.' They understood it had been a tough call on me to be disqualified, but it didn't ease their pain. Ironically, Nigeria was also disqualified and England took the gold.

Everyone else went home, but Maurie and Nick wanted me to go back to Europe for two more races. Two plane trips in two days finally got me to Paris for the grand prix final and another clash with Pérec. I was exhausted and wasn't expecting too much when I lined up on her outside in lane six. After just over a hundred metres, she was already alongside me. My plan was not to let her get past me for as long as I could, so I accelerated. I kept with her entering the straight, but the effort eventually took its toll and I started to overstride near the finish, allowing Pérec victory in front of her adoring home crowd. As I desperately gasped for air at the finish line, I looked for the clock. 50.04s. Wow! Another massive personal best and another Australian record!

A sense of fulfilment swept over me that night. I had exceeded my own expectations. I was a Commonwealth Games gold medallist and ranked number two in the world for 400m and number four in the 200m. I had well and truly arrived in the big time.

It wasn't until I got home and saw the thousands of letters and faxes that I began to comprehend the full impact of having carried the Aboriginal flag at the Games. 'I'm ninety-four years old and I live in Cape York,' one woman wrote. 'I've seen all these things happen with stolen children, being moved from our homes, seen cruelty and sadness, and when I saw you run around with that flag, for the first time in my life I felt it was worth it all to be an Aborigine.' The letter summed up everything, and tears welled in my eyes as I read it.

The demands from newspapers, magazines, television and radio stations were overwhelming: Nick's phone never stopped ringing. Little Aboriginal kids would come up to me when I visited schools and say, 'Look, I'm Cathy Freeman', and sprint around the playground.

On the business side, sponsors were suddenly queuing up. Telstra and Ford had been the main partners of the Games team and they'd chosen me to be the face of the team, which meant I did a television ad and received a car to drive around in. Nick had just signed a big new deal with Nike that extended beyond the 1996 Olympics. Kellogg's even wanted to put my face on one of their breakfast cereal boxes.

Nick and I were invited to afternoon tea with the Prime Minister. I didn't know what to call him – Prime Minister, Mr Keating or Paul – and ended up using all three during our twenty-minute get-together. He told us he had been a good swimmer at school. Although we had a pleasant time, this sort of official function wasn't my cup of tea.

That October, Nick and I escaped to the Top End for a much-needed holiday. It was a chance to take a breath and assess what we'd been through and what lay ahead. Athletically I had made great strides, and everything was now focused on further improvment for the 1996 Atlanta Olympics. On a personal level, though, our relationship was changing. I had sensed, even before the Commonwealth Games, that something was wrong. Nick was no longer my boyfriend, more my controller. He had taken on so many roles in my life – father-figure, older brother, friend, lover, coach, manager, motivator, dietician – and the lines had become blurred. He was very protective and didn't like me seeing my girlfriends. I was convinced that he was obsessed with Freeman the athlete, not Freeman the woman. It had reached a point where I knew I needed to take a break.

We had flown to the Kimberleys and were staying on a beautiful property. After a day of crocodile watching and fishing, our hosts had set up a candlelit dinner for us on the balcony under the stars. It was very romantic, and after some small talk Nick started to talk about the future. As I looked out on the beautiful night sky, I suddenly realised where the conversation was heading. *My God, he's going to ask me to marry him.*

'Don't ask me, Nick,' I said.

He seemed shocked, and then he quickly changed the conversation. I knew from that moment that our personal relationship was doomed. I'd told him several times that I loved him, and I had, but I was young and he had been my first serious boyfriend. We were now growing apart, and the only thing keeping us together was our joint pursuit of my Olympic dream.

CHAPTER 9
Madness in Gothenburg

I had become a prisoner.

That's what my life started to feel like in the months after the 1994 Commonwealth Games. Everywhere I went, people recognised me. They'd whistle at me as I walked down the street, or stop me in shops and ask for an autograph. It was madness. I loved dancing, and Nick and I would often go to a nightclub, but now we'd only last ten minutes before being mobbed. It started to affect my personality. I began to feel uncomfortable around people, especially in groups, and even resorted to buying a wig of long, dark-brown hair to wear when I went shopping.

Ironically, there was one positive spin-off: no more discrimination problems at Australia Post. There weren't any customers snubbing the black girl behind the counter now; in fact, everyone wanted to be served by me. It got to the point where I had to be moved to the main office and a role in the public relations department. That was weird, given my feelings about the media, yet here I was writing press releases. I worked alongside a guy called Mark, who was really helpful, and we got on famously. Often we'd get to go on daytrips, such as going out to interview a local artist about a new stamp release for the in-house magazine. Mark would always let me drive and we'd talk and laugh all the way. But it was also a frustrating job, because there were times when I didn't really know what I was doing there.

The 1995 domestic season was a bit of a disaster. I came back to training four kilos, or about nine pounds, overweight – I was usually 51kg, about eight stone – and had really lost my drive. I'd been through so much over the last four years that I felt like I needed time out. Gainsford was beating me every time and I was just longing to get overseas and away from all the attention. News of Gainsford's victory in the 200m at the world indoor championships didn't help. As I was coming home from training I heard Neil Mitchell on radio station 3AW say, 'Melinda Gainsford's gone right past Cathy Freeman.'

Nick came up with the University of California in Los Angeles, the same track Pérec trained on, as the location for our training camp. We took off in May, and Mark Holcombe, a world junior 800m finalist, came along as my training partner. Fort and Nick had realised that I needed to be pushed in training and that most girls were unable to keep up with the specialised training programme I was now used to. They knew I was better at chasing, and that's what the stronger guys made me do.

We saw Pérec a few times and I chatted with her briefly, but you couldn't call it friendly. One day her coach, John Smith, yelled from the other side of the track, 'Don't speak to the enemy.' It was such bullshit, but that was the way the Americans and Pérec liked to play it. They couldn't relate to my easy-going, laid-back personality.

It was in LA that Arthur Tunstall reared his ugly head again. Word got to us from Australia about a joke he'd told about me and famous Aboriginal boxer Lionel Rose, along the lines that we'd pinch the pearly gates from heaven given half a chance. I couldn't believe it. I'd done all this work to try to prove to people that Aborigines can achieve great things, and here was this stupid man reviving the old cliché that all blacks are petty thieves. Several Australian television crews arrived at the track wanting comment and I told them I had no respect for Tunstall. Two weeks later he released an apology, but the damage had been done.

Nick and I made a quick return home to Brisbane in June for my brother Norman's twenty-first birthday. Nick and I had been clashing a lot, and everything boiled over at the party. It was about midnight, and I wanted to keep partying with all my friends and family.

'You're not going out until four a.m., drinking and carrying on,' Nick said to me. 'The world championships are only a couple of months away.'

Everything with Nick revolved around training and racing. He didn't understand that my family came before anything else.

'What will one night matter?' I yelled at him.

But he wouldn't budge, and eventually I relented and again missed out on just being myself. I didn't want to be Cathy Freeman the super-star athlete that night; I just wanted to be Catherine Freeman the sister, the daughter, the cousin, the black girl going crazy on the dance floor. Sadly, he could never understand that.

The final race before the Gothenburg world championships was at Monte Carlo – one last crack at Pérec. I'd been plagued by a niggly calf injury and was in desperate need of a confidence boost. I drew lane three, on the inside of Pérec, and as we moved into the home bend I sensed that something was wrong. Her usual style was to push it from the start and set up such a gap that it was inevitably too hard to pick her up. This time I was right next to her, so I surged with 150 metres to go. She couldn't go with me and I cruised home to score my first vic-tory over the great French runner. It was her first loss over the distance in five years.

I was so excited, although the victory was tarnished when I realised Pérec had virtually given up after I passed her and finished fifth, with fellow Aussie Renee Poetschka getting second. Gothenburg couldn't come quickly enough. I had shattered Pérec's illusion of greatness and was convinced I could do it again. I became obsessed with beating her. When we got to Gothenburg, I began to have trouble sleeping. I was consumed with winning the world title. I could feel myself losing my mind. Even when I went to the toilet I was thinking about it.

Getting through to the final was not a problem, but being ready for the final was a whole different thing. Again I had hardly slept, and I woke early. The race wasn't until seven p.m. so I tried to kill time by ringing my mum, not once but twice, to see if hearing her voice would calm me down. It didn't. I was clearly on edge and I snapped at Nick when he tried to help. 'You don't know what it's like, you don't know how it feels.' It felt like the day was going on forever and I constantly looked at the clock. When we left the apartment and headed to the track, I was walking so fast that Nick and Fort couldn't keep up. I was on a mission.

I saw Pérec over the other side of the warm-up track and was struck by how calm she looked. Fort tried to run through the race plan with me but I wasn't really listening. I didn't need to: I knew how to beat her now and the others weren't even a factor. When we got on to the track I saw my Aboriginal flag in the crowd. Instead of thinking about the race, I was thinking about what it was going to be like to be the world champion.

As we were called to the blocks, I froze. 'On your marks,' the starter said. Then it hit me. *I am shitting myself.* The gun went off and I bolted. I went as hard as I could.

It felt exhilarating to be moving so quickly. As we headed down the back straight, I had already blown most of them away.

I can win this. I'm going to be the world champion.

At the top of the straight I was level with Pérec.

OK, time to do what you did to her in Monte Carlo. Go, girl!

With eighty metres to go, something happened. It was a feeling I hadn't experienced in a long time. No. Please, no. I hit the wall.

I'm not going to be world champion.

It was like I was going in slow motion. My legs and arms felt like cement. With thirty metres remaining I could only watch as Pauline Davis and then Jearl Miles ran past me.

I'm not even going to get a medal.

I'd stuffed up completely, in exactly the same way as I had at the Olympic trials in Adelaide three years earlier. I couldn't believe I'd done it again. My body was in so much pain. As I made my way back through the mixed zone, I could tell by the looks on some of the Australian team officials' faces that I had disappointed them. Though I was shattered, somewhere in the back of my mind there was a growing sense of relief. It was over. For the past week I'd driven myself crazy thinking about this race.

Nick tried hard to hide his disappointment. 'I think you showed today you'll be a champion one day because you took it on,' he said. 'You didn't have the strength or condition to do it, but you had the heart to do it. You ran to try to win.'

Despite beating Miles and Davis in subsequent races in Europe, I just couldn't get the disappointment of Gothenburg out of my head. It seemed to have affected Nick as well, and I was glad when the season finally came to a close. We had one final business appointment on the way home, at Nike headquarters in Portland, Oregon. All of Nike's major stars had been called to an Olympic summit to outline plans for Atlanta. It was pretty intimidating being around guys like Michael Jordan, Michael Johnson and Carl Lewis.

One night I was about to go to bed when the phone rang in our room. It was two Nike girls I'd met earlier in the day and they wanted me to go out for a drink. I wasn't going to, and then they put Michael Johnson on the phone. In his deep voice he said, 'Cathy, you're coming out. C'mon.' How could I say no to Michael Johnson? Anyway, Nick was out somewhere with other Nike guys.

'Yeah, I'm coming,' I quickly said, and rushed downstairs.

We walked down the street to a bar and Michael got tequila for everybody. I'd never had one before and turned to the group, asking, 'How do you drink it?' This blond-haired guy who worked for Nike took my glass and said he'd show me. His name was Alexander Bodecker, but everyone called him Sandy. It turned out that he was a big track and field fan and we started talking and then had a dance. He was a very relaxed and funny guy. He offered to show me around the bar and we soon found a quiet corner to talk. We talked for hours, and it didn't strike me until we said goodbye that he was keen for the night to continue. I declined.

Nick had got wind of my visit to the bar and the next morning questioned me about Alexander. I told him nothing had happened, even though the name Alexander Bodecker was certainly now stuck in my mind.

Things degenerated further when Nick and I got back to Australia, and in November I told him I wanted to move out. We simply had nothing left to talk about other than athletics. I was intrigued by my mystery Nike friend from America and decided to write him a letter. Only a day after I sent it, a letter from Alexander arrived. He was very keen to keep in contact and I felt the same way.

Nick and I had just bought a house in Richmond Terrace, Richmond, only a block from Miller Street, so I moved in there with my friend Tiff Cherry. I wasn't ready to break away completely, not with the Olympics the following year. Nick and I agreed on this and we actually began to get along better, sharing meals most nights. He regularly stayed over. When Nick bought another house in Richmond, in Stanley Street, we decided to move into it together. My breakaway had lasted less than two months.

All my energies, negative and positive, were focused on chasing my Olympic dream in Atlanta. Nothing else mattered.

CHAPTER 10
THE SPRINTER'S MARATHON

If Fort told me to do fifty sit-ups, I would do sixty; if training started at eight a.m., I'd be there at 7.45. I was obsessed. I knew that to achieve my dream I simply had to train harder. I became a perfection-ist. I'd finish my warm-up lap on the very blade of grass I'd started from. There was no cutting corners. My stepfather's favourite saying was 'If you're going to do something, you've got to do it properly.' Now I was starting to put Bruce's words into action.

The more experience you get, the more motivated you become, and I knew I now had that desire to do things better than before. Gothenburg was still a major mental hurdle. I had several sessions with sports psychologist Jeff Simons because I was worried about the next time I lined up on the blocks in a big race. His message helped, but really I was in a holding pattern waiting for that day to come again.

After three months of solid training I was bursting at the seams to get back into racing and was happy to hear that Nick had arranged for Sandie Richards, the bronze medallist at the 1994 Commonwealth Games, to come out to Australia. There could be no cruising – as some-times tended to be the case early in the domestic season – with Richards around. She was one of the best in the world, so I had to be ready.

Our first clash was at the Melbourne Track Classic at Olympic Park on a perfect night in late February 1996. When I warmed up on the oval across the road with my training partner, Pat Seal, I felt really light and could sense electricity flowing through my body. I knew I was ready for something special.

Richards was on my outside in lane five and she always went out hard in her races. I kept in touch with her until the bottom of the back straight, and then made my move. It felt like I glided up the straight with the biggest crowd I had ever seen at Olympic Park going crazy. As I crossed the line I looked straight at the electronic clock: 49.85s. I had done it! I punched the air with joy and started jumping around and laughing. I had finally done it. I had become the first Australian woman to break the fifty-second barrier.

As I jogged a victory lap to show my appreciation to the wonderful crowd I spotted several Aboriginal flags. I was so pumped. Those girls overseas had better take me seriously now. I had known that until I could show I could run a sub-fifty I wasn't going to be able to challenge Pérec. This now put me well and truly in that ballpark. When I spoke to Nick later, as usual I tried hard to find a negative about the run. 'Do you think I've peaked too soon?' I asked. He laughed, and said that running 49 seconds was just the start of things to come. I hoped so.

I claimed the 100m and 200m titles at the national championships in the absence of the injured Melinda Gainsford, and then ran 50.21s at the grand prix final in Brisbane to win the Female Athlete of the Year award. With an intense six-week training block in Atlanta coming up, I jumped at the chance to compete in a 400m professional race at the Stawell Gift. It was the change of pace I needed, a bit of fun in a beautiful little town in central Victoria. I loved the bush and anything to do with nature, so driving through the picturesque country with the smell of the gum trees everywhere instantly soothed my mind and soul. Running at Stawell on the grass track brought back memories of my childhood at Melaleuca Park in Mackay. I called it pure running. While some people didn't enjoy the handicap format, I loved the thrill of the chase, especially when I was in top shape.

On the start line I adjusted the backmarker's red sash and cleaned my wraparound sunglasses. I scanned the field to try to get my bearings and find the front markers. This wasn't as easy as it sounds because they were a long way away – about forty metres around the bend. With no lanes, no stagger and no starting blocks, this was going to be interesting. The race was all about control and not panicking. After two hundred metres I had yet to catch any of the front markers and could sense that the crowd had given up on me. When you race on tartan tracks you tend to float across the surface; on grass you get the opportunity to really dig the spikes into the turf and use the power of your body. It is an awesome feeling, and as I was approaching the final sweeping bend I was flying. I started picking up the girls one by one. The home straight at Stawell is not your regulation one hundred metres, it's a lot less, and when I came wide on the final turn the leader was still fifteen metres ahead. With each stride I could hear the crowd booming. As they were lifting, I was lifting, and again I experienced that floating sensation. One girl veered out and tried to elbow me out of the way, but nothing was going to stop me this day. Like a good racehorse I seem to have a nose for the finish line, and in the last couple of strides I drove and caught the final girl.

The crowd went nuts. I knew this was one of the best moments of my sporting life. It felt like I had been running on air, like something was moving me around the track. I was still gasping for breath when a television interviewer told me my time. I thought she said 54.8 seconds, but it was actually 50.48. I did a victory lap and didn't want the moment to end. I loved the feeling of knowing that, with the Olympics just over three months away, I was in the best shape of my life.

The moment we arrived in Atlanta in April, I knew it was a recipe for disaster. For six weeks Nick and I, Fort and Mark Holcombe, my training partner on this trip, had to stay in a tiny two-bedroom apartment. Nick and I slept upstairs in one room; Mark was on a sofa bed in the second bedroom, which was only separated from the lounge room by a divider; and Fort slept on another couch in the lounge. I hated being around men all the time. For years I'd shared houses with them and here I was again, living in their pockets. I felt claustrophobic, and Nick's intensity and manic control over everything I did was really driving me crazy. He had stepped up his role as the food police, and it was so infuriating. I was forced to sneak out and buy some chocolate donuts to fulfil my cravings.

There was tension everywhere. It escalated when Sonia O'Sullivan, Ireland's 5,000m world champion, began ringing the apartment looking for Nick. She was splitting up with her coach and having problems with her preparation. It didn't bother me that she was ringing Nick for advice, but she would never talk to me – it was always urgent that she spoke to Nick. He was very secretive if I questioned him about what she wanted and I knew there was more to it than he was telling me. When I pushed him one day in the apartment he went wild and started packing his suitcase.

'Right, that's it! I'm going,' he said.

'Fine,' I yelled back at him.

Fort went after Nick and took him to an Irish pub down the road to talk him out of it. Mark turned to me and said, 'Do you want to stay or go home?'

'We're not going anywhere. We're training.'

I half suspected the dramatic walkout had been one of Nick's games. He returned later that day after a long talk with Fort and once again we agreed to put everything aside until after the Olympics.

Through all this turmoil my training at Atlanta had been sensational. I knew this not only because Nick and Fort weren't complaining, but also because of the look on Maurie Plant's face when he arrived in town. We were all down at the track and I had just finished my warm-up, so I took off my tracksuit. Maurie took one look at me in my little tights and sports top and went, 'Ohhhhhh.' I was ripped and he'd never seen me in that sort of shape – his eyes nearly popped out of his head. When he realised I was looking at him, he turned quickly to Nick and pretended to be talking. I'd always used other people's reactions as guides throughout my career. Even back at primary school, I knew I was a good runner because of the excitement my running generated in adults. Now that the Olympics were only a couple of months away, Maurie's look was the confirmation I needed that I was ready.

My first race in the US was against Pérec, and you could tell we were both just sizing each other up. I ran the race in a way that was the total opposite of Gothenburg. I was very slow out, so much so that I cruised home with plenty in the tank. Pérec won in 50.17s, I was second in 50.39. I then raced in Eugene, Oregon, and afterwards Nick and I went to visit the Nike headquarters in Portland. It is an enormous complex, like a village of buildings, and I was following Nick around from meeting to meeting.

'Hello, Miss Freeman,' a familiar voice boomed as I got to the top of the stairs.

I turned around, and sitting down opposite the stairwell was Alexander Bodecker. I immediately tensed up.

'Oh, hi,' I managed to get out. I could sense Nick's eyes burning through the back of my head. 'I got your letters.'

'I didn't get yours,' he said.

I half laughed and suddenly wished I could click my fingers and disappear. Alexander obviously sensed how uncomfortable the moment was and quickly told me where his office was 'if I wanted to visit'. Later, I slipped away and went looking for Alexander's office but he wasn't there – which, in the circumstances, was probably a good thing. I couldn't deal with any of it, with the Atlanta countdown at six weeks.

The previous year Nick and I had bought a house in Hampton Hill, London. It was a perfect location for us, near training facilities and surrounded by parks. We'd been able to do this because the demand for my services had grown so much in the corporate world. My sponsors now included Qantas, Schweppes, Telstra, Ford, Australia Post, Nike, News Ltd and Channel 7. The London base was one of several real estate purchases we'd undertaken, the most significant being a new house for my parents in Brisbane. I deliberately left the business side to Nick because it still blew my mind that people would pay large sums of money to be associated with Cathy Freeman.

I was getting paranoid about injury and had eased training for a week because of a sore foot. My next race was in Gateshead on England's north-east coast, and on the trip up I decided it was time to bury the ghost of Gothenburg. I had to stop being scared about what had happened last year and simply go for it. I had to push myself to run the first two hundred metres fast. If I didn't do it now, I never would. The last thing I wanted to be worrying about in an Olympic final was hitting the wall.

Conditions weren't perfect in Gateshead – there was a very blustery wind – but I was happy to see leading British athlete Sally Gunnell in the field. At the gun, I flew out of the blocks and pushed the first two hundred metres as planned. As the bend approached I closed my eyes and attacked. Yes! No wall. I cruised into the straight and just kept going to win by fifteen metres from Gunnell in 49.96s. I was so happy I'd finally nailed it. After four years of running 400s I had just run the almost perfect race. The struggle had always been in my mind because running the 400m is a balancing act. If you go out too hard, like I did at Gothenburg, you blow up; if you go out too slow, you're going to lose. Finding the balance and building the confidence takes a long time and requires a fair bit of bravery.

My greatest asset is my ability to relax. Some people call the 400m the sprinter's marathon, and other runners often joke about why I decided to specialise in the hardest event on the programme. In the 100m or 200m it's just a matter of going hell for leather, but in the 400m tactics are critical. You have to find within yourself the ability to cruise at high speed for 250 metres and then be able to go up a gear and attack the final 150. Backing your own judgement is crucial. You need to know instinctively what is too much and what's not enough in the first part of a 400m race. That knowledge only comes over time and through many hours of practice. No one can write it down on a whiteboard, you just have to feel it.

Reacting to the conditions of the race is also important, whether that be someone coming up on your inside or the weather. Not losing your cool if someone challenges you in the back straight is harder than it sounds. Your instinct is to race them right there and try to keep ahead, but the problem is you can't go from third gear to fifth in a couple of strides. This is where being relaxed is so important. You have to be able to stick to your race tactics and have the patience to know that if you do, you'll get that girl who just went past. Like most things in life, the fastest way to learn to do it right is to completely stuff it up a few times. Gothenburg had been my biggest lesson; Gateshead was my graduation.

A mild bout of food poisoning interrupted my preparation for the Oslo grand prix. Despite still not feeling well I clocked 49.81s, a new Australian record. This made me even more convinced that I was damn fit. Nick had collected a number of Pérec's races on video so we spent a day watching them, as well as some of my races, to formulate a plan to topple the French queen. To have a chance of beating her, the key was to be within touch after two hundred metres, because that's where Pérec won most of her races – by flying early and breaking the hearts of her opponents.

In my last race before the Olympics, at Crystal Palace on 12 July, I wanted to have a practice run of my Pérec plan. I started brilliantly, and by the end of the first bend I was already at good speed. I maintained that down the back straight and then went up a gear around the final bend and had the race won Pérec-style at the top of the straight. I felt very relaxed, and the time was another personal best and Australian record: 49.59s. I was ready.

CHAPTER 11
THE BIG MISTAKE

I decided to keep a Games diary when we arrived in Atlanta. On day one I wrote down my objectives for the next eight days: avoid media, crowds and stress; more importantly, avoid another Gothenburg.

It definitely helped that I'd stayed in Atlanta a few months earlier. I knew my way around the city and was at ease with my surroundings. It was a very different experience from my first Olympics in Barcelona. This time I felt in control.

Nick always liked to use mind games to motivate me in training. He knew how ultra-competitive I was so he'd always come up with remarks my competitors might have said or results from overseas to which he knew I would react. Nick also liked to come up with something that would stick in my mind for our race plan. Over a hot chocolate in a café next to Phipps Plaza, a fancy shopping precinct I liked to visit, Nick explained how he had written out a six-point race plan. I told him that was too much and we needed to condense it.

'What about coming up with an acronym, like in that Nicolas Cage film we saw?' I suggested.

The film was *Kiss of Death*. We'd first seen it in LA the year before and then hired it on video in London more recently. The two main actors in the film have a long discussion about inventing a kind of acronym for themselves. I liked the idea.

After a few minutes, Nick came up with the word FLAG. He wrote the explanation down on the back of a Visa card receipt: '1st 100m – Fly away from your blocks, quick over first 30m; 2nd 100m – Leg speed, quick, quick, quick; 3rd 100m – Attack; Home straight – Grind every last ounce of energy out of you all the way through the line.' He then wrote, 'Run your own race, stay calm, no mistakes.'

'I'm not sure about "Grind", it feels like slow and under pressure,' I said. 'You're trying hard but not getting anywhere, that's what grind means to me. What about G for Go?'

But Nick didn't want me to be running slowly early in the race waiting for the 'Go' signal at the top of the straight, so we decided both could work.

Bruce and Mum had come over to Atlanta and were staying near our apartment with an African-American Baha'i family. I took Mum to the opening ceremony of the Games and sat in the stands with her. It seemed to drag on for ever and, unfortunately, by the time Muhammad Ali was lighting the flame we were already home and climbing into bed. I couldn't afford to stay out any longer. My friend Peta Powell had also come over, which was a perfect diversion for me. We sunbaked by the swimming pool at the apartment, went shopping together and just talked about girlie things. I loved being able to do that again.

I checked into the athletes' village on the Wednesday, two days before the first heat. I liked getting away from Nick and everyone, and being around the other athletes got me into race mode and helped me relax. The other bonus was that my masseur, Garry Miritis, was with the Australian team and based in the village. For the past five years he'd been treating my little aches and pains and he'd become a fixture in my pre-race routine.

My first venture into the Olympic stadium for the opening round of the 400m was an enjoyable one. I wasn't nervous, and I even spotted my parents in the crowd near the 100m start. I ran a controlled race and finished second to Nigerian Olabisi Afolabi in 51.99s. I met Nick for dinner and then watched Susie O'Neill on TV as she won gold in the 200m butterfly. I really got a buzz out of watching fellow Aussies kicking arse and couldn't believe the American broadcasters didn't show Kieren Perkins' 1,500m gold medal swim.

The next morning my preparation for the second round was rocked when I found out a bomb had exploded in Centennial Olympic Park, killing two people. Oh, my God. Where were Mum and Bruce? Where was Nick? I frantically tried to contact them and eventually got on to Nick, who reassured me everyone was safe. By the time my second-round race came around I had managed to get my focus back. I won it in the fast time of 50.43s and was pleasantly surprised by how easy it felt.

Nick and I had established an after-race routine where I'd go and eat with him back at the apartment so I could debrief and Nick could quash the negatives that inevitably crept into my mind after each race. As the semi-final wasn't until eight p.m., and we both still felt uneasy about the Gothenburg experience, Nick took me to the zoo to distract me for the afternoon. By the time we got back to the village my mind was relaxed and ready to switch on. I'd decided to wear a special pair of running shoes with the Aboriginal flag on them. I had brought a flag to Atlanta – Aboriginal on one side and Australian on the other – but it was against Olympic rules to fly anything other than the recognised flag of your country. To do so could mean disqualification. That was something I wasn't going to risk, so in conjunction with Nike, Nick and I had come up with the shoes idea.

It was a tough semi-final, with German Grit Breuer, Yusuf and Richards the main dangers. I again ran a controlled race to win in 50.32s. When I was in the mixed zone, the area where we collect our gear and sit down after the race, I looked up at the screen and saw that Pérec had won the second semi-final. No surprise there, but I couldn't believe the time: 49.19s. Wow! That was faster than I had ever run. Her time played on my mind until I walked out of the village to meet Nick at a nearby petrol station. It was eleven p.m., and we sat down on the footpath to talk.

'Gee, Pérec was impressive,' I said. He agreed, but was more interested in congratulating me on making my first Olympic final.

Shopping was the diversionary tactic for the final, and I enjoyed dragging Nick from store to store the next morning. As I was trying on some shorts in front of the mirror, I turned to him and asked, 'How do you think I'll go?'

'I think you'll run well,' he said.

'No, be more specific,' I demanded.

He thought if I ran to my best I could finish first or second.

'I think I'll be second,' I said.

There are times when you say something and afterwards you're not really sure why you said it. That was the feeling that hit me then. Second! Maybe I was trying to ease the expectation, making sure in my head that there wasn't any Gothenburg-like pressure.

Suddenly, Nick became positive. 'I don't know about that,' he said, before pointing out that Pérec had never been tested under pressure and tonight was our chance to do that.

After a lunch of toast and honey, Nick took me back to the village to prepare for the 7.35 p.m. final. This was our last point of contact before my big race, but there were no emotional goodbyes. There was really nothing left to say; we both knew I was as ready as I could be. I tried on a new pair of spikes because the shoes with the Aboriginal flag had an errant stitch that hurt my toe. I put them in my bag and made sure I also had the Visa card receipt with FLAG written on the back. I then caught the bus to the warm-up track with Fort and my room-mate, Lauren Hewitt.

As usual, I went over to Garry a couple of times with sore spots that always seemed to appear as the race anxiety began to build up. I knew the clock was ticking and my time was coming around quickly. I was nervous but relaxed at the same time. I just wanted it to be different to Gothenburg. After the second call for the women's 400m final, I walked into the open marquee where my bag was checked, and went over the race plan one last time with Fort. As the bus pulled up to take us to the stadium I turned to Fort and said, 'Hug me, Fort, hug me. Just keep hugging me.' For a moment I lingered in his arms. I needed that assurance that whatever happened in the next thirty minutes there would be people waiting for me when it was all over.

On the bus I had brief eye contact with Sandie Richards, but there was no talking. Each of us dealt with our nerves in our own special way. I had this overwhelming feeling of wanting to get on with it. As we filed into the stadium it was almost like I was hypnotised. I was so focused I couldn't really hear the crowd around me. I was determined to keep everything calm. I went through my routine of setting up the blocks and did a few run-throughs. Then I stripped off my leggings, adjusted my number and began nervously kicking the track. I was in lane four, with Pérec on my inside. I knew I had to push it in the first two hundred metres and try to keep her at bay.

Don't let her dictate the race.

I started urgently and entered the back straight at a nice cruising speed. As we approached the two-hundred-metre mark I realised Pérec still hadn't passed me.

Yes! First part of the plan executed perfectly.

At that moment, Pérec made her move and got within half a metre.

Time for A – Attack. Go, girl!

As we came around the bend with 120 metres to go I caught Nigerian Falilat Ogunkoya in lane five.

I've got the silver.

At the top of the straight, the stagger came into play and Pérec was suddenly half a metre in front. With eighty metres to go I gave it everything and moved up on equal terms with her. For what seemed like an eternity I was at her elbow. She was so tall and her stride so long, but still I was going at her. If she kicked, I kicked. Then, with ten metres left, I suddenly lost some form.

No, no! She is too strong. No! No!

I knew it was over and could only watch as Pérec won by three metres. As I crossed the line I clapped my hands, congratulating myself on not doing a Gothenburg. Then I saw the clock: 48.63s. Unbelievable! That was the time I had been looking at on my mirror for the past four years. Pérec had run 48.25s. Ogunkoya was third in 49.10s.

I found an Australian flag in the crowd, and then saw Nick, who had tears in his eyes as we hugged. We had been through so much but I loved him for everything he'd done. I knew I wouldn't have been there without him. My head was spinning. I was in shock. I was in a place I had never been before, a state of euphoria that I didn't know existed. Nick urged me to stay out there and soak up the moment.

As we prepared for the medal ceremony I realised I'd forgotten to bring my team tracksuit and I had to borrow Debbie Flintoff-King's bottoms and distance runner Carolyn Schuwalow's top. I couldn't believe it when Pérec produced a beauty kit from her bag and started putting make-up on. She lent me some lipstick, eye shadow and mascara and even helped doll me up. I couldn't stop smiling as I stood in front of the world with an Olympic silver medal around my neck.

Hours of media interviews followed, which Maurie and David Culbert, the former long-jumper who was working as a liaison officer with the Australian Olympic Committee, shepherded me through until we arrived at a Nike party at two a.m. There were only twenty people there, including my parents and a surprise guest, Raelene Boyle. I'd been in regular contact with her while she was recovering from breast cancer and I was so happy to see her there. At four a.m. Nick drove me back to the village.

On the way I asked him, 'Are you disappointed? Did you think I was only running for second?'

He laughed it off and said anybody who ran such a great time wasn't running for second.

I didn't tell him, but something was eating away in the back of my mind. I was thinking I might have given Pérec too much respect. Something inside me had been satisfied with second. The silver medal fitted the stepping-stone theory I had followed in my career; winning the gold was too big a jump at this stage. I hadn't backed myself enough to make that quantum leap.

When I walked into the common room at the village I found Louise McPaul in her pyjamas watching television. She had won a silver medal in the javelin three days earlier but was still on a high and unable to sleep. I sat with her and chatted for a while before eventually heading to bed as the new day dawned. When Louise had won her medal, the team had plastered signs and posters all over the wall and the door of her room. I looked at them again as I made my way to my room. I was hoping the team might have done the same for me. They hadn't. There was nothing on my door or in the room. It hurt. I'd always sensed some sort of estrangement between the other Australian athletes and Cathy Freeman. I don't know whether it was jealousy or because they didn't like Nick. I knew that part was true for some of them, but I thought they'd still be excited for me.

Once in bed I again reviewed the race in my mind, with exactly the same result. Why did I say to myself 'I've got the silver' when I passed Ogunkoya? For that millionth of a second I had become weak, and it really annoyed me. I hadn't been ready for gold. Next time I would be.

I was stuffed. Whatever I did, I couldn't get myself fired up for the 200m. Despite only going through the motions I made the semi-finals, but I knew there'd be no repeat of the Commonwealth Games this time. On the bus to the stadium for the semi-final I was seated across from Pérec. Our eyes met and I mouthed, 'I'm tired.' No response. It was like she was staring right through me. I soon realised that while I had lost my focus, Pérec was in the zone again. No matter what tricks I played with myself, when the gun went off I still didn't have anything there. My body was tired. As I crossed the line in sixth I was so relieved it was over. While Pérec was winning the 200m gold, I was out party-ing, boogying away at a nightclub.

After a few days off, it was back to business in London to continue racing on the European circuit. Maurie and Nick were desperate for me to defeat Pérec before the season was over and they reasoned that she'd be at her most vulnerable now because of the heavy social commit-ments that come with being a dual Olympic gold medallist. The rematch came in Brussels, nearly a month after the Olympics. A couple of hours before the race, Pérec was riding in the back of an open car as part of a parade of champions to mark the twentieth anniversary of the meet. Already, in the hotel, American sprinter Gwen Torrence had come up to me and said, 'Girl, this is it. Mary-Jo, she's going down tonight.' Nick was just as confident.

Once again I was drawn on the outside of Pérec in lane five. The game plan was exactly the same as Atlanta: start strong and don't let Pérec pass you in the first two hundred metres. I executed the plan to perfection, and as I came into the straight she still wasn't there. I went for it, and with twenty metres to go I sensed Pérec break. She gave up, and I cruised home to victory in 49.48s. Nick was so excited, he urged me to do a victory lap.

In the drug-testing room afterwards Pérec had an ice pack on her hamstring and was being consoled by her coach, John Smith. She looked distressed. I went over to comfort her but she didn't want to talk. As soon as I got back to the hotel I gave Mum a special wake-up call back in Australia. The magnitude of the victory was starting to sink in. It was only the second time in six years that Pérec had been defeated in the 400m, and both times I had done it. Unlike Monte Carlo a year earlier, Pérec had given everything, yet I had beaten her.

Rematch number two was at the grand prix final in Milan with a cheque for US$78,000 going to the winner. I was excited. I wanted to prove that Brussels couldn't be put down as just an off-night for Pérec. I wanted to get her scalp in the biggest event of the season. As usual, Pérec looked switched on in the warm-up, but when we were all called to make our entrance on to the track she was nowhere to be found. Everyone was looking around for her when an official approached us and said that she had withdrawn. I felt myself deflate. I'd been so pumped to race her again that suddenly all the adrenalin just flowed out. Luckily I was able to regroup before the start of the race, and after a short battle with Ogunkoya in the straight, I pulled away to win in 49.60s.

Tokyo was the last stop on the circuit, and after again defeating Ogunkoya I went along to the end-of-season party. This was the one opportunity of the year to chill out, have a few drinks and get to know some of your rivals. Everyone gets dressed up, and I was embarrassed about how I looked compared with the likes of Pérec, Gwen Torrence and Merlene Ottey. I was enjoying a few glasses of wine when Pérec approached and started laughing at my dress. 'Cathy, your dress is too long, too long.' I laughed, pointed at her tiny mini-skirt and said, 'And yours is too short.' For the first time we started chatting. We talked about our families, how many brothers and sisters we each had. It was great. Later, the party broke up into small groups in different rooms and I was harassed by a drunk Russian pole vaulter. He kept trying to kiss me, even though former 400m British champion Roger Black repeatedly told him that my boyfriend was in the room.

On the way home to Australia, we decided to stop over in Hong Kong for some shopping and also to catch up with Ben Crowe, one of the head Nike guys. I had just signed a new deal with Nike that took me through to the Sydney Olympics. As Nick and I got out of the lift at the Nike offices in Hong Kong, who should be standing there but Alexander Bodecker. I nearly died. This guy kept bobbing up in my life. We chatted, and he ended up coming to lunch with us and some other Nike people. That was pretty weird. As we said our goodbyes, I couldn't help but wonder when and where this Alexander Bodecker would pop up next.

CHAPTER 12
LOST AND ALONE

'Hey, what are you doing?' I asked Nick as I walked into his office, which was set up in a downstairs room of our Stanley Street house. 'Writing to Marshy,' he said, before quickly turning off the computer as I peered over his shoulder.

'Oh,' I said, thinking there couldn't be anything too top secret in an e-mail to sprinter Damien Marsh.

He got up and walked out without saying anything. It was very strange, and it got me thinking. Sonia O'Sullivan had been ringing up even more frequently since we'd got home from overseas three months before. She and Nick would sometimes talk for up to an hour. My woman's intuition told me something was going on.

A couple of days later, Nick was out at some business meetings and I was about to head down the street when I walked past his office. The computer caught my eye and suddenly I remembered the look on Nick's face when I'd interrupted his e-mail writing. It was time to do a bit of investigating. I started up the computer. I didn't have any idea what I was looking for and I'd only just started using e-mail so I wasn't quite sure how to operate it. After a few minutes I stumbled across the inbox and began flicking through. There were a few from Nick's accountant and Nike, and then bingo, a long e-mail from Sonia O'Sullivan. I clicked on open.

I don't know what I'd been expecting, but what appeared on the screen made me suddenly want to be physically sick. It was virtually a love letter. Sonia was explaining how she had all these feelings for Nick and that she desperately wanted them to start a life together. I started crying. I knew our relationship was over and I had been thinking about leaving, yet seeing this ripped a hole in my heart. How could he be doing this behind my back? How long had this been going on? When was he planning to ship me out and move her in?

I had to get out of there, but where could I go? For God's sake, this was my home. I didn't have anywhere else. I rang my best friend, Peta. 'Can you come and get me?' I asked her. She was about to go and pick up her new car, and said she would come round after that. With each minute I stayed in the house, I became more upset. I rang Peta again. 'Peta, can you come and get me now?' I said, sobbing.

'OK, get your stuff together and you can move in here with me,' she said.

I quickly grabbed a bag full of clothes and waited outside.

It was nearly four months since I'd stood on the podium at Atlanta with an Olympic silver medal around my neck. Now my life was unravelling around me.

For the next few weeks I slept in the spare room at Peta's. I started drinking and smoking heavily and going out to nightclubs and bars – the Saloon Bar in South Yarra was one of our favourites. I was on a path to self-destruction. I just didn't care. I was nearly 24 and for the first time I could do anything I wanted. More significantly, I was driven to do things I knew would annoy Nick the most.

I got into the habit of opening a bottle of red wine and a packet of cigarettes before Peta even got home from work. Each cigarette felt so good, and the more we talked, the more I drank and smoked. She agreed that I had to completely separate myself from Nick but it simply wasn't that easy. The following week I had to go with him to a Nike conference in Hawaii. I couldn't get out of it and I was dreading being alone with him again. I was suddenly really drunk, and again the tears started. 'Peta, I'm going to be sick,' I said to her. She quickly helped me down into the backyard and sat me on the ground with a bucket. As I vomited, she held the hair out of my face. When I'd finished, I just slumped to the ground and started crying. What was happening to me?

The last place I wanted to be just before Christmas was stuck in Hawaii with Nick at some sales conference. He kept emphasising how important it was for me to be there as one of the company's major stars in the South Pacific region. To make the whole thing even more bizarre, we were forced to share a hotel room. I was determined to avoid Nick as much as possible and had started to wonder whether I might run into Alexander Bodecker again.

At the end of the first day I headed to the gym for a work-out and as I was coming in the entrance I spotted my new friend. I liked the smile that lit up his face when he saw me. We chatted for a while and I managed to slip in that I had split up with Nick. He was doing a sales pitch on soccer and invited me to go along and meet some of the soccer stars. I found myself enjoying his company. He was very kind, a real gentleman. Spending time with him was a welcome diversion from my woes back home in Australia. When we left, I knew there was some serious chemistry with my Nike mystery man.

I didn't see her at first; I only saw Nick at the front gate of the Stanley Street house as Maurie pulled the car into the kerb. Nick was talking to someone inside the house, and just as he turned to see us arriving, Sonia O'Sullivan walked out. My eyes nearly popped out of my head. What the hell was she doing in my house? How dare they? I just sat there stunned for a moment. I didn't know what I was going to do. When I get angry I have these feelings of unbelievable strength, and as I pushed open the door I felt like I could pick up the car and turn it over.

'Just get back in the car,' Maurie said firmly. He tried to grab my arm. 'Get back in the car.'

I looked at the pair of them and was filled with hatred. Then it struck me: I'd been brought here for a reason. This was Nick's way of letting me know Sonia was in town. He couldn't just tell me straight out, he had to play games and get Maurie to drive me round so he'd be on hand to control me. But I knew this wasn't the right place or time to make a scene, so I got back in the car and we drove off in silence.

No matter how hard I tried I couldn't get the sight of Sonia out of my head. Now I knew she was here, the next thing I needed to know was in what capacity. Was she here to do some training? Was she staying downstairs like a lot of overseas athletes had in the past? Or had she replaced me in Nick's bed? After driving around the city for hours that night I pulled up at the other end of the street from Nick's place in case someone recognised my car. I crept along the footpath and looked for any signs of life inside the house. There were no lights on, and then I checked my watch and realised why – it was three a.m. I reached over and opened the rubbish bin. I don't know what I was hoping to find, maybe some used condoms, but all I could see was food scraps. A car driving past startled me. Imagine if someone caught me, Cathy Freeman, Olympic silver medallist, sifting through a rubbish bin in the middle of the night. I shut the bin and ran back to my car. I was losing my mind.

As each day passed my anger kept building. Nick still hadn't told me anything. I needed some answers, so I decided to confront him. I went round early in the morning and knocked on the door. He was still half asleep when he answered it and I pushed past him. Before he could do anything I was up the stairs and into the bedroom. Even though I'd thought so much about it over the past few days, I still wasn't ready for what I found. Sonia's clothes were hanging where mine had hung; her shoes were next to the bed where mine had lived. I looked into the bathroom and her toothbrush and toiletries were on the shelf in exactly the same spot where I'd put mine.

All my anger suddenly boiled over and I punched the mirror. It shattered on the floor and blood started streaming from a deep cut on my hand. I knew what a cleanliness freak Nick was and how much he hated any marks on the walls, so I started to smear blood all over the place. He lunged at me and grabbed me around the waist. I was going crazy and anything I could get my hands on I pitched in his direction. 'How could you do this to me, you bastard?' I yelled as I grabbed a vase and hurled it. One minute this had been my house, the next minute it was hers. 'Where is she, Nick?' He'd managed to wrestle me out of the bedroom and into the hallway. By this time we both had blood all over us. My rage was now turning to tears so I went downstairs and headed for the door. 'I hate you!' I yelled, and with that I ran to my car and drove off. I parked outside Peta's and stayed in the car because I couldn't stop crying. I was falling apart.

The next day Fort came and got me and we went furniture shopping for my new house in Lyndhurst Street, Richmond, which Nick had at least helped me buy. Fort sensed something was wrong, but I certainly wasn't offering any explanations. I decided to move in later in the week, although most of the furniture was yet to arrive. I'd been at Peta's for nearly two months and I thought getting my own place would help me to get my life started again. I was wrong. The house felt so empty, and for the first time in my life it hit me – I was alone.

I slumped against the wall and began to cry. I must have stayed in the one spot for hours. I couldn't move. I couldn't do anything. I had been with Nick for over seven years. So many questions kept popping into my head. Why doesn't he love me any more? Who is going to be there for me now? I could feel myself falling deeper and deeper into depression. As I looked around the empty room, I had an overwhelming urge to end everything. I didn't want to be there. I didn't want to be in this world any more. I didn't want to be Cathy Freeman. I had never thought about death before, but right at that moment I had an understanding of why people took their lives. They saw suicide as the only way out. How was I going to get out of all this? How could I just disappear?

A noise outside shook me back to reality. Suddenly I was scared. My God, I couldn't believe I was thinking about suicide. I had to speak to my mother. I had to hear her voice. *Please pick up, Mum, please.* After five rings I was beginning to freak out again, but she finally answered.

'Mum, I want to come home,' I said before she even had a chance to say hello. Then the tears started.

'I know Nick has hurt you,' she said, 'but you've got to take this thing, turn it around and make it into a positive. Show him that you're not going to give him the satisfaction of you not realising your dreams.'

Mum wanted to come down to Melbourne straight away but I didn't want her to see me like this. I had to sort through this myself. The one thing that was becoming more and more clear to me was that I had lost the desire to run. A couple of days later, Maurie and Kate came over to see the new place. Fort was also around, along with my friend Nova Peris-Kneebone. We were all sitting out in the courtyard when I announced, 'I don't feel like running this year.'

I think they'd been expecting it, but Maurie was determined to change my mind. 'It will be very hard to come back,' he said.

'Well, what about taking the 1997 domestic season off?' I said.

'I don't think that's a very good idea,' he said firmly.

The next day I went down to the track again to meet Maurie. I argued that Pérec had taken 1993 off after she had won the Olympics in 1992. He pointed out that she took a break after she'd won a gold medal, not silver. Plus there were the obligations I had with my new sponsors and advertisers. 'It's not worth throwing it away,' he said. 'Believe it or not, Nick only wants to try to help you.'

Bruce and Mum organised to have my finances audited. I'd always left that side of my life to Nick and his accountant, Peter Jess. I had trusted them with it, but that trust had been broken. After the Olympics I had asked Jess for answers to ten simple questions about my finances. I was sick of not being taken seriously. I could tell Jess and Nick thought it was a joke when I produced those questions for my accountant but they failed to realise that the days of keeping Freeman in the dark were coming to an end, like a lot of other things.

Severing all my ties with Nick wasn't going to be easy. The major complication in the whole process was that, in partnership with Nike, Nick had set up an athletes management group under the banner of the Melbourne Track Club (MTC). It was designed to get more exposure and sponsorship for lesser-known athletes. The reality was that without me as the face of the club it would fall apart: Nike would pull out, and all those athletes would be affected. Nick had also quit his job at the *Herald Sun* to run the new venture. It was his livelihood, and even though he had hurt me so much I wasn't a vindictive person. It was bizarre. I hated him with a passion one minute, and then the next I'd be looking out for his welfare. Our ties were going to take a bit of breaking.

I had been driving Peta nuts talking about my meeting with Alexander in Hawaii. She finally got sick of it and pushed the phone towards me. 'Just ring him,' she said.

As I dialled the number I felt more nervous than I did before a big race. What if he didn't remember me? What was I going to say? After what seemed like a dozen rings I was just starting to relax, thinking I could simply leave a quick message on an answering machine, when he picked up.

'Hello,' he said. For a couple of seconds I couldn't speak. 'Hello?'

'Hi, Alexander, it's Catherine Freeman. I hope you don't mind me calling,' I said.

He laughed. My fears that he wouldn't remember me were quickly eased. He couldn't believe the timing of my call: he travelled so much with his job and I had rung on a rare night when he was at home in his Portland apartment. Again I found myself relaxed with him and we talked for a couple of hours without realising the time. I promised to let him know when I was next over there. A couple of days later a package arrived in the mail from Alexander with a few CDs and other little bits and pieces, including a letter that again stressed how much he wanted to see me. It was nice to feel that eagerness from someone again, and I decided to send him a package of my own.

Though my heart wasn't in it, I kept turning up for training. Maurie talked me into going to New Zealand to race and asked if I minded if Nick came. I knew Nick was determined to get some sort of working relationship happening again. 'Sure,' I said, thinking that with Maurie there as well it should be OK. We made it to New Zealand well enough, but it didn't take long before Nick and I were at each other's throats. On the track I won the 100m and then defeated my old sparring partner, Ogunkoya, in the 200m, which at least showed me I hadn't lost everything in the past month.

The Victorian championships were next, and by then my motivation had dropped again. I shared the sprints with training partner Lauren Hewitt and won the 200m in 24.10s, a ridiculously slow time. I couldn't remember the last time I'd run so badly. A fifth place in the 100m behind Gainsford-Taylor in Hobart followed, and then, in front of my home crowd at the Nike Classic, on 20 February, I only managed second to Gainsford-Taylor in the 200m. Afterwards I saw Nick and Sonia together, smiling and carrying on. I had begun to see them together regularly at Olympic Park for training and it was driving me crazy. The press were also hounding me for comment about this Pauline Hanson woman who had started a racist political party, One Nation. Everything was getting too much for me again. I needed to get away.

It was nearly midnight, but I rang Fort and told him to come and pick me up the next morning because I was going back to Brisbane. I decided to take my dog Frankie with me, even though hurdler Kyle Vander Kuyp had moved in, because I wasn't planning on returning for some time. Fort said he would organise some training partners for me up there. I just needed Mum and the rest of my family around me. I needed to feel Mum's love and have her hold me in her arms because I knew I was safe there. She was a very strong woman, and if ever I needed to feed off that strength it was now.

One of Mum's favourite sayings was 'Time heals all wounds.' I was enjoying my time away, but then Nick rang and spoke to Mum. One of my sponsors was thinking of pulling out if I wasn't going to run this year. I didn't care, but I could tell Mum was worried about money issues and I got the impression she was siding with Nick, which really annoyed me. I stewed on it for a couple of days and then I was chosen as Telstra's Sports Personality of the Year, an award I was to receive from Prime Minister John Howard in Melbourne. Again I had no interest in going, but Mum explained the political ramifications of a Cathy Freeman no-show. I knew she was right. It would make headlines, and suddenly I'd be this black crusader against the white government. I just didn't need all this in my life.

Nick sent Fort and Peter Jess's daughter, Zoe, who was working for MTC, up to Brisbane to collect me. The national titles were in Melbourne in the first week of March and if I was going to return it had to be now if I was to be ready. I tried to be more positive on my return to training, and by the time of the nationals, even though I was a bit out of shape, I had convinced myself that I would win the 400m and the 200m against Gainsford-Taylor. I jogged through the 400m in a slow 52.09s and then, despite closing late, couldn't catch Gainsford-Taylor in the 200m.

I was back competing, but my attitude still wasn't good. Nick and Maurie could sense this and suggested that I go to South Africa for a couple of races where maybe the change of scenery would rekindle my fire. Nick asked if I wanted him to come. Despite our personal relationship having broken down, I knew that the best thing for my running was to have him still involved. The move worked. I won my three races, including an impressive 50.70s run to beat Ogunkoya. I was besotted by the beauty of South Africa; watching lions prowl in the wild and following apes up a mountainside was a tonic for me, and I could momentarily forget my troubles. In Cape Town we visited the cell where Nelson Mandela had spent something like eighteen years. I was freaked out. I couldn't believe he had remained sane. And it made me reflect on the state of my own mind.

The trip wasn't without the usual Nick troubles. We seemed to take it in turns to blow up. One day he would say he couldn't manage me, then the next I would tell him I wanted him out. In the end we agreed that the best thing for both of us was to stay together in a professional sense. It sounded good in theory, and it would be put to the test immediately. A six-week training camp in El Paso, Texas, was next on the agenda in preparation for the Athens world championships.

CHAPTER 13
SHAVING THE PAST

'Just tell me what's going on!' I screamed at Nick.

I wanted to kill him. I was going nuts. We had only arrived in El Paso the previous day but with Nick and I having to share an apartment it was just a matter of time before it got ugly.

'C'mon, you bastard, tell me!'

Then I did something I'd only done once before: I punched Nick in the face. The force of the blow stunned him. The previous time had been years before when I was drunk and jealous. This time I was in a rage because I'd had enough of all the secrecy surrounding him and Sonia O'Sullivan. I desperately wanted some closure to our relationship and I needed to hear the truth come from his mouth. It was driving me crazy.

I ran into my room and started wrecking furniture. A chest of drawers went first, then a vase. 'What the hell is going on?' I yelled again as I punched a hole in the wall. It hurt like hell and I slumped to the floor.

'That's it, Catherine. I'm going,' Nick said as he headed back into the other room. He was going to Philadelphia, where Sonia was training.

'Well, I'm all alone now, aren't I?' I said.

The phone rang. I heard Nick answer it, and then he appeared in the doorway of my room. 'It's for you, it's Sandy,' he snarled. I had rung Alexander at his office to let him know I was in America but he wasn't there so I'd left the El Paso number. The look on Nick's face ignited my anger again and I reached over and grabbed a pot plant.

'Fuck off, you bastard,' I said as I hurled it at him. The pot shattered against the wall and narrowly missed him. By the time I got to the phone, the line was dead.

Nick didn't leave straight away. He couldn't, because my three training partners, Jason Richardson, Cameron McKenzie and Mark Moresi, weren't arriving until the end of the week. Nick rang Maurie and told him to get Fort over to America because he was leaving. I refused to do any training so we had ourselves a stand-off. When the guys finally arrived and had settled in, Nick called them together and told them what was required. Then he vanished.

Richo took over Nick's room in my apartment. The next morning we were both in the kitchen having breakfast. 'I'm going to quit,' I told him. He almost fell off his chair. He'd flown halfway around the world and in the space of twelve hours the coach/manager had walked out and now the athlete wanted out too.

'Fine, so you want to be home with your family,' he said. 'That's great. You'll go home, see your mum and kiss your nephew. You'll sit around, and after a few days you'll start thinking about Athens. After a few weeks you'll be going stir-crazy. You might think you're unhappy here, but it won't be anything to how you'll feel back there.'

Richo's point was valid, but I still wasn't convinced. I rang Mum and she immediately wanted to fly to Texas to comfort me, but again I said I would sort it out. Psychologist Jeff Simons, who had helped me during the break-up, was next, and he ensured that the penny dropped. He simply asked me to imagine what it would be like sitting on my couch at home watching the Athens world championships on TV. I knew the answer. It would be terrible. I'd hate myself.

Then Fort arrived, and I started to focus on my training. I thrived in the competitive environment with the boys. We all really clicked and enjoyed each other's company. My nick-name became 'Conchita' after a local called me that during a shopping trip into town.

I had managed to find a street map of Portland, as I was interested in where Alexander lived. One night he rang on his way home from work. I told him I had the map and he began to describe the streets he was driving down so I could follow. He was going to dinner with some Nike friends and he kept me on the line. I chatted to him while they ate and he even put me on to a couple of them. Then I followed him on my map as he drove home. I had no trouble saying anything to him and in the end we were both laughing at how our first date had been a three-hour phone call following Alexander's movements around Portland.

Before I'd left Australia, Alexander had called to invite me to a soccer match Nike was putting on between Brazil and Mexico in Miami. He had left a message with Kyle, who'd failed to pass it on. It turned out that the invitation was still open and I gladly accepted a chance to escape from El Paso. We had to go to the official function before the game, and as we arrived at the marquee Alexander had to go back to check something with the driver. As he ran down the road I couldn't help but laugh because he looked like someone out of *Miami Vice* with his bleached blond hair, dark sunglasses and cool suit and tie.

It was a great evening, and it was so nice to have some male affection after the disaster my relationship with Nick had become. We stayed the night in a beautiful hotel and I couldn't believe it when I got back to the room after the match and found the light flashing on the telephone. It was a message from my mother. 'Catherine, darling, this is your mother here. I hope you're all right. I'm just a bit worried about you.' I laughed. *Don't worry, Mum, I'm in good hands.*

When I awoke the next morning I knew there was something special with Alexander. What I couldn't understand was why I seemed to attract older men. Nick was thirteen years older than me and my new boyfriend was more like twenty years older.

We hooked up again in Eugene, Oregon, where I was competing in the 200m at the Prefontaine meet. I was so excited to see Alexander again that I was like a giggling schoolgirl and I really wasn't tuned in for the race. Subsequently I finished third in the very slow time of 23.09s. But I was so happy because the camp at El Paso was over and we were staying in Portland for ten days so I was able to hang out with Alexander. Fort returned to Australia, and in his absence my intensity towards training declined. I was having such a good time away from the track that I suddenly didn't want to spend as much time on it. By the time Richo, Cameron, Mark and I left for London, where I would meet Nick again, I knew my form had slipped since El Paso.

Nick and I hadn't spoken for six weeks, and when he saw me at the airport he was shocked at how much weight I'd put on. I was about a stone above my racing weight and Nick instantly blamed Richo and the boys for letting me blow out. I didn't particularly care what he thought because I had a new man in my life.

Slowly I got my head back around training, helped by the big group of Melbourne Track Club athletes who had also settled in London to prepare for the world championships, which were just over two months away. One day a group of us went shopping in Camden Town. Again I was with the boys: Richo, Kyle Vander Kuyp and Rohan Robinson. The first thing they all did was get their hair cut. Well, in reality they got their heads shaved. As the afternoon progressed, I thought more and more about getting a haircut of my own. We were at the markets when I spotted a tiny hairdressing booth. I turned to Richo and said, 'I want my hair cut. I want to get it like yours.' I wanted to shave off all my hair as a symbolic way of getting rid of the past. I was going through a major change in my life and I just thought, what the hell!

Rohan's jaw dropped. 'You can't do it. You're a role model. No, you can't.' But Richo, in typical fashion, was all gung-ho about it. 'Yeah, all right, let's do it.' As we were piling into the shop, a beautiful young girl with collar-length hair came in and said to the barber, 'Shave it off.' Richo said she was an angel sent down from heaven to show me the way. The girl looked great afterwards, so I sat down and we started with the number five blade. At number four, Kyle walked out saying he couldn't watch any more. The boys were all yelling and the crowds outside had started staring, trying to find out what all the commotion was about. I stopped at 1.5. It felt awesome. I felt masculine and suddenly aggressive. It was like, 'Fuck you, world, I can do what I want. I don't have to answer to anybody and I don't care what anyone thinks.' I also had my nose pierced.

I was shocked by the different reactions my new look caused on the circuit. It seemed to make a bigger impression on guys. Garry Miritis said I looked like a dickhead, while sprinter Frankie Fredericks was in shock. 'What have you done?' he kept muttering, because his grandmother had told him that a woman's beauty resides in her hair. My main concern was how Alexander would react. I invited him to come and watch me race in Oslo. The stakes had suddenly become very high because my lead-up form had been ordinary and with the world championships just a month away I needed to pull out something special, a confidence booster.

The day before the Oslo meet there is a tradition where the athletes all gather for a strawberries and cream party. Alexander was flying in that afternoon so I arranged to meet him there. The party was at a small apple orchard, and I was standing with Nick and Maurie when I saw Alexander walk in. I deliberately moved behind some trees as he started looking around. I was like a big cat in the jungle spying on its prey. I was scared about how he was going to react to my shaved head. Some guys like only girlie girls. Right now, I was the furthest thing from that.

'Hi,' I said as I sprang from behind a tree. A big smile appeared on his face and we hugged. He said nothing about my hair and just started chatting away. He was a gentleman, through and through.

I enjoyed performing in front of loved ones as it brought out something extra in me, and I was determined to impress Alexander. Nick, who had politely greeted Alexander the previous day at the party, was up to his old tricks, trying to fire me up before the race. He said Pérec had been quoted saying she thought I was out of shape and couldn't win in Athens. She had also apparently said that she wasn't going to run the 400m there, preferring the 200m.

Nick wanted me to go out hard. On the blocks I surveyed the field and realised that most of my main rivals were missing: no Richards, Ogunkoya or Miles. *Gee, I had better win this thing or I'll look stupid.* I started well and was moving fast at the two-hundred-metre mark when I heard Nick yell out, 'Yes!' I must have been on target for a good time so I attacked the bend and held it together down the straight. When I glanced at the clock, I couldn't believe it: 49.39s. Yes! I was back in town. Maybe I wasn't as unfit as everyone had thought. I ran over to Maurie and hugged him, then threw my victory flowers to Alexander in the crowd before embracing Nick as he arrived at the finish line. I hadn't experienced such an adrenalin rush since Atlanta, and I knew then that the hunger was back.

CHAPTER 14
THE BIG GREEN LIGHT

Nick and Fort had never really got on from day one. When I had arrived in London overweight Nick had gone off his tree and virtually sacked Fort via a fax. He'd told me about this, and I was so caught up in my own little world that I wasn't fazed. The one and only thing that I really trusted Nick with was his decision-making involving my running. I liked Fort and he'd been good to me, but I thought I was probably at the point where it was possible for me and Nick to steer the ship ourselves.

Athens was a beautiful city and I really enjoyed the Greek people, who seemed to have a special affection for Australians. I roomed with 1,500m runner Margaret Crowley in the team hotel and had to rise at five a.m. to prepare for my first heat of the world championships, which was at the ridiculous time of eight a.m. I was still half asleep and ran a muddling stop-start race to finish second to Jamaica's Lorraine Graham. The key was to conserve energy, as the second heat would be run that evening – or so we thought. The team coaches seemed to think otherwise, and for what seemed like hours they debated this with Nick. It was frustrating because I didn't know whether to switch off and relax or start focusing on the evening race. Eventually it was confirmed that I had to run again later.

While I was waiting I saw Sonia O'Sullivan, and I instantly became agitated. Since I had returned to Europe and been working with Nick, she had been absent, so I'd used the out-of-sight, out-of-mind theory. Now, as I watched her run around the track, all the hurt from six months ago came flooding back.

At the warm-up track I started to play games with Nick. I just wanted to annoy him. 'Is this my water?' I asked him. Athletes are very particular about water bottles because of the fear of spiking.

'Yes,' he said.

'Are you sure?' I pushed.

'Yeah, I'm pretty sure.'

I kept at it. 'Are you absolutely sure that's my water?'

His anger rising, Nick said, 'Well, not absolutely sure because I've taken my eyes off it for a few seconds, but I'm pretty sure.'

'Well, how do you expect me to drink it? I might get poisoned.'

With that, Nick turned and walked off in search of another water bottle.

Victory number one.

Again I felt very comfortable in the second heat, and near the line I sensed that Jearl Miles-Clark was desperate to win it so I slowed to allow her through. Nick was furious, saying that I needed to win to ensure a good lane. 'I don't give a stuff about the heats,' I screamed, and stormed off. The final was all I worried about.

As the bus pulled up at the team hotel I saw Alexander standing out the front and my mood suddenly brightened. He was my ray of sunshine. I needed to talk to someone, as Nick and I were no longer communicating; every time we tried to talk it would get personal and end up in a row. Alexander and I had dinner together and just talked about anything other than the following night's semi-final.

The next morning I met Nick for our regular coffee to hatch a game plan for the finals. What happened next was the last thing I was expecting. Normally this talk would be about race directions, with some confidence-boosting; instead, Nick launched into a tirade about how I was running poorly and not listening to instructions, and accused me of playing games between him and Alexander. He even brought Sonia into it.

I'd had enough of all this fighting and I didn't care any more. I didn't care that I was the favourite to win the world championships. 'I'm going home. I'm not going to run,' I said. He didn't even comfort me then, instead continuing on about how I needed to change my attitude.

'God damn you, Nick, why are you getting personal?' I screamed. 'I've had enough of all this.' I got up and ran out of the coffee shop.

As I walked into the hotel I was trying to cover my eyes so no one would realise that I was on the verge of tears. I found a hiding spot in a booth in the darkest corner of the lounge. What was happening to me? I needed to get out of there. I didn't care if I never ran again.

Just as I was thinking about how I could get a plane home, I saw Nick and Alexander walk into the lounge together. They were locked in what looked like a serious conversation and they were heading my way. What the hell had my ex-boyfriend and new boyfriend been talking about?

'I met Sandy outside,' Nick said. 'He knows what *I'm* about. Enjoy your lunch.' He then turned and walked out.

Alexander slid into the booth next to me and grabbed my hand. 'I believe you can do it,' he said quietly. I could feel my anxiety subside. 'You're doing this for yourself, not for anybody else, so all you have to do is go out and do your best.' It was like music to my ears. Here was someone who didn't have a vested interest in me, someone who wasn't concerned about sponsors or contracts. He was only worried about me. 'Don't let any of these other distractions come in,' he said.

We talked for nearly an hour, and when we'd finished I realised that I needed to run these next two races for myself, for my own peace of mind and wellbeing, and not for Nick or anyone else.

At five p.m. I met Nick downstairs and it was business as usual. I asked him about the field and what he thought. His message was that I was to finish first or second and ensure a good lane in the final. Run the first 250 metres hard and then decide what's required after that, he told me, but, 'Don't kill yourself.'

Once again I executed the plan perfectly from lane three, and as we neared the bend I had already collared Miles-Clark in four and Ogunkoya in five.

OK, ease it up now.

Around the bend I switched off, knowing that the stagger would keep me in the lead.

Nice and easy, Freeman. Save it for tomorrow.

With thirty metres to go I was still coasting when suddenly they both surged on my outside. As I had slowed so much I took a while to kick back into gear, and my late rush on the line wasn't enough. Miles-Clark won in 50.05s, a hundredth faster than Ogunkoya, with me another whisker away in 50.11.

Oops.

I was on my way to get a massage when an official told me my lane for the final: lane one. I couldn't believe it. I'd never run a final from lane one before. This was going to be interesting. I had just started getting my hamstrings massaged when Nick arrived.

'I've got lane one,' I said.

'Yeah, that's a good lane, no worries,' he said casually.

'But everyone says it's a bad lane,' I said.

'Who is everyone? Look, what lane do we train in?' Nick said.

Fair enough, I thought, and we didn't speak about it again until the following day at the warm-up track.

I was very worried about lane one. The key was going to be my start, and I knew that was not my best asset and never had been. Nick started reeling off stats. Michael Johnson had run the fastest ever 400m from lane one in a relay, and I'd set an Australian record from lane one in Monaco back in 1994. He got me to do some starts. Even though they weren't feeling great, he kept encouraging me. 'That's the best one yet,' he said after I had almost fallen out of the blocks. I wondered what he was up to, but maybe the starts weren't as bad as I thought.

The race plan was to really go for it at the steeplechase water jump, which was adjacent to lane one at the 150-metre mark. 'At the water jump, there's a big green light,' Nick said. We then jogged a couple of laps of the warm-up track and each time I went past the water jump I surged. I wanted to make sure that it was in my head.

In the call room, Sandie Richards, who'd spent three weeks training with us in London, whispered to me, 'You can do it.' But the demons were circling, and they got worse once I was on the track at my blocks. The other runners seemed so far away from me and my lane looked so tight with the white rail running along the edge and a large yellow track clock sticking out where I thought I might hit it.

C'mon, Freeman. Remember what the psych told you, just concentrate on what you can do.

The start was good and clean by my standards, but after 150 metres I seemed to be even further away from the other girls because Tatyana Alekseyeva, the Russian in lane two, had flown and nearly caught Ogunkoya in lane three.

I'm not in this race. Where's the water jump?

As soon as I passed the water jump, I felt strong. There was plenty in the tank, and I knew I was going to need it.

You're coming at them. Don't panic. You've got them.

When the stagger kicked in as we entered the straight there was a line of four of us: Richards, Miles-Clark, Ogunkoya and me.

No one ever runs you down, Freeman. You're half a metre ahead, and don't forget, there is no Pérec.

At the fifty-metre mark I sensed Ogunkoya drop back, but Richards and Miles-Clark were still pushing.

Stay in rhythm.

With ten metres to go I sensed a late charge from Richards.

Dip at the line, girl. Dip!

Yes, I'd done it. Well, I thought I'd done it. Sandie and Jearl came over to me and we had a group hug. I was sure I'd won but I needed confirmation before I was going to do anything. I looked over to Maurie, who had his BBC monitor in front of him, and he gave the thumbs up. I had won my first world championship from lane one. Lane one! I just wanted to scream. I had run 49.77s to nose out Richards (49.79) and Miles-Clark (49.90).

What now? Unlike the Commonwealth Games, and to an extent, Atlanta, I hadn't really thought about flags or anything like that; I'd been too busy trying to stay sane and actually get to the start line. Then I heard someone yelling my name, so I turned round and saw Kate Plant and one of Nick's friends walking towards me with the Aboriginal and Australian flags.

An Australian Aborigine was the best in the world. The world!

I couldn't believe I'd done it. How the hell had I pulled this off after the worst ten months of my life? I could feel everything catching up with me. My heart was racing and I was very emotional when Channel

7 reporter Pat Welsh grabbed me for an interview.

'I've had a beep! beep! beep! beep! hard year and there were times when I didn't think I was going to make it,' I said.

If only you knew the half of it.

PART THREE: NEW DIRECTIONS

CHAPTER 15
THE CLIPPING OF WINGS

The sun shining through the window made me stir. As I lay there in the sanctuary of my own home with my cats playing on the end of the bed, I began to analyse my life and my running. 'Fancy – little ol' me, world champion,' I said to the empty room. It had been a couple of months since I'd stood on the podium at Athens with the gold medal around my neck.

Never before had I looked at my life in terms of parts and sections, but now I was alone, a 24-year-old single woman who also just happened to be an Olympic silver medallist and world 400m champion. I'd come so far in such a short time, not only in my running but also in my personal life. I had already lived a very full life with so much personal satisfaction. The funny thing was, I had been winging it. I'd just let things roll along, happy to be doing something I loved. I'd never thought about the money or looked at running as a career. I was always just a little black girl who could run fast. Nick and others had directed my life and I had winged my way to the top of the world. All I'd had to do was run. For some reason, as I lay looking out at a beautiful Melbourne spring morning, I knew it was never going to be that way again.

Times were changing. I was no longer a little girl, I was a young woman, and I had to start thinking about the future rather than letting each day roll into the next. This new philosophy would be put to the test when Alexander arrived the next day for his first visit to Australia. Our relationship had been going on for just over six months but we hadn't spent more than two or three days in a row with each other during that time. How would we react to being in each other's pockets for a few weeks? What would sharing a bathroom with him be like? These silly little questions were about to be answered.

After a couple of days in Melbourne we headed up to Brisbane, and then across to the Northern Territory. Alexander had this wonderful capacity to relate to people, especially the younger children, and he took meeting my family in his stride. I could tell that they were a bit wary of him, but that was understandable. They hadn't met too many middle-aged, white, American men before, let alone one who was their daughter's/sister's lover. Colour or age weren't an issue for me; it was all about the person and what was inside.

Alexander's stay seemed to fly past, and the thing that struck me afterwards was how easy it had been. A couple of weeks after he left we had one of our long phone conversations and we got on to the topic of marriage. He was asking whether I had ever thought about it.

'I'm not scared of marriage,' I said.

As I was telling Peta about the conversation she put up her hand to stop me. 'You know he's going to ask you,' she said.

I immediately went red and started shaking my head. 'No, he won't.'

She started laughing. 'He will. I'm telling you he will.'

Alexander's work schedule didn't allow him to return to Australia until just before Christmas. He had a sales meeting in Singapore and then he flew into Melbourne. It seemed such a long time since we had been together. I'd realised in his absence how happy he made me when he was around.

We were just getting settled in bed when he asked if I could go downstairs and get his bag. I didn't see why he couldn't get it himself, but I decided to keep the peace and do it for him. I plonked it on his side of the bed and climbed back in. I heard him rustling through the bag, then he said, 'I've got something I want to ask you.'

What the hell does he want me to do now?

'OK, what?' I said sleepily.

'I want to spend the rest of my life with you. Will you marry me?'

I was stunned. He wants to marry me. *He wants me to be his wife. Oh, my God.* 'Yes,' I said as I hugged him. I was so excited that I sat up and started bouncing up and down. 'Yes, yes, yes!' I kept yelling.

Then, suddenly, I was overwhelmed with self-doubt. I turned to him and said, 'Why did you pick me? Why me? Surely you can find somebody better.'

Alexander smiled and reached out for me. 'I want *you*.'

All my life I had wanted to hear those three words. Then he pulled out a small square box that held a glittering diamond, a beautiful single stone, which I was to design my engagement ring around. I was stunned by how perfect this moment was.

My little brother Garth, his girlfriend Lisa and their baby boy Damon were staying with me at the time. I raced downstairs to tell them. I wanted to tell the world that I was getting married. I wanted to shout it from the rooftops. Garth and Lisa convinced me otherwise and thought it would be better to tell Mum and the family in person when we went up to Mackay the next day for Christmas.

When we got there Bruce was still in the Territory, so we took Mum and little George, Gavin's youngest son, who was staying at Mum's, out for lunch at a small deli. Alexander kept waiting for the right time to tell her but George wasn't keen on sitting still for long and one of us was constantly up trying to keep him under control. Eventually, I just said, 'Mum, Alexander and I are getting married.' She seemed a bit taken aback because she had only met Alexander once before, but she realised I was happy and for her that was all that mattered.

Then we all went round to one of my uncle's houses where the rest of the family had gathered for the afternoon. As soon as we walked in, I blurted it out, 'We're engaged.' My brother Norman, who never shows any emotion and doesn't really say much, came up to Alexander and gave him a hug. He was genuinely excited for us, and as I watched them embrace I was hit by a reality check. Twelve months ago I was having suicidal thoughts; now here I was, surrounded by my family and my new fiancé.

How the hell did you do it, Freeman?

Right at that moment, I loved life.

CHAPTER 16
Cos I'm Free

It was no surprise that our little excursion around Melbourne ended up at the Queen Victoria Market, the mecca for bargain shopping in Melbourne. Alexander and my cousin Kelvin were with me to indulge my passion, and as I was roaming through the market stalls a sign across the road caught my eye. It was a tattoo parlour. I already had a tattoo on the inside of my ankle, a tiny rose, which I'd been talked into getting back in 1993 by one of Garth's girlfriends. She'd really wanted to get a tattoo but hadn't wanted to go by herself, so I'd gone along and, as my nickname from school was Flowers, picked out the rose.

I had thought about getting another tattoo after I'd had my head shaved during my identity crisis. I wanted to get something to illustrate my new freedom. The idea had resurfaced, thanks mainly to a song I just couldn't get out of my head: 'Cos I'm free, to do what I want, any old time.' It was so catchy. Another part of the chorus was 'Don't be afraid of your freedom'.

I turned to Alexander and Kelvin. 'C'mon, let's go over there.' They both looked at where I was pointing and smiled. I explained to the lady tattooist that I wanted the words 'Cos I'm free' on my right bicep. I could relate to those words. Whether you are black, white, rich, poor, uneducated or educated, you should have the freedom to express yourself, the freedom to love yourself and to enjoy your own space. You should feel free just to be who you are and be proud of it. As I watched the lady go to work with the needle, I knew this was the perfect statement for me. I'd always been a free spirit and I wasn't going to change for anyone. A lot of people, particularly Aborigines, are scared to show their true colours for fear of the consequences. They are trapped. I no longer was. This new sense of freedom had come over me with the realisation that I was finally breaking away from the stranglehold Nick had on my life. I was starting a new, exciting chapter in my life with a new man.

I didn't know what to say to Nick about the engagement. How would I tell him? Even though our relationship was well and truly over, there was still a bond between us that made it awkward. It finally came to a head at training when he sensed I was nervous about something. 'Alexander and I are engaged,' I said as we walked a lap of Olympic Park. He didn't seem too shocked and mumbled something about congratulations. We finished the lap in silence.

Later that week we were having lunch together when it came up again. I sensed he wanted to say something.

'Look, you haven't had any other boyfriends,' Nick said. 'You were with me for so long, you got really upset, don't you think this could be a rebound thing? You don't think you need a bit more time? I mean, he's from another country and he's a lot older than you, and even me.'

I knew that what he had just said summed up the feelings of my friends and even my family. What they couldn't understand was that I'd lived my life on gut instincts and everything felt right about Alexander. The timing and the age were irrelevant; I was happy, and I now realised that was all that mattered.

A call on Nick's mobile the next day as I was jogging around the football field opposite Olympic Park raised my happiness to a whole new level. A big smile broke out on Nick's face as he handed me the phone. 'It's for you, it's the Australia Day Council.'

I didn't understand, and it still didn't quite register when the voice on the other end said, 'Congratulations, Cathy, you've been chosen as Australian of the Year.' I started laughing. This was big. A little Aboriginal girl from Mackay was the 1997 Australian of the Year.

'Me? Why me?' I said to Nick. 'They could have chosen so many other people, yet they chose me.'

'You're a great Australian,' he said as I started jumping around like a little girl.

'I guess I'm making history.'

I had to go to Perth to accept the honour from Prime Minister John Howard. At least I got to buy a new dress and to doll myself up. I even had to style my hair, because it had started to grow out, much to the pleasure of my mother, who had been horrified by the shaved look. When I got up to accept the award I was momentarily lost for words. 'Wow! Wow!' was all I could say. This was a moment I would always treasure, and I told the audience that it meant far more to me than my world championship gold medal.

Unfortunately, Alexander was unable to share that moment with me as he'd had to go back to the States. He was the head of Nike's soccer arm and they were building up for the 1998 World Cup in France in the middle of the year. We really hadn't spent much time together since our engagement so I was dying to get over to America to start training.

My first race in the US was again in Eugene, Oregon, where I ran a surprisingly fast 50.02s. I was enjoying training and certainly didn't have any of the motivational problems of the previous year. Nick had mapped out a two-year plan leading into the Sydney Olympics and I was determined to make sure I followed it every step of the way.

In June 1998 we moved to London and I saw more of Alexander because he was coming and going from France, where the World Cup was about to begin. I went over for the opening game, Brazil v. Scotland, which was a nice couple of days away from the grind of training. I then went off racing. The first stop was Lucerne, where I won comfortably in 50.35s. Oslo was next. It was one of my favourite tracks because I always seemed to run fast there. I was feeling light before the race and there was some electricity flowing through my limbs. Just before we were to go out for the race, I was putting on my spikes when I pulled the tongue out of my left shoe. I had forgotten to bring my spare pair of spikes, and with only five minutes to go I told Nick I'd just tighten the laces. No big deal.

I got off to a good start and ran aggressively down the back straight. Twelve months earlier I'd run 49.39s here and I was definitely fitter now. I really wanted a special time. I already had Ogunkoya and Breuer covered as I rounded the home bend, but just as I was coming off it I felt a crunch and sharp pain in my left foot. I was suddenly gripped with fear. What had I done? What should I do? I continued on down the straight but with each stride my brain was registering more and more that there was a serious problem with my foot. I managed to finish the race, fourth in 50.92s, and afterwards Nick seemed just as perplexed as I was about what had happened. I iced the foot and we discussed whether maybe the missing tongue had left the foot unstable. I was really worried and I rang Alexander as soon as I got back to the hotel. I was very paranoid about injury and always had any little aches or sore spots treated straight away. I knew this was on a whole different level.

We flew back to London and after a couple of days the discomfort had settled down, but my anxiety levels hadn't. Nick didn't believe the injury was serious and I sensed a similar sentiment in Maurie and others – that it was just a slight hiccup along the way that would soon be rectified. I wished they would listen to me because I was worried about the Commonwealth Games.

Alexander made a surprise visit. He'd been about to go and watch the junior tournament Nike had organised for the World Cup, but instead of getting on the bus he got in a taxi to the station and caught the train from Paris to London. I was so happy to see him. I felt like he was the only one who understood me. He had the ability to say things that instantly soothed my mind. My next race in Rome was only a few days away and I was petrified about it. What if the injury was serious? What would happen if I couldn't run? I kept asking Alexander these questions. The day before I was to fly to Rome to race, Alexander was scheduled to return to Paris for the World Cup final, Brazil v. France. I had started organising my bags when he came into the bedroom and said, 'I'm coming with you.'

'But what about the World Cup?' I asked.

'You need me right now, Catherine, so I want to be here,' he said.

He was willing to sacrifice the event he'd been working towards for two years to be with me. I tried to change his mind but it was set. I loved him so much. Alexander gave his finals tickets to Nick and Peter Jess, so while they were enjoying the World Cup final we were on our way to Rome in search of some answers.

I was still having trouble putting much weight on to the foot, and when I tried to do some warm-up drills at the track the pain was unbearable. It was stupid even attempting to race with all these doubts swirling around inside my head. We went and saw three different doctors, but several X-rays later still nothing. However, the last doctor also took an MRI scan, which showed a bone bruise and a small bone cyst underneath the foot at the base of the big toe. He was confident it would heal within a couple of weeks. I wasn't so sure. The funny thing was I could walk around without any problems; it was only when I ran and put pressure on my toes that there was pain.

Rome was beautiful, and Alexander and I went for a long walk to try to get my mind off the injury. That night we went to the stadium to watch the events. I am not a good spectator and I was feeling more and more uncomfortable as the night went on. When the announcer started reading out the field and the girls began to walk on to the track for the 400m, I started crying. I couldn't watch. I got up and left. Alexander caught up with me at the bottom of the stairs where I had slumped with my hands covering my face. The Commonwealth Games were in a couple of months and I desperately wanted to run. I was worried I would never be able to run again.

When I got back to London, Mum and Bruce had arrived. They were on their retirement trip around the world. It was good to see them but with each day I was getting more and more frustrated about just sitting around being unable to train or do anything. My best friend, Peta, also arrived to give moral support. Everyone had a theory about what I should be doing, Nick telling me to get out there and test the foot while the doctor was recommending more rest. In desperation they flew my personal physician, Dr Peter Fuller, over from Melbourne, hoping that a familiar face would help ease my concerns. He gave me a cortisone injection, but it didn't work. The next step was a CAT scan, and finally we had some answers: a burst ligament in my toe had ripped a flake off the bone which had created persistent bruising in the joint.

Seven weeks after Oslo, I announced I wasn't going to the Commonwealth Games. Again I got teary when I thought about what I was missing out on: wearing the green and gold again. It really sucked.

There was only one solution: I had to get away, far away.

In my own little way I'm a bit of an adventurer, and I knew exactly where I wanted to go – Iceland. For some reason, Iceland had stuck in my mind after I'd seen some pictures in a travel magazine. It was described as the closest thing to the moon because of its barren landscape. The beauty about it was that I couldn't get any further away from the world of track and field if I tried. The Arctic Circle sounded like the perfect place, so I packed a bag and off I went by myself on the four-hour flight from London.

I quickly found out why it's called Iceland. I was frozen stiff. I virtually buried myself in clothes, my daily ensemble including underwear, long black tights, leather pants, knee-high boots, singlet, skivvy, turtle-neck sweater, a big sports jacket, gloves and a hat. I stayed for a week in the capital, Reykjavik, and did tours from there each day. The place was so beautiful and had a really romantic feel about it. I loved the volcanic craters, waterfalls and thermal pools – I could have happily stayed for months. I made friends with a Scottish couple and I couldn't get over how much the guy sounded like Sean Connery. The local bus driver recognised me and insisted on taking me for a look at the local athletics track.

I had a tiny television in my room but the reception was very bad with the wind howling outside. The only time the Commonwealth Games entered my mind was when I had the TV on, and once, through a snowy haze on the screen, I could make out a news report saying that Ato Boldon had won the men's 100m.

When I got back to London, Alexander was there finishing up his business with Nike because he had decided to take a leave of absence. He was burnt out and desperately wanted to spend more time with me. We flew to the States for a holiday in Alaska where one of Alexander's friends had a cabin up in the national park. It was perfect. The cabin had no running water or heating and an outdoor toilet. I loved being so far away from civilisation. We spent five days hiking and exploring before borrowing a 4WD and driving up to Anchorage for a four-day fishing and bear-watching trip. Alexander is a fishing freak and he taught me how to fly-fish, which was a lot of fun. I didn't want to leave this world. It was so easy, most unlike the real world I lived in.

Eventually, though, we had to head back to reality. We flew to Portland because Alexander wanted me to see Stan James, the orthopaedic surgeon who had helped Michael Jordan with his foot problems. His analysis was exactly what I wanted to hear. He confirmed the micro-fracture and said that taking time off had been absolutely the right thing to do. Now all that was left was to get my nerve back on the track. Somehow, I knew that wasn't going to be easy.

CHAPTER 17
GETTING THE GROOVE BACK

'Hi, Fort, it's Freeman. I need to talk to you. How about some dinner tomorrow night?'

I had never resolved what had happened with my ex-coach. Our split had happened through Nick without Fort and I actually talking to each other. It had been weird, but that was how most relationships involving my running worked. Nick set everything up, Nick controlled everything, and I just did what I had to do – run fast. As the 1999 season dawned, I decided I needed the old firm back, the team that had made me successful in 1996. That meant I needed Fort. I dearly hoped he felt he needed me again as well.

We met at my favourite Thai restaurant in Richmond. He must have known what it was about, but he did a good job of hiding it during the initial chitchat.

'Fort, I wouldn't mind you coaching me again,' I said.

He looked up from his rice and shook his head. 'No, no, no. I don't want you again,' he said, smiling. His attempt at keeping a straight face wasn't very successful, and I knew I had him back. I'd written to him late in the previous year, basically apologising for the way I'd treated him. I'd thanked him for his help over the years and explained how, in hindsight, our falling-out was just a case of the pressure getting the better of all of us.

'I want Nick to be involved too. Is that a problem?' I asked. I knew this was the potential deal-breaker, but I was convinced a working relationship was possible.

After a long pause, Fort looked up. 'Not really,' he said.

Team Freeman was back together. However, I'd decided there would be one major difference: I didn't want Nick or his accountant in control of my financial affairs any more. Our relationship had changed so much that I no longer wanted Nick to have that much influence over me. I knew I needed his athletics expertise but I wanted independence. I had grown increasingly frustrated by Nick and Jess's refusal to keep me up to speed. It was eating away at me, and it had reached the point where I'd regularly take off in the car and just drive around Melbourne for a couple of hours, thinking about everything. Still, I knew I needed help if I was going to break free of MTC. My first stop was the Victorian Institute of Sport and its director, Frank Pyke. I also turned to Australian head coach Chris Wardlaw. He had been a good friend for many years and was often the link in keeping peace between Nick and Fort. Most of all, I trusted him.

All the business problems plus the anxiety over my injury combined to leave me struggling on the track. My head wasn't right. I still didn't have confidence in my foot and we'd already had to back off training because of some aches. I was putting my foot in a bucket of ice for thirty minutes after each session. All these insecurities manifested themselves before a low-key 400m race on 14 January as part of the Tattersalls series at Olympic Park. I didn't want to be there. Fort insisted that I run, and after an hour of going back and forth I made it to the blocks. I ran like I was in a confused state and actually switched off at the top of the straight, allowing Lee Naylor to pass. Luckily, I had enough time to fight back and win, but it was the scare I needed. I realised I had to get my act together.

An even bigger scare came three weeks later at the Canberra grand prix. I lost my 200m heat and then, in the final against Australia's latest sprinting sensation, Tania Van Heer, I pulled out of the race with sixty metres to go. I'd felt a pain in my left quad and panicked, thinking it was Oslo all over again. It turned out to be just a twinge but I was glad I hadn't risked it. We made some slight adjustments to my programme in an attempt to stop the constant niggles I was feeling in my legs and everything seemed to get back on track over the next few weeks until Fort relayed some gossip to Alexander one morning at training.

'Have you heard Nick's news?' Alexander said later.

'What news?' I said.

'Sonia is pregnant.'

His words hit me like a sledgehammer. I couldn't believe what I'd just been told.

'Are you all right?' Alexander asked.

'Yeah, fine. I've got to go.'

I ran to my car and drove around for a while. Why hadn't Nick told me himself? The more I thought, the more confused I got. *Why her? Why wasn't it me? Oh my God, don't tell me I'm still in love with him.* I went home in a daze. The moment I saw my cousin Kelvin, I started crying. 'I don't know what's wrong with me,' I said.

I'd never really looked at Sonia and Nick as a long-term couple. I had actually confronted them once at Stanley Street, as part of my attempted closure of our relationship, and asked them, 'Do you love each other?' They hadn't responded. Now I felt left out. Nick had been my first love and we had a special bond. But I was losing him. He was having a baby with another woman.

While Alexander was in the shower I snuck out and drove to Peta's house because I couldn't be around Alexander with these thoughts going through my head. I had totally forgotten it was Valentine's Day, and when Peta's boyfriend answered the door I quickly picked up that he was annoyed at me for interrupting their romantic day. I didn't stay long and again drove around for a while. I decided I had to talk to Nick. For some reason I was worried about him. It was bizarre, but I wanted to know his feelings so I rang his mobile.

'Hi, it's me,' I said. 'I heard Sonia is pregnant. Are you all right?'

He said he'd planned on telling me in person but just hadn't got the chance.

It took a couple of days, but finally sanity prevailed and I was able to let go of the whole Nick–Sonia baby episode. After the initial emotions had subsided, I began to realise how much better off we both were apart. I was engaged to a wonderful man and Nick was going to become a father.

Next was the Sydney grand prix on 20 February at the Olympic warm-up track. The day before the meet I got the chance to visit the

Olympic stadium and walk on the new, springy Mondo surface. I stood at the finish line and looked around the empty stands, trying to picture what it would be like in eighteen months' time. I felt a tingling in my toes. I was standing in the place where I would live out my dream. I was still buzzing the next night when I got to the blocks for the 400m. My form had been ordinary because of my self-doubts regarding the injury. However, with all the Olympic talk of the past few days, I was energised.

I'm Catherine Freeman, I'm supposed to be here!

I ran like the Freeman of old. I attacked the back straight and turned for home well ahead of Britain's Commonwealth Games silver medal-list Alison Curbishley. It was exhilarating, and I was shocked when I crossed the line and the clock had stopped at 50.76s. I threw my arms up in the air in a victory salute. It wasn't for winning the race but for winning the battle with my own mind and body. There was no way I was in fifty-second shape, yet I had done it.

During the following week I suffered for my gut-busting effort in Sydney. I felt sick as my body slowly recovered. Maurie and Nick then talked me into going to the world indoor titles in Tokyo to run in a 4 x 400m relay. I repeated my dislike for indoors, but they said it would do me good to get away with the other girls and get a taste of international competition again. I was hopeless on the tight track, but we still managed to win a silver medal. The trip gave me a chance to get to know Tania Van Heer, and I immediately liked the way she left her competitive nature out on the track. She was more interested in talking about animals than track and field, which worked for me.

Back in Melbourne in March, the national titles were at Olympic Park and the press was talking up my clash with Tania because she had shown some impressive form over the 400m. In the warm-up I found myself a bit on edge and sounded Nick out.

'Do you definitely think I can win this?'

'You're the world champion, you don't lose races like this,' he said. 'Tania's talented but you can't just turn up and beat Cathy Freeman in the national titles.'

Exactly. She has to pay her dues. It's time to let everyone know who is still the queen.

I was in lane four, with Tania on my inside. I went out strongly, and it was obvious at the end of the back straight that her tactic was to attack around the bend. She had run very conservatively and that gave me a chance to put a nice gap between us. As we entered the straight, Tania loomed briefly, but I held her off to win in 50.94s.

The queen lives.

Team Freeman then relocated to the Couran Cove resort on South Stradbroke Island for a three-week training camp. The complex, run by world distance champion Ron Clarke, had its own 180m track and all the facilities, including sand dunes, which I ran up and down every morning. Several of Fort's other athletes – Evette Cordy, Susan Andrews, Alistair Stevenson and Cameron McKenzie – also spent time up there. However, the trap for me was the closeness to my family. A short boat ride and I was on the Gold Coast, with my parents just an hour down the road in Brisbane. My visits to them cut into valuable training time.

Nick only came up to the training camp a couple of times; with Alexander now very much in the picture, he was staying more at arm's length. This made it easier for us to maintain our working relationship, no matter how weird the situation appeared to the outside world. It was as though we were obligated to stay together to see through this dream we'd shared for the past eight years. However, my move to loosen Nick's grip on my finances went up a notch when I returned to Melbourne and had lunch with marathoner Steve Moneghetti. I'd known Mona for years, and Chris Wardlaw had recommended I talk to him as he had gone down the self-management path. They both stressed that the process was going to take time, but just before I headed to London for the European season I made the first positive step towards independence. I had been introduced to accountant Alistair Hamblin by the Victorian Institute of Sport and I authorised him to begin collating all the relevant information from Jess and Co. Nick was furious and blew his top with Chris and Mona when he found out they were advising me.

I was glad to get to London in mid-May to begin my build-up towards the Seville world championships. It was a relief to leave the financial mess at home. Nick had found me a new training partner, an

800m runner named Jai Thomas, the boyfriend of national 1,500m champion Sarah Jamieson. After an ordinary 200m run in Slovenia, we went to Seville for a 400m race, which I won in 51.06s. Maurie always liked me to have a race at the championship venue a couple of months beforehand because it enabled us to familiarise ourselves with the landscape and explore the city for the best accommodation and restaurants.

My next major assignment was in Athens, the scene of my world championship triumph two years earlier. All the big names were there, and I thrived on the electric atmosphere created by Maurice Greene breaking the world 100m record. I ran in the 200m and was disturbed by my unplaced run. I'd been pumped up beforehand but nothing happened during the race; I just couldn't sprint with them. I left Greece with my spirits flagging and the realisation that I had lost my speed.

I bumped into Marie-José Pérec at the next meet in Stockholm and was struck by how different she was. The usual air of superiority was missing, although I suspected it was partly because of the illness she had suffered over the past twelve months. Pérec had been laid low by the Epstein-Barr virus, a form of glandular fever, and was only now attempting to get back on the track. She was happy to chat and explained how she wouldn't be running in Seville but would be coming to Sydney next year. I desperately wanted her to be in Sydney. I not only wanted to win the Olympic gold medal, I wanted to bring Pérec down in the process. But before I could get too far ahead of myself I needed to get my act together.

It was nearly twelve months since I had hurt my foot but it still played on my mind. I had stepped up my training, and as I arrived in Gateshead, England, for my next race I was particularly nervous. This was supposed to be a low-key event and the only real challenger I was expecting was Sandie Richards, who was also on the comeback trail from injury. However, just as we were getting on the plane, word reached us that Richards had withdrawn and the promoters had replaced her with Nigerians Falilat Ogunkoya and Charity Opara, ranked numbers one and two in the world in my absence the previous year.

By the time our race came round there were puddles all over the track. I knew this was going to be a dogfight and I wasn't sure whether

I was ready. I was two lanes inside Ogunkoya so it wasn't until we had only a hundred metres to go that I reached her, and then we matched strides most of the way down the straight. Fally is so much bigger and stronger than me that she's always hard to beat in a straight-out slog-fest, which this race had become. Finally I edged about half a metre ahead and somehow hung on to win in 50.66s. As soon as I crossed the line I bent over in pain; I couldn't breathe or speak. I so wanted to cel-ebrate because I knew my confidence was back. It had taken me seven months to finally feel as though I hadn't lost it. After all the problems I'd had that season, I still came out in my first big international race and knocked off the world number one.

Monaco and the beautiful Louis II Stadium were next. It was my favourite track on the European circuit and I had that sixth sense before the race that this would be a good one. Ogunkoya was there again, and she had just run the season's fastest time, 49.62s, to win the Nigerian championships. Rather than be worried, that news excited me. I hadn't gone under fifty seconds since the Athens world champi-onships – tonight was the race to change that.

I was on the inside of Ogunkoya and went out hard early, catching her in the back straight. I had got to her so quickly that I then eased up, fearing I might hit the wall later. This allowed Fally to draw level, and with forty metres to go I went for it. Just as I edged away I felt my legs tighten. Luckily, I was close enough to the finish line to carry on and just get there in 49.76s.

No, Freeman, you haven't lost it!

Unfortunately, our performances on the track took a back seat to the series of positive drug tests that had rocked the sport. It saddened me because I had known Linford Christie and Merlene Ottey, both of whom tested positive, from my early days on the circuit. Merlene's positive test especially shook me because she'd been my hero; I still had the photo taken with her back at the 1990 Commonwealth Games. A year later, however, Ottey had her ban lifted by the IAAF. I couldn't understand the whole drug situation: to me it was a simple choice of right and wrong. Drugs are cheating – how could you not know that's wrong?

I've never been offered drugs or been associated with anyone that has done drugs. I remember when I had my head shaved back in 1997 and had built up my shoulders and upper body, people said that I was on drugs. Unfortunately it has got to the stage where if you are successful at track and field it is automatically assumed that you are cheating.

Back in London I had my final lead-up race at Crystal Palace, where I again defeated Ogunkoya. We had a week before we were due to head to Spain. What was expected to be a low-key time changed significantly when I had the most amazing dream. In it, a voice was booming through my head saying, 'Live for the moment, Catherine. Don't live to regret not doing anything.' It startled me, and I woke up expecting to see someone standing over me with a microphone. There was no one there except Alexander, sound asleep next to me. I didn't wake him, deciding instead I would wait for the right moment. It wasn't until the next day that it became too much. We were getting out of the car at the train station and I said, 'Hon, I want to get married.'

'Now?' he said.

I slowly nodded and smiled. Maybe it was the insecurities that had been with me all my life, but there was still a part of me that was scared Alexander didn't really want to marry me. I was convinced that's what the dream was about, so I now had to make it happen. Alexander sensed my determination and went along with everything as I began writing down in a notebook what was required if we were to make the wedding happen before Seville. He began scanning the Internet to find out the regulations in different countries and whether medical clearances were required to get a marriage licence. Over the next couple of days we investigated flying to Las Vegas or getting Concorde to take us to places like Gibraltar or the Bahamas.

While I was getting a massage from Garry Miritis, I told him Alexander and I were considering eloping.

'I think you should at least ask your mum if she wants to come,' he said.

I mentioned that to Alexander, who was straight on the phone to Brisbane to find out if Mum's passport was up to date. That night, as Alexander explained his latest plan, I grabbed his hand and made him stop.

'You know, maybe we'd better wait until after the world championships,' I said.

I could tell he was relieved. It had been pure madness even considering getting married without at least Mum and Bruce there. I knew Alexander thought as much, but he'd gone along with everything because he knew how determined I was once I got something into my head. We decided not to waste the week's work and agreed that the big day would come after Seville.

Just before we left for Spain I found myself alone with Nick and decided to tell him.

'Alexander and I are going to get married after Seville,' I said.

He seemed surprised. 'Do you think that's wise?' he said. 'Wouldn't it be better if you just focused solely on the Olympics and put things like that on hold for twelve months?'

I should have known that's what he'd think. It was always business before pleasure with Nick; he was always thinking about the bottom line.

'You only get one chance like Sydney,' he continued. 'It's never going to come around again.'

I turned and walked away.

CHAPTER 18
HOT AND BOTHERED

'Oh my God, it's so hot,' Lee Naylor screamed as we got off the bus at the warm-up track.

Seville was a beautiful city, but there was one major problem: it was hot, damned hot. The daily heatwave seemed to peak in the late afternoon so we'd train in the morning and then escape back to our air-conditioned hotel rooms. I took the opportunity to be part of the opening ceremony – I'd been given the honour of carrying the Australian flag – because my first race wasn't until two days later. It was certainly the most relaxed I'd felt at the start of a major championship, and I enjoyed it so much that I took time to hang out with some of the other athletes.

The first of many difficulties that were to confront me in Seville happened on the morning of my heat: I began to get my period. I couldn't believe it. I'd forgotten to take my birth-control pill one day the week before and that had set everything off. So here I was about to start the world championships with a bloated stomach and no energy. The heat was so intense that as I jogged around my mouth and throat were dry and my chest was sore. But I didn't want to over-drink before my race. To add to my rising anxiety, as I waited for our heat I saw a young Russian girl, who had gone out really hard in the previous race, collapse on the track at the finish line.

By the time I got on to the blocks I was feeling terrible. I was in lane eight, and I proceeded to completely stuff up my race plans. Instead of going out hard for three hundred metres and then cruising home, I ran a fast hundred and turned off along the straight before nearly being floored at the two-hundred-metre mark by a gust of heat from an open exit in the stadium. I really slowed down, and by the time we entered the straight the rest of the field was alongside me. I then had to work hard to hold out Nigerian Olabisi Afolabi in 51.49s. For a few minutes afterwards I felt like I could hardly breathe. We found out later it was actually 47°C on the track!

Even though we could hardly stand each other at the time, Nick was still fulfilling his role as manager and motivator. It was funny, because if we talked athletics and nothing else we were fine. Unfortunately our conversations inevitably became personal, but the next day at lunch Nick's focus was on the second round and how he wanted me to finish one or two and be guaranteed a good draw in the semi-final. The dangers, Afolabi and Grit Breuer, were both on my inside and Nick didn't want me to let them get too far ahead at the top of the straight.

From lane six, I again started well and then switched off at the two-hundred-metre mark as I'd done in the earlier round. It was like I was daydreaming, because by the time I realised I was cruising the other two had shot five metres clear. With every bound I was closing, but I had left my run too late and missed the runner-up spot by two-hundredths of a second. I'd mucked up because I'd been lazy, and I was about to pay the ultimate price.

Assistant team manager Geoff Rowe approached me at dinner that night with the bad news. I don't know whether he was trying to be funny but it irritated me how casually he informed me that I was in lane eight for the semi-final. I started freaking out the second he had uttered the words. Lane eight! Lane eight! I was the defending world champion and here I was in the outside lane, the worst possible, in the goddamn semi-final. I wasn't even going to make the final.

I tried to sleep, but just as I'd be nodding off it would come screaming back into my mind. Lane eight! I tried getting up and drinking some water but that didn't help. I was then up and down to the toilet. I was driving myself crazy. I started thinking about all this other personal stuff like how Nick had said I shouldn't get married. It was all starting to pile up and I just wanted to be in another place. The next morning I saw Lisa-Marie Vizaniari outside the hotel getting into a taxi.

She was going home because she'd failed to qualify for the discus final. I was so jealous. I wanted to get into the taxi with her and on to that plane. As we were saying goodbye, I whispered to her, 'I want to go with you, I want to go with you.' I was in a state of panic and I could sense tears were about to flow, so I rushed back upstairs to my room.

Nick wanted to meet me downstairs for lunch to talk tactics. 'Listen, Cathy, you're stuffing this up the same way you did in Athens,' he said as soon as we sat down. 'If you don't run the semi-final properly you'll be in lane one or lane eight for the final. That Lorraine Graham, she's no donkey, and she'll beat you. You've got a chance tonight to finish her off. If you run properly, come out there like you really mean it, like you did in Oslo, like you did in Athens, then it will be in their heads that they can't beat you.'

I was still anxious when I got back to my room. There was too much happening. My mind was spinning. The wedding. Nick and Alexander. A knock on the door interrupted yet another debrief with Alexander. It was Maurie. He would always come and see me before a big race and offer one of his pearls of wisdom.

'Maurie, I'm glad you're here. I need to ask you a favour,' Alexander said. 'I need you to talk to Nick. He keeps telling Catherine that we shouldn't get married.'

I was lying on the bed, and Maurie looked straight at me. 'No, I won't,' he said. 'I'm certain that is none of my business or Nick's, but I'm also certain that with the semi-final in a few hours maybe we should be putting our thoughts to something else. I'm just here to tell you, Catherine, that we believe in you.'

Maurie was right. Everything could wait. I had a world championship title to defend and if I was even going to get a chance to do that I was going to have to run the race of my life.

I met Nick at the warm-up track and we walked two laps of the outside lane to help me visualise what I needed to do. Nick's theory was that I had to keep the others out of sight. 'You've got to run like a scared bunny,' he said. If ever I needed to flick on my focus switch, it was tonight.

I was relieved when I entered the stadium and sensed that both mind and body were ready. I knew I had to start well. The first two hundred metres would be critical and, thankfully, I got out smoothly. As I neared the final bend I could sense that the Russian in lane seven was closing as the stagger began to take effect.

Don't let her get ahead. See no one.

With a hundred metres to go, the field straightened and I knew I was behind. I didn't know if it was one metre or two because it was so hard to calculate from the outside.

Go now, Freeman. Run scared.

When I went for it there was plenty there so I started to power down the straight. I was calling on energy from deep inside and I was lifting. All that was left with fifty metres to go was Breuer, who looked to be a couple of metres clear.

I'm flying again. That wonderful feeling is happening again.

With a couple of long bounds I grabbed Breuer and hit the line first, giving myself a quick clap as I saw the time of 49.76s. My mind was so strong. Like Pérec in Atlanta, I'd blown them away in the semi-finals.

If they couldn't beat me today, they never would.

Rest days are never much fun at major championships. Again I didn't sleep well and tried to kill some time playing cards with Steve Moneghetti and marathon runner Kerryn McCann. Alexander suggested a movie, so we went to see Julia Roberts and Hugh Grant in *Notting Hill* with Richo and his fiancée, 5,000m runner Kate Anderson.

No matter how hard you try, you inevitably spend the day of a final watching the clock. I tried to amuse myself with laundry, a massage and going down for a two-hour nap in the afternoon. The final wasn't until 8.30 p.m. and we left for the track about three hours before then. I'd drawn lane five, with Ogunkoya on my inside and Breuer in lane six. Nick didn't want me to be too far behind entering the straight – two metres was fine, but not five.

'You can only beat yourself here,' he said. 'If you run the right race, if you don't make a mistake, there is no way you can lose.'

After giving Fort a quick hug at the call room, I walked into the second call room under the stadium. My mind had been fried after the semi-final drama and I knew I wasn't fully wound up for the final. As we walked out on to the track I scarcely acknowledged the crowd and didn't hear my name getting read out, as I was trying everything to get focused for the next fifty seconds. If I could do that, I would be world champion again.

I exploded from the blocks and was within two metres of Breuer by the start of the back straight. By the two-hundred-metre mark I was alongside her, and I knew she was gone.

Coming around the bend, the only girl I hadn't passed was the other German, Anja Rucker, over in lane eight. Then Ogunkoya made her move and for ten metres we matched strides before I began to pull away.

You've done it, Freeman.

Hang on. I could sense someone still there. It was Rucker on the outside. She was coming home hard.

Push it now. She won't catch you.

My nose for the finish line was again perfect, and I held Rucker at bay to win the gold medal in 49.67s, the German getting the silver in 49.74s and Lorraine Graham bronze in 49.92s. I slumped forward with my hands on my knees. There was no feeling of excitement or joy. I was just relieved it was over. I couldn't even smile. I knew a huge weight had just been lifted from my shoulders, but as I turned and looked towards Maurie, who was trackside with the BBC, I could only think of one thing: the Sydney Olympics. Defending my world championship crown was only a stepping stone on the journey to my ultimate dream, and that was now just over a year away.

A photographer handed me the Australian flag and gestured for me to run a victory lap. I didn't feel like celebrating this moment and instead stood near the finish line with the flag draped around my shoulders. Nick came over and urged me to show some elation, but I was struggling with my breathing again because of the heat. I stayed out on the side of the track near the mixed zone to watch the men's 400m. I almost got more of a buzz out of Michael Johnson breaking the world record than my own achievement. I was so emotionally flat.

Once again I had forgotten my team tracksuit and had to borrow one – three sizes too big – from team manager Peter Brukner for the medal ceremony. Nick suggested I should try to show the world I was happy or it might be misinterpreted by the press. 'That would be acting,' I said. But as I stepped up on to the dais, I jumped around and waved my hands with the biggest smile on my face. After the gold medal was around my neck, I made sure I turned to the crowd in the back straight to show everyone how happy I was. By the time the last couple of lines of 'Advance Australia Fair' were being played, I was genuinely enjoying myself. The relief had finally turned to exhilaration and I could even sense tears forming as I looked up at the crowd for one last wave. A little Aboriginal girl was again the best in the world.

We celebrated at a Nike party until four a.m., then at nine the next morning I had a press conference, where I again faced the inevitable stream of questions about the plight of the Aboriginal people back home and the Stolen Generation debate. I played a straight bat to all of them because by that point all I wanted to do was get back to the hotel and rest.

The semi-final of the relay was the next day, but in the morning I had to go to an IAAF function with Nick. Alexander and I met him in the foyer of the hotel but I'd forgotten to put on a Nike top so Nick suggested I go upstairs and change. As I was coming back down the stairs I heard raised voices and then saw Alexander rush at Nick and shove him backwards. Nick dropped his computer bag and shaped up to punch Alexander.

'Righto, let's go,' he said.

I was stunned. I couldn't believe what I was seeing. My fiancé and my ex-boyfriend were having a fight in the hotel lobby.

'What's going on?' I yelled. 'What's wrong?'

'I'll tell you what's wrong,' Alexander said. 'He's calling you a liar.'

'I'm not calling you a liar,' Nick said.

'She says you keep telling her that we shouldn't get married,' Alexander said as Nick came at him.

'Stop it!' I screamed. Thankfully, one of the Australian team coaches, Keith Connor, and a couple of other people intervened and separated the two men in my life.

I couldn't stay and turned to walk out. I got into the taxi that was waiting for us and Nick followed me. I didn't know where Alexander had gone, but the place was going crazy. As Nick went to climb into the car a security guard came and grabbed him; they wanted to talk to him inside. I got out of the taxi and went back upstairs, where I found a very upset Alexander. The tension between the pair had been simmering away from the moment Alexander had arrived on the scene. I'd known it would only be a matter of time before something like this happened. But what were we going to do now? How were we going to make this thing work? I couldn't think about that – I had a relay to run.

The semi-final went without incident, but the same couldn't be said about the lead-up to the final.

'Well, what are we doing?' I said to Jackie Byrnes, the 4 x 400m relay coach.

The team meeting was in chaos. With just four hours until the final the coaches had decided to make a last-minute change and included Lauren Hewitt, who'd made the final of the 200m, at the expense of Susan Andrews. We hadn't been consulted or even told this might be happening so when the news was delivered it rattled the team. 'Oh, this is crap,' Lee Naylor said. Tamsyn Lewis, who had run in the heat as a late replacement for Tania Van Heer, said, 'I can't put up with this any more, I'm going to find Susan.' Tania was also distraught for Susan.

I had just been sitting there fuming at all the bullshit that was flying around. I knew that if this was the decision then we had to move on and get our tactics sorted out because time was running out. I turned to Lauren and asked, 'OK then, what are you going to do?' I could see that she was scared and it obviously wasn't her idea to be part of the relay. I was sick and tired of something going wrong with our relay teams. I was getting more and more frustrated with Byrnes, who was also Melinda Gainsford-Taylor's coach, because there was just no communication between us. I had run the relay heat, which was my fifth 400m in six days, while most of my main rivals rested up for the final. She hadn't once asked how I was feeling or whether my body was standing up. I could already feel some warning signs and was just hoping I could make it through. Eventually I walked out of the meeting and went back to my room. When I emerged an hour later to get on the bus, Lauren had pulled out and Susan was back in. All that confusion had been for nothing and had only managed to upset everyone. I wondered what effect it would have on us because I knew I was tired. I really thrived on being involved in a team and I just hoped the spirit between us stayed strong.

Tania ran a good first leg, and when she changed to Lee we were fourth. Lee ran a great leg, and by the time Susan got the baton we were in third place, about fifteen metres behind the US and Russia. The nervous tension started to rise as I watched Susan surge at the leaders down the back straight. Unfortunately the effort took its toll, and by the time I got the baton we were back in sixth. When I looked up I saw that third-placed Grit Breuer was about twenty metres away.

As I rounded the first bend I suddenly felt my ham-strings tighten. They were screaming out to me and I knew I couldn't push it. It was clear we weren't going to win a medal and there was no way I was going to risk any damage with the Sydney Olympics just twelve months away. I kept going but only held sixth place. I knew I'd run a shocker but I didn't have a choice. Maybe if we'd been closer I might have at least tested it, but the last thing I needed was a serious injury to cap off a tumultuous world championships.

I caught up with the girls and apologised. 'My legs were just gone,' I said to Lee.

'You don't win a world championship without it taking everything out of you,' she said.

I appreciated her comments, and she repeated them to the waiting media, explaining how we couldn't always rely on me to win a medal and that we needed to be able to rest our number one runner during the heats. The girls were great and so understanding that it helped to ease the pain I felt at not being able to produce my best effort.

Fort came down and saw me and we were on our way to get a massage at the warm-up track when Jackie Byrnes confronted us.

'That was a bullshit run, Cathy,' she yelled. 'I think you owe those girls an apology.'

She was really in my face. I was shocked, and didn't know what to say.

Fort quickly stepped in. 'Don't you think you should find out if there's a cause before you say stupid things like that?' he said.

'All right, what is it, then?' she barked back at us.

Normally I'm pretty fiery when someone confronts me in this way, but I was exhausted, and my anger turned to tears. 'Don't worry about it,' I said as I began to cry, and Fort motioned for Jackie to leave us alone. I became semi-hysterical. I was laughing then crying, but most of all I was furious. 'How dare she?' I kept yelling as I began to kick wastepaper bins over at the warm-up track. Garry Miritis tried to calm me down as we jogged a lap but I wanted to vent my anger. By the time I got back to the hotel I was shattered. I showered, and then Lee and Lauren arrived to see how I was because they'd heard about the confrontation. I just wanted to get out of Seville. It had been nothing but a nightmare, even though I'd somehow found the strength to defend my world championship title. That gave me great confidence, because I knew the pressure was going to be magnified a thousand times going into the Olympics on my home soil as the gold medal favourite.

Alexander had already gone back to the States and I had to fly back to London with Nick. He hadn't come down to the track for the relays so I hadn't seen him since his argument with Alexander. We agreed we needed to discuss how everything was going to work next year when we got back, but for now Maurie had a couple of races planned in Europe. He always liked me to continue racing after major championships. The first race was in Italy, but only a couple of minutes into my warm-up I knew something was wrong. I had an ear infection, though it wasn't affecting me that much, and I just couldn't shake this feeling of emptiness. I didn't want to run. It was obvious I'd reached the end of my tether.

'I can't do this,' I told Maurie.

He didn't argue the point and quickly made up a story about a hamstring niggle to appease the event promoter. My head and body were fried so I pulled out of all my other scheduled races and returned to London to meet up with Alexander, who was busy planning our wedding.

CHAPTER 19
THE WEDDING

'He is not to come training.' Nick's voice rose slightly for empha-sis. 'If we have a training camp he is to stay away.'

I was sitting in a café called the Italian Place in Teddington across from Nick and Maurie. They wanted Alexander to stay out of the equation.

'If you want to get married, just do it after the Olympics,' Nick con-tinued. 'If you're going to be together for ever, why can't it wait another twelve months? You don't need a big adjustment in your life right now. We can't stop you, but that's what we think. But he has got to keep out of things so we can get our job done.'

I knew a lot of what they were saying made sense, but Alexander was pretty determined to make it happen now. After my initial freak-out dream about getting married, I was at the stage where I really didn't think the timing was a big deal.

My dream was to get married by the ocean, barefoot on the sand, with beautiful white horses as part of the ceremony. Our tight time frame didn't allow for such extravagances, but Alexander had found the perfect location on the Internet, a place called Half-Moon Bay in San Francisco. Both of us wanted it to be a private and intimate gath-ering, and our only guests were to be Mum and Bruce and three of Alexander's best friends: Mark, John and Roger. We set the date for 19 September, which gave us two weeks to get back to the States, pick out a dress in Portland and then drive to LA to collect my parents. Everything had been organised over the Net: the details for the service, the flowers, the cake and the photographer. The only downside was that my brothers weren't going to be there to celebrate my wedding day. It was an impossible task to get them and their families over to the other side of the world in such a short time. Two weeks certainly wasn't long enough for them to arrange passports, book leave from their jobs and organise care for their children. I rang each of them back home in Australia and explained the circumstances. They all understood, which meant so much to me, and we promised to have a good, old-fashioned Freeman family celebration when I returned.

On the flight to the States my ear infection got worse, and when we arrived in Portland I went straight to a medical clinic. I was in agony. My head felt like it was going to explode and they had to fill me up with painkillers and antibiotics. I returned the next night because the infection had actually worsened and it was placing our wedding arrangements in jeopardy. Alexander wanted to hire a car and drive up the coast to San Francisco so we could take in the beautiful scenery along the way. It was a great idea, but I spent most of that time in a fog because my head was filled with drugs. I really couldn't enjoy anything and was beginning to wonder what else could possibly go wrong. I didn't have to wait long.

When we arrived in San Francisco, we found out that our secret wedding was no longer a secret and the media was camped outside the hotel. This really pissed me off because only a small group of my closest friends knew anything about it. It was Bruce who first alerted us to the problem; he'd overheard a conversation between two photographers outside the hotel about whether they'd spotted Cathy Freeman. When notes from press organisations started being left under our door, Alexander arranged for us to escape out the back. To throw the hounds off the scent, the management kept our names on the guest list. We then checked into a nearby hotel under a pseudonym.

I'm not a very fussy person, and that was the way I approached the purchase of my wedding dress, picking the first one I tried on in Portland. It was powdery pink, strapless and very feminine. I asked Alexander what he thought in the shop and he liked it, so that was the end of that. I also got some earrings and a bracelet to complete the outfit. I knew it would be too raunchy for Mum, and as we were getting ready she said, 'Alexander chose the dress, did he?' I glared at her and explained that it was my selection, quickly ending the discussion.

I'd had a couple of panic attacks the night before. I was so not the marrying type, and suddenly it dawned on me that I wouldn't be able to be with another man again. I'd never looked at it in that way. Was I ready to be a married woman? These questions raced through my mind until I sat down and talked through it all with Alexander.

The setting was ideal. The ceremony was to take place on the top of the sand dunes and, magically, a school of dolphins appeared in the water as we were getting ready. There had been a delay because I'd sent Alexander back to the hotel as I wanted to change my shoes. It was a bit overcast so the lady celebrant had lent me a cream-coloured, Japanese, woven shawl that went perfectly with my dress. But I was wearing black high-heeled shoes and now wanted to swap them for a pair of pink sandals that were back at the hotel.

As we started the short walk towards the sand dunes I counted the number of people who were part of my wedding day. I smiled when I recalled how one of the suggestions after our engagement was to hold the wedding in a marquee at Melaleuca Park, my childhood athletics track which was now known as Cathy Freeman Athletic Park. What a drama that would have been: hundreds of guests and probably as many security guards. At Half-Moon Bay there were eleven people, including me and Alexander: Bruce and Mum, the three guys, the celebrant, plus a couple and their son who were taking care of the photography and video recording. Suddenly I was racked with guilt and sadness that all of my family wasn't with me. I turned to Mum, and she had already started nodding before I'd even uttered the words, 'I wish the boys were here.' It was like she knew exactly what I was thinking.

The celebrant moved quickly through the vows as I held hands with Alexander. He was wearing cream linen pants and jacket, a light-blue shirt and a small pink flower that matched my bouquet. He was starting to choke up, and beside me Mum already had her handkerchief out, wiping away the tears. I kept giggling because I felt so happy. I'd tried not to have any pre-conceptions about the day or how I should feel when I uttered the words 'I do', or felt the ring slide on to my finger. Both key moments came and went with a minimum of fuss, a couple of laughs and big smiles.

After the ceremony we posed for some photos on the sand before heading back to get changed for a celebratory lunch. I was so happy that common sense had prevailed and we hadn't eloped because I'm sure Mum would never have forgiven me. The restaurant overlooked the water and everyone chilled out and soaked up the beautiful surroundings. I went for a walk along the beach alone and couldn't get out of my head something that Bruce had said to me earlier, 'Your wedding day is supposed to be the happiest day of your life!'

It had been.

As darkness filled the cabin I reached up and turned on the small light above my head. I searched the seat pocket for something to write on, and the best I could come up with was a brown paper bag. It was time to write my annual goal-setting list. Every year since 1994 I'd used the twenty-odd hours in the plane coming home from Europe or the States at the end of the season to assess and plan my goals for the year ahead. As I flattened out the bag it suddenly dawned on me that there had never been a more critical list than the one I was about to write.

I wrote four words in capital letters along the top: SYDNEY 2000 OLYMPIC GAMES. I stared at them for what seemed like minutes before breaking my trance by flicking up the window-shade and looking out into the darkness. The next twelve months were the most important of my life. I knew I had to commit like never before, and that meant sacrifices had to be made.

As soon as I started to write the word 'sacrifice' I looked at the sparkling diamond ring on my wedding finger. I'd already made one big sacrifice – no honeymoon. I was travelling home to Australia without my new husband. Seated next to me were Mum and Bruce, who were both sound asleep. We just didn't have time for a holiday because I wanted to get back home and start training on 4 October, and Alexander had to finish up some work in the States. So here I was, not even past my first fortnight as a married woman, husbandless on a plane flying over the Pacific Ocean.

The list began to take shape. I had to be very strict with my diet and cut out treats like chocolate and red wine with my dinner. Training was the other main focus. At the bottom of the paper bag I wrote, again in capital letters, I WILL TRAIN LIKE I HAVE NEVER TRAINED BEFORE, and then double-underlined it. That was the key. Under the heading 'Lifestyle Goals', I wrote the word INDEPENDENCE. I knew I had to get out of MTC and take control of all sections of my life before the Olympics. This was going to be the most challenging goal of the lot.

CHAPTER 20
THE COUNTDOWN BEGINS

From day one of my training back in Melbourne I felt on, which in athletics-speak means I was focused. My training programme ran six days a week and generally involved three track sessions, two workouts on the hills, two to three weights sessions, and circuit exercises five times a week. My rest day was usually on the Saturday.

The hill sessions took place either at Jolimont, just outside the Melbourne Cricket Ground, or down by the beach at Black Rock. These were tough workouts, sprinting three to four hundred metres up the incline between eight and ten times. Further into the session we'd increase the speed and decrease the time between reps.

Early in the season my training was geared towards strength and general aerobic fitness. Initially the track sessions were more about volume: reps up to 500m, or reps of 6 x 300m with a two-minute rest, or 10 x 200m with a one-minute rest. We didn't actually run many 400s in training, but tended to focus on the times and rest breaks between reps to simulate the effort required in a 400m race. Later we added in speed work, which involved sets of 120m and 150m to 200m run at a faster pace with fewer reps. An example of a really tough session would be 3 x 300m followed by a 200m just two minutes after the 300m. The weights focused on building explosive strength in my quads and hamstrings, core stability in my stomach and lower back, and power in my arms. I can lift 3 x 70kg on the bench press, which isn't bad for a girl of just over eight stone (or 53–54kg). As we got closer to competition, I dropped down to only one weights session a week. Circuit involved five or six different exercises to strengthen my stomach, including sit-ups, push-ups and dips. I usually did these in the morning. Stretching was obviously very important, and I spent between thirty and forty minutes before each session loosening my body.

To complement all this work I had to maintain a good diet, and mine was devised with the help of the Victorian Institute of Sport nutritionist. It was a mixture of higher protein base, some carbohydrates and low fat. I also used supplements, which provided more vitamins and minerals, because the food alone just didn't give me enough. These helped with my energy levels and recovery rate. It's really important to go into each session as recovered as possible and not be tired, because that's when you are at risk of injury. I tried to eat two hours before training, usually some muesli with honey for breakfast, and some juice. I snacked a lot rather than having big meals because it helps the recovery process. Lunch was light, something like rice cakes with salmon and light cream cheese, a salad or a healthy sandwich such as turkey with cranberry sauce. I never had butter or extra sauces and tried to stay away from red meat, only eating it every now and then. I preferred chicken, although it had to be skinless and free-range. I also ate a lot of fish and steamed vegetables.

The Sydney Olympics acted as powerful motivation for me; I followed everything in my programme to the letter and quickly settled into a good routine. Most of the action had been happening off the track, Athletics Australia having called all the relay girls in to discuss the Jackie Byrnes incident in Seville. Several of the others had complained about her, and while I didn't like to get involved in the politics of it all, I said I'd prefer not to have to work with her again. A week later Byrnes was replaced by John Quinn, Essendon Football Club's fitness adviser and the new coach of Lauren Hewitt.

Alexander and I had also found a new home. The search really didn't take that long because Alexander immediately fell in love with a five-bedroomed house in Kew that was very private and had beautiful views of the Yarra River. I was easily convinced.

A low-key state league meet at Olympic Park on Thursday, 18 November kicked off my Olympic campaign. I ran in a 4 x 400m relay for my club, Ringwood United, and couldn't believe how excited I felt at being back out there. A couple more state league meets followed before I debuted onto the grand prix circuit at the Zatopek Classic in Melbourne on 6 December. We decided that I'd run the 100m because we were concentrating on my speed, but my sprint debut didn't go according to plan. I thought someone had moved at the start so I sat back waiting for the second gun and a false start. When it didn't come, I looked up and I was already metres behind the others. I hate losing at the best of times, especially the first big race of my Olympic campaign, so I really pushed it and luckily got there by a whisker in 12.05s.

We moved into the new house just before Christmas, and to celebrate arranged for all my family to come down from Queensland for a couple of weeks. I loved having my nieces and nephews around me. We had seventeen of the Freeman clan bunked down in Kew that Christmas.

On 29 December I flew to Tasmania to race in two handicap events at the Devonport Gift. The 400m was run that night, and after giving what seemed like a hundred metres to some of the other girls I only managed to finish eighth. I was more fired up for the 200m the following night, where I was pitted against Tania Van Heer. Despite a two-metre handicap in her favour, I surged late on the grass track and caught her on the line to win in 23.73s. I was pretty happy with it, and my training partner, Jai, admitted he didn't think I was going to beat Tania because of the handicap. On the plane back to Melbourne, I thought about what Jai had said and realised that the Freeman of twelve months ago wouldn't have won that race. Mentally and physically I was already different. I was beginning to like the new version.

The first grand prix meeting of 2000 was in Canberra on 15 January, and I ran the 200m/400m double. I just failed to pip Melinda Gainsford-Taylor for second behind Lauren Hewitt in the 200m, while I comfortably won the 400m in 50.91s. You could already sense the excitement of the Olympic year among the athletes; the chase was on for qualifying times and personal bests. I chalked up one of my own in training, Nick telling me that at 35.9s I'd clocked the fastest three hundred metres of my career. I then went out and got my revenge on Hewitt at the Victorian championships in early February, winning the

200m in 23.19s. I stuck with the 200m for the next two grand prix events, in Brisbane and Sydney, finishing third and second respectively, both behind Gainsford-Taylor.

I was really pumped about the domestic season, and the reason why was next on the agenda: the national championships were being held on the Olympic track in Sydney. This was what I'd been waiting for since I'd started back in October – the chance to perform and familiarise myself with the stadium where in seven months' time I'd be chasing my dream. We called it a 'dry run' for the Olympics. The key to being able to perform to the best of my ability at these Games, in my home country, was to learn to control my emotions and think of Sydney as just another track. The day before the championships were to start, I did a warm-up inside the stadium. It felt awesome, even electric, and this was with nobody in the stands. There was a tingling in my toes and an extra bounce in my body as we strode along the new surface.

For the opening round, two thousand school kids were brought in to cheer, and I was struck by how loud they were. If they could do that, what sort of noise would more than a hundred thousand people make? It was very blustery for the race, which I won easily in a slow 54.05s. At a press conference afterwards I couldn't put into words how great it had felt to run inside the stadium. All I kept saying was 'Ahhh'.

I made a conscious effort to take notice of all the procedures during the rounds, from the first call room to how long it took to walk through the tunnel underneath the stadium, the size of the small warm-up area under the stand and the entry point on to the track. Every step was important. For the final, the nerves really hit when I started taking off my tracksuit next to the blocks. The field was strong with the inclusion of Mexican Ana Guevara, who Nick and Maurie thought would be a contender later in the year. This only fuelled my desire. No way was I going to get beaten in my dress rehearsal for the Olympics.

I raced with a rhythm and strength I rarely possessed so early in the season and by the top of the straight I had killed off the others. Guevara chased hard but I was gliding towards the finish line, and as I crossed I looked straight at the clock to my left: 50.00s. Wow! The adrenalin of the Olympic stadium had pushed me to within a whisker of breaking fifty seconds and it was still only February. I couldn't help but wonder what I might be capable of by September. Everyone around me was genuinely excited and it was good to know we were heading in the right direction.

The 200m heats were the next day and already Jai, Nick and Maurie were getting inside my head about beating my old sparring partner Melinda Gainsford-Taylor. I still didn't think I had my speed back, but by the time Sunday came round the constant encouragement had started to work. The final was one of the last events of the championships and my sixth race in four days. Melinda had also had a tough campaign in the 100m, plus, as my team kept pushing, she was coming back from a knee injury. 'She's vulnerable,' Nick said.

I hadn't beaten Melinda in Australia for over five years. When racing Melinda, the key was not to panic, because she inevitably ran a great bend and at some stage in the straight would look to have a winning break. The question was whether you could close that gap over the final twenty or thirty metres. The start went as predicted. I was on the outside of Melinda, and when the stagger took shape as we entered the straight the gap was at least five metres. By the fifty-metre mark I could sense myself building and had crept a little closer; at twenty metres a little closer still.

It's happening again. I'm flying.

She was stopping, and a couple of strides from the line I grabbed her.

Yes! I've still got it.

I'd got there by two-hundredths of a second in 22.78s. I lingered out on the track for a little longer than usual. I loved it out there, and I was already connecting to the vibe and spirit inside this magnificent stadium. I couldn't wait to return.

The dynamics of my team had changed over the past few months, with Jai taking a more significant role. Nick was spending less and less time at training and Jai had become his messenger boy. In the warm-up before races Jai was now the one who talked tactics, and I sensed this was becoming increasingly frustrating for Fort. The issue reared its head at the Melbourne grand prix on 2 March. Guevara was again my only threat in the 400m, and before the race Jai was adamant that I should go out hard and get past the Mexican by the middle of the back straight. I didn't argue: these people were in my team because I trusted their judgement. But when I got out on to the track a hint of doubt rushed over me on seeing that Guevara was in lane five, two lanes away on my outside.

From the gun I charged out and really raced the first 150 metres. At Olympic Park the back straight is usually as packed as the main grandstand and I could hear the excitement of the crowd as I ranged up to Guevara exactly as we'd planned. I worked the bend hard and straightened with a significant lead, but with sixty metres to go I suddenly felt different. My legs were getting heavy and my stride was out. I had pushed it too much at the start and was now paying the price. With twenty metres to go I started to worry about Guevara; I couldn't feel her, but I could sense by the rising sound of the crowd that she was coming.

C'mon, Freeman, no one runs you down, especially on your home turf.

Luckily the line was looming and I had enough left to get there first in 50.31s; Guevara had closed to within a couple of metres, clocking 50.41. But I was shaken. I had made myself vulnerable and I was determined that should never happen again. My anger was matched by Fort's. 'What was that?' he asked. I just shrugged my shoulders and looked over at Jai and Nick, who were locked in an intense discussion. I didn't need this and walked away, looking for Garry and his massage table. Although it wasn't the ideal finish to the domestic season, I was relieved that we could now focus on a solid two-month training block before leaving for Europe.

Back in December 1999 I'd made a quick trip over to America to attend a Nike Olympic summit. One of the key reasons for the get-together was to unveil the Nike swift suit, a full-body running outfit with hood that was going to be available for selected athletes to use at the Olympics. It was certainly impressive, and when Danny Hopkins from Nike rang to tell me he had a test model in Melbourne for me to try on, I was excited. He came down to training at Sandringham the next morning with a video camera to capture my every movement in the new suit.

Above left: One of the funniest people I ever knew – my father, Norman.

Above right: How good is this? Kicking back in the front yard of our family home in Burston Street, Mackay.

Left: One tough, no-nonsense woman. My mother, Cecelia, and me aged four.

I never stopped smiling as a kid. Life in tropical Mackay was free and easy, and I was always running round barefoot with my brothers and cousins.

My inspiration. My older sister, Anne-Marie, had cerebral palsy and couldn't walk or talk, but she could light up a room with her big brown eyes and magical smile.

Mum and Bruce's wedding day in 1982. I was nine and thought I looked pretty good. Even my younger brothers, Norman and Gareth, looked the part.

Above: My brother Norman, on the left in the white singlet, and me at a local competition. He was a very talented sprinter but his real passion was Rugby League.

Left: With my first coach, Mike Danila. I'm holding the 1990 Young Australian of the Year Award. After just six months with Mike I made it into my first Australian team. We won gold in the 4 x 100m relay at the Auckland Commonwealth Games.

Opposite: One of my proudest moments. Showing the world the Aboriginal flag after my victory in the 400m.

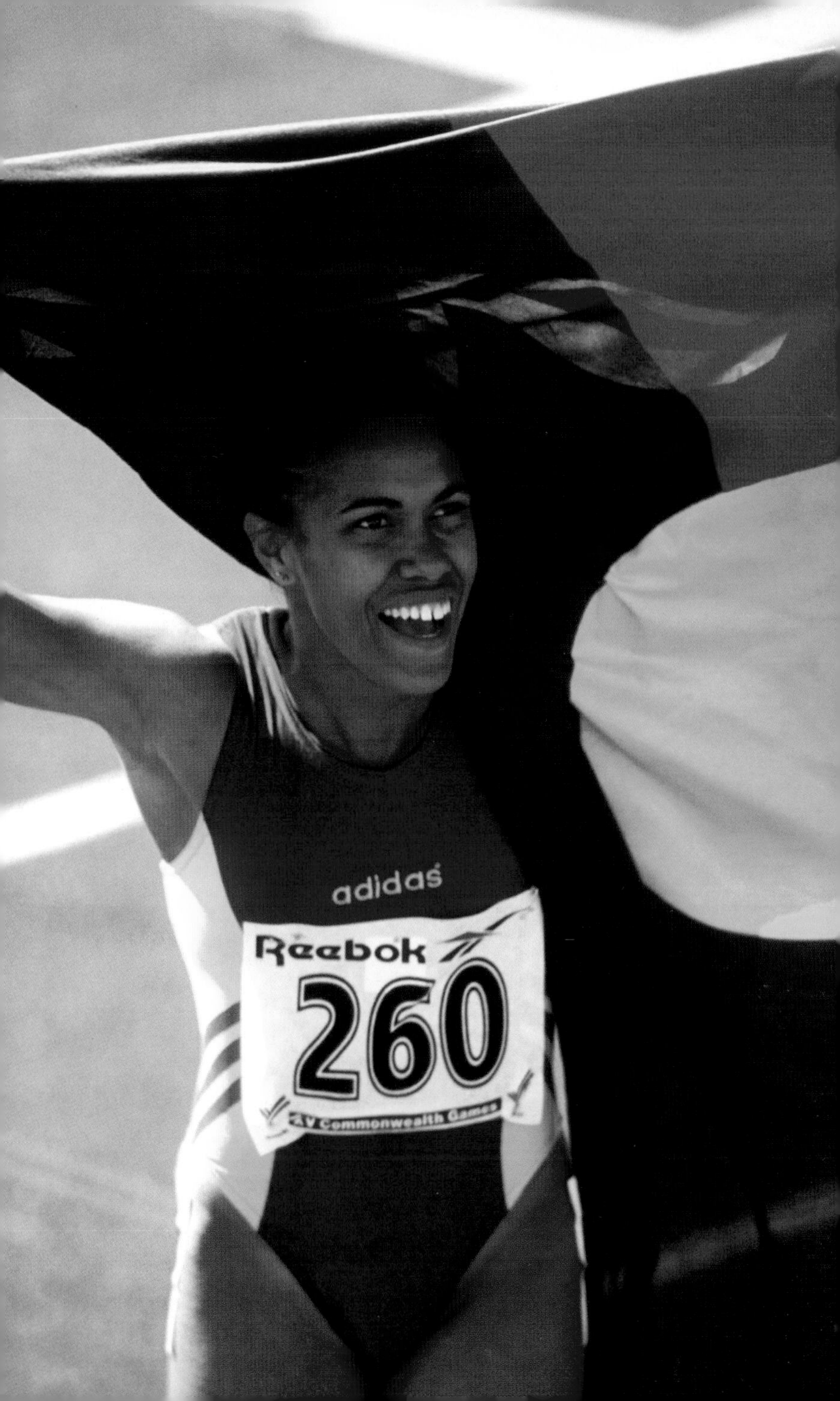
adidas
Reebok
260
XV Commonwealth Games

© Al Bello/Getty

Opposite: An historic moment for our country but I was worried about getting soaked – leading up to Sydney I'd been dogged by a cold I couldn't shake. Relief at doing my part without a mistake was short-lived when the cauldron hit a snag.

Above and below: With 80m to go I knew I'd won the gold medal. I had blocked out everything else until then but halfway down the straight the roar of the crowd burst through my senses – I felt like they were carrying me in their arms to the finish line.

© Mark Horsburgh/Sport the Library

Above: Good old Fort. We have had our ups and downs but I owe a lot to my long-term coach, Peter Fortune.

Below: Time to move on. I've retired, and life is taking me in a new exciting direction. Where exactly? Only time will tell …

At first it felt weird, but with each run-through I began to feel more and more comfortable. I could hear the wind whistling across my ears with the hood on and it actually felt like I was cutting through the air. I felt lighter and faster in it. The only problem, which I joked about with Danny, was that I hated standing out, and there was no way of missing me in the swift suit. I came to the conclusion that I would only wear it on a very special occasion. And I already knew exactly what that occasion would be.

CHAPTER 21
END OF THE ROAD

When I opened the front door Alexander was sitting on the couch waiting for me. I threw my bag down on the floor and looked over at him. He had a strange expression on his face.

'What's wrong?' I asked.

He picked up a magazine and pushed it my way. 'Have you seen this?'

I suddenly froze. 'Oh my God,' I said slowly. On the cover of the 27 March *Woman's Day* magazine was a picture of me. Inside was a four-page spread headlined CATHY'S EX-LOVER BREAKS HIS SILENCE. I couldn't believe it. What had Nick done? I felt weak and had to sit down next to Alexander. There were pictures of Nick and Sonia with their six-month-old daughter, Ciara, but the whole article was about my relationship with Nick. This was the man who for years had shielded me from the media, had gone out of his way to ensure our relationship was kept out of the papers, yet he was now revealing all to a goddamn women's magazine.

I felt betrayed. I pitched the magazine across the room. 'That's it,' I said to Alexander, 'It's over. MTC and Catherine Freeman are no more.'

I was consumed with anger, and later that night I rang Chris Wardlaw. 'Rab, I've had enough,' I said. We'd already had several meetings about the mechanics of splitting with MTC. I told him that process now had to be fast-tracked.

My anger hadn't subsided by the time I got to the track the next morning. Jai and Fort quickly picked up my vibe and not much was said until Nick showed up. He had just got back from the world cross-country titles.

'What do you want?' I snarled at him.

'I've just come to see how training is going,' he said.

How could he stand there and pretend to care?

'Get out of here. You make me sick,' I said, and walked off.

I met with Rab at the Pavilion Café in the Fitzroy Gardens to formulate a game plan. I deliberately went on my own because I knew there were people out there who would think Alexander was pushing me into this, which couldn't have been further from the truth. If anything, he was concerned about me making sweeping changes so close to the Olympics. But this was my life and I was finally going to fix it. I agreed with Rab's suggestion that Nick should stay on as my athletics manager and we would pay for his services. I'd also appoint a separate business manager and media manager.

I had ignored the reality of my bizarre work set-up with Nick for a long time. I'd been more concerned about running and training than getting my life in order. I'd been lazy because MTC was like a security blanket to me. I had seen it as too hard to change, even though there was mistrust between me, Nick and Jess. For a long time people believed that I didn't have a mind of my own. I'd seen an article about MTC, written twelve months before, which described Nick as the 'godfather' and quoted him as saying his assistants had to do everything for me because I couldn't find my own way to the airport to catch a plane. That made me so angry. Who the hell did he think he was?

Rab arranged a meeting with Nick at the Observatory Café in the Botanical Gardens, around lunchtime on Saturday, 8 April. We arrived first, and as I sipped my coffee I wondered which way the next couple of hours would go. I had a gut feeling I was about to say goodbye to the man who had guided my career for ten years.

It was fortunate that Rab and Nick were friends from way back. Rab slipped perfectly into the role of mediator.

'Nick, I don't want to be a part of MTC but I'm happy for you to be my athletics manager,' I said.

He shook his head. 'I'm not going to do that. It has to be the way it is now, the way it's been in the past, with me deciding everything.'

No, no, no! Don't you understand? I'm 27 now, not seventeen. It's my life, and I want control of it.

Debate raged back and forth for a good hour about Jess, de facto relationships, asset splitting, contracts, management fees and who owned what. I hated how in every discussion he would bring up personal baggage. I finally lost my cool and went at him about the *Woman's Day* article. He just sat there and listened, then quietly said, 'You know I would do anything for you.'

I was shocked by this response. I couldn't understand where that had come from. I might have thought that in the past but he was now doing the complete opposite.

'That is bullshit, Nick, absolute bullshit,' I said. 'I wouldn't ask you for help if you were the last person on this earth.'

Rab reminded us that the last thing either of us needed was for this to end up in the courts. 'You guys are crazy if you're going to give all your money to lawyers,' he said. That was about the only thing we did agree.

Nick couldn't see my point about how the basis of the MTC set-up was to manage athletes, which was his occupation, and that I was willing to let him continue doing that job. Why couldn't we put all this personal stuff about the finances behind us until after the Olympics and just focus on training?

'It's either all or nothing,' he said.

We'd come to a stalemate.

'I'm sorry, Nick, it's not all,' I said.

Then something very strange happened. It was one of those moments where through instinct you're drawn into an action. We both got up out of our seats and hugged. For a split second, MTC and all the other bad stuff between us disappeared. It was closure. It was to be the final gesture of our partnership.

That night Alexander had arranged for Steve Miller, a former athletics coach who was heading up Nike's preparation for the Olympics, to fly down from Sydney and spend the night. I'd also known Steve for years and it was good to get an outsider's perspective on my situation. He stressed that everything that needed to be in place for me to be successful could be done with minimal stress and disruption. 'It's just a leap of faith,' he said.

I knew that in Rab I had the perfect person; I could trust him to bring this whole thing together. Despite the outcome of the meeting he was still hopeful of changing Nick's mind and getting him on board for the Olympics. I was happy to go along with him until the phone rang one Sunday afternoon. It was Steve calling Alexander from the airport to inform us of an extraordinary confrontation he'd just had with Nick. Somehow Nick had found out about Steve's visit and had waited at the airport for him. Steve described him as like a person from another planet, a madman. 'He said a lot of crazy things to Steve,' Alexander explained. 'One of them was, "Freeman will not make it to the start line without me."'

The sentence floored me. He still believed I couldn't do anything without him. *That arrogant control freak, I'm going to make sure he eats those words.*

I was starting to freak out about the whole situation when I got a call from Mum. She'd just received a fax from Nick that contained all these ramblings about how everything was about to collapse because I was getting rid of him. She was very upset. I told her not to worry because we'd sort everything out. Then I hung up and immediately dialled Rab's number.

'Rab, it's Freeman,' I said. 'Thanks for everything you've done but I don't want anything to do with him.'

Nick had gone too far this time. There was no coming back.

A couple of days later Alexander and I met with Rab and Fort to discuss our next move. Rab had Nick's detailed plan leading up to Sydney written down. 'The whole plan is in place, the only thing is Nick's not here,' he said. Alexander had spoken to some of his contacts in track and field in the States about training venues and accommodation because the only change we wanted to make was to head to Los Angeles instead of straight to London as Nick had outlined. More importantly, as Rab pointed out, we needed to know if the rest of Team Freeman were with me or not. Jai, Maurie and Garry were all close friends of Nick's and Jai was also an employee of MTC. I wasn't sure of any of them because I knew how controlling and manipulative Nick could be.

We agreed that there was only one way to find out – confront them. A meeting was arranged for Good Friday at the regular spot, the Pavilion Café in the Fitzroy Gardens.

I didn't like what I was becoming. This wasn't me. I hated confrontations. I'd always find ways of being flexible for others. And these people were my friends. But time was running out. I could no longer afford to be nice. My Olympic dream was on the brink of collapsing, and I wasn't going to let that happen.

I arrived alone for the meeting just before ten a.m. and Rab gave me some cheat notes that he'd prepared for me. I knew I wouldn't need them because all I was seeking was some straight answers about Team Freeman's allegiances.

Once everyone had arrived, Rab began the meeting. 'Catherine has decided she is no longer involved with Nick and the Melbourne Track Club,' he said. I surveyed their faces and noticed that Jai looked particularly nervous. 'The plan for the lead-up to the Olympics is already in place and we're not going to change that at this stage, apart from going to America instead of England.' He then asked Maurie to list the proposed race schedule. Rab went through every detail, then added, 'I don't think this is the optimum situation, but I think things can sort of work out.'

I then laid it all on the table. 'Look, guys, I'm out of MTC and you're either with me or you're not. I need you, but we're running out of time here. If you're not with me, you're out and I'll get someone else.'

My statement was met with silence.

I turned to Jai. 'I'm going to America. I want you there as my training partner.'

'I can't,' he said slowly. 'I'm not prepared to go to America and train because I have to think about Sarah.' It turned out that Nick had arranged accommodation in London for Jai and his girlfriend, Sarah Jamieson, who was in the running for an Olympic berth in the 1,500m. If Jai pulled out now it could jeopardise Sarah's position.

'I own half of this company so aren't I your boss as well?' I said.

Maurie interjected. 'I don't think that's relevant in this case.'

I glared at him, then asked Jai how much Nick was paying him. 'I'll pay you more if that's what you want.'

Garry was next. We'd been through so much together and really loved each other, but I knew that if anyone was going to fire up it would be him, because we'd had some massive arguments before. 'I don't know why you want to change a winning team,' he said. 'It's like messing with a Formula One team.'

I was getting more and more annoyed. I needed these guys to understand why I was doing this. If they didn't believe I could do it without Nick, then I didn't want them around.

'Look, I'm trying to win a gold medal here and I'm not going to let anything get in my way,' I told them as the meeting ended.

The three of them left, and I sat with Fort and Rab for another couple of hours. Jai and Garry were out as far as I was concerned, but Rab wanted me to think about it for 24 hours. Through Alexander's contacts we'd arranged to train at the University of California in Los Angeles with John Smith's HSI (Handling Speed Intelligently) group, which included world 100m record-holder Maurice Greene, Ato Boldon and Inger Miller. Everything was organised at that end, we just needed to sort out our end.

The more I thought about the Jai situation, the more upset I became. He had always been there for me and claimed to be my friend, and for him to do this to me just really hurt. You spend a lot of time with your training partner and it's a special relationship. We all knew Nick pulled the strings with Jai and that's why Nick was so dangerous – he gave and gave and made people feel like they owed him.

That night I prayed for the first time in a long time. Nothing was going right for me. The Olympics were just over five months away and my preparation was in chaos. I so badly wanted to get away from everyone and everything. I actually felt like I was going crazy and started saying my prayers out loud. 'God, please help me,' I said. 'I'm giving myself up to you, God. I feel helpless. Why has it all gone wrong? I'm begging you, God, please help me.'

On Easter Monday we all met at the Stawell Gift. I still enjoyed making the trek up there to watch the final because the place had so many good memories for me. I met Rab and Fort and we sat down on the hill together. I had decided Jai was definitely out. 'I think you'd better start looking for a new training partner for me,' I said to Rab. He smiled. I think he'd already set those wheels in motion. He and Fort had sounded out 400m hurdler Evette Cordy and 200m/400m runner Scott Thom about coming over to the States for the first part of my training. The search for a full-time replacement for Jai would begin immediately.

CHAPTER 22
A FEW TWISTS AND TURNS

Instead of goal setting on the plane over to LA, I used the time to try to get my head right. I had to leave behind the mess of MTC and get my focus back on training and racing. Plus, the bar had just been raised with Marion Jones clocking the fastest 400m for two years – 49.59s – at the Mt SAC Relays in California.

I knew I'd made the right decision the moment I walked on to the track with the HSI guys. They were so loud and energetic, so committed and motivated, I immediately found myself feeding off them. I wanted to be around athletes who were also going to be under pressure in Sydney. Maurice Greene was the favourite for the 100m and each of us could relate to what the other was going through. Back home there was no one I could talk to or train with who had any idea of the pressure that came with being me. These guys understood.

It was a very stimulating environment, and I thrived on it. I'd jump in and do some starts and speed work with them and then go back to my normal programme with Fort, who had come over for the first ten days. After one particularly tough session, John Smith said, 'You just ran that session faster than some of my guys can run.' I really respected John because he was a former world record holder and had coached so many great athletes. I enjoyed picking his brain and sharing thoughts with him. He had the greatest respect for Pérec, and he'd talk about how if she wanted to do something she'd let nothing stand in her way. It was her absolutely ruthless determination that he admired. Right now she had her eyes on my Olympic gold medal, but instead of being worried about that I couldn't wait to go head to head with Pérec again.

Even the thought of it got my heart racing.

While we were in LA, I had a strange phone call from John Coates, the boss of the Australian Olympic Committee, saying he was in town and wanted to catch up. I'd known him for many years and figured he was just checking in to see how everything was going. We met at a tiny Italian restaurant, and as the dinner progressed I sensed that John was nervous about something. Finally he brought up the reason for his visit – the Games' opening ceremony. 'We're trying to figure out a way of celebrating the past and the present and the future in what we're doing,' he said slowly. 'We would be very proud and honoured if you lit the cauldron.'

It took me a couple of seconds to comprehend what John had just asked me, and then I nearly leapt over the table into his lap. 'Yes, yes, yes! Though I'll understand if you change your mind.'

A smile appeared on John's face. 'And of course you're sworn to secrecy,' he said. 'You can't tell anyone.'

I had never really thought about the opening ceremony. I was so focused on getting my body and mind ready to win Olympic gold that none of this had come under my radar. I knew what a statement it would make for reconciliation to have an Aborigine light the flame at the Sydney Games, but I had to treat it as a peripheral issue. Yes, it was exciting and a great honour, but I couldn't get carried away with it. There was a time and a place for everything, and right now I had to focus on being ready to run the fastest race of my life.

But the next morning at training I could feel myself getting more and more uptight. I was trying so hard to hide my excitement that I'd actually gone totally the other way and wasn't saying anything to anyone. Then, halfway through our warm-up, I stopped. Evette and Scott both looked at me strangely. I had to tell somebody; I needed to share the news in order to share the pressure. 'I'm lighting the flame,' I said. Scott just stared at me and didn't utter a word while Evette started screaming and hugging me. Both of them reassured me that it was a great honour and that I deserved to be the one doing it. I had actually thought swimming legend Dawn Fraser would be the one. After our brief celebration I made Evette and Scott swear that they wouldn't tell a soul. I didn't want to think about what would happen if John Coates found out what I'd just done. One day I hoped to get the chance to explain why I'd chosen my sanity over his secret.

After weeks of speed work with Maurice and co. I was looking forward to resuming racing in the 100m/200m in Modesto, California, because it would give me a good indication of how far I had progressed. After my blocks slipped in the 100m, I recovered to finish fifth in 11.26s, just two-hundredths outside the personal best I'd set back in 1994. I didn't make the same mistake in the 200m, winning easily in 22.82s after Inger Miller had pulled out before the race.

With a week to go in LA I developed a niggle in my hamstring abductor. There was no way I was going to risk pushing it, and although I had it looked at by a couple of local masseurs, I knew I needed to see the man who knew my body better than I did. I had wanted Garry out of the equation because of his allegiance to Nick, but in the end I agreed that he simply couldn't be replaced. He was going to meet us in Bath, our first European destination. A plan to go to France with hurdler Colin Jackson's group had been stalled after the French government found out about my involvement and thought it unwise to be helping out the main danger to their darling of the track, Pérec.

Evette and Scott had to return to Australia, so John Smith helped us out in our search for a new training partner. Tom was a tall, strapping white college boy who was a high 46-second 400m runner and a low 21-second 200m runner. He came out for a couple of pool and track sessions and seemed to be exactly what we needed.

My training with HSI had made headlines back home because they'd included me on their website as the latest member of the team. So now everyone in Australia thought I'd dumped my coach just a few months before the Games and had defected to America where I'd live and train from now on. Wrong! John, and particularly Ato Boldon, had thrown the idea around and I thought I might do something with those guys in the future, but my home base would always be in Australia with Fort. He'd been there through the good and the bad, and I didn't want anything like this to become an issue in the lead-up to Sydney. A few quick phone calls and the story was straightened out for the following day's newspapers.

I always called Garry 'Kyriacos', which was his real first name, but I should call him a magician because once again, after just one session with him in Bath on the afternoon we arrived, I was fixed. I don't know how he did it or whether it was a mental thing, but Garry came up with the answers and that's why I needed him every step of the way. I couldn't race without him. My speedy recovery meant that we pressed on with the race schedule that began later in the week in Turin, Italy.

The next night I was relaxing with Alexander on the couch in the apartment when Tom appeared at the doorway. I looked up and got a fright. Something was seriously wrong: he was sweating profusely, his shaved head had turned bright pink and he was shaking.

'Tom, are you all right?' I asked as I sat up straight.

'Guys, I can't handle this, I can't handle this,' he said. 'I can't be here any more, I'm freaking out. I don't know what's wrong with me.'

I'd never seen anything like it before. It appeared to me he was having a nervous breakdown. Apparently Tom hadn't slept since we'd left the States two days before. 'I'm so sorry, I'm so sorry,' he kept saying. Alexander was furious and took Tom outside to try to talk some sense into him. I slumped back into the couch. 'This is just great,' I said to the empty room, and then I started laughing. I had to see the funny side of it or else I would start crying. What else could possibly go wrong? I'd lost my long-term manager and two training partners in the last two months. When was this madness going to end? I began to think about Tom and realised I'd already had some doubts about him. He was one of those people who used negative terms all the time. Everything was a 'goddamn disaster'. Funnily enough, that was exactly the right phrase to describe Tom.

By the time we climbed into bed I was starting to panic. I could feel the pressure building. How was I going to push myself with no training partner? I felt like I was on a ferris wheel that had just stopped and we were in limbo, swaying in the breeze. The problem was I didn't know which way we were going to fall.

The next morning Tom was gone, back to the States, never to be seen again. The SOS for a replacement had already been sent to Rab back in Australia. I'm not one to dwell on negatives; people are strange beings, and we had to live with that and move on. That was the message I was trying to get across to Alexander, Fort and Garry as we prepared for our trip to Turin.

The plan was to drive from Bath to Heathrow, where we had to drop off a hire car, and then continue on together in the remaining car to the airport at Stansted. What we didn't bargain for was the traffic jam to end all traffic jams on the M25. Unless you're a local and know the lie of the land, once you get stuck on the M25 you are there for ever. For over a hundred kilometres we crawled along. I just switched off. My ability to sleep anywhere at any time was a major bonus, plus I figured it was no use concerning myself with traffic jams as I already had enough problems. It came as no surprise that by the time we got to Stansted we'd missed our flight. We debated whether to turn around and go back to Bath or try to find somewhere locally to stay for the night and fly to Turin in the morning. Eventually it was agreed that as we'd already done the hard yards, things could only improve from here.

We reasoned that finding accommodation would be the easy part of the exercise. How wrong we were. Every hotel and pub in Stansted was booked out. Tom Cruise and Nicole Kidman were filming a movie in the area and they'd taken all the accommodation. Even I was starting to lose it now. After driving around for a while we found a beautiful castle about thirty minutes away in the countryside. It was an amazing place, but I didn't want to know what it was costing us for the night.

The next morning we made sure we were at the airport early and checked in with plenty of time up our sleeves. The race wasn't until later that afternoon, and as I looked out of the window of the plane and we started to move off, my concerns began to ease. But we'd only gone about thirty metres down the runway when the plane suddenly stopped. The captain announced that there had been a malfunction and we had to return to the terminal. Surely this was all a joke, a big set-up; surely a camera crew was going to pop up from behind the seat and yell, 'Surprise!' It was now getting too bizarre to be true. 'Can you bloody believe it?' was all Garry could say.

Two hours later, we took off. By this time I was thinking that if I got through this trip, the Olympics would be a piece of cake. Somehow the flight went without incident and we landed safely in Turin, although Garry's medical kit didn't arrive, which caused yet another delay. Eventually it was located, and we then went in search of our hotel, which turned out to be very old and basic. Through all the mayhem we'd forgotten to eat, so Alexander went in search of food while I tried to get my head around running – there was now less than two hours until my event. I'd never competed at Turin before, and the moment I saw the track I realised why. The warm-up area was basically just a patch of dirt, the track itself was porous, and to top everything off it was raining. I did my best to stick to my regular warm-up but I was really starting to feel ordinary.

When I got down on the blocks at the start, I started to feel dizzy. I wobbled a bit and thought about putting my hand up to alert the starter but didn't get the chance because the gun went off. It was amazing how my body clicked into what it was trained to do and took charge of the situation. I felt like I was on auto-pilot: my brain wasn't thinking but my body was working. For those 51.2 seconds I could have been anywhere. I wasn't worried about the time; I was just happy that despite the numerous hurdles that had been thrown my way on this trip I'd still been able to produce on the track. That was the type of mind-set I was going to need in Sydney.

Amazingly, we arrived back in Bath in one piece and stayed there for another week before moving to our London base in Windsor, which would be home for the next two months. Rab had found me a training partner who would meet us in London. His name was Sean McLoughlan, a state league runner from Western Australia who had trained with 400m runner Susan Andrews, another of Fort's athletes.

This wasn't the only piece of news that had arrived from home. Nick and Jess were taking legal action against me for breach of contract over my split from MTC. Alexander had been in regular contact with our lawyers because we knew it wasn't going to be a simple break, but that didn't help ease the pain when the Supreme Court bombshell dropped. 'Why is he doing it now?' I kept asking. 'Can't all this wait until the end of the year?' I was in shock. The man who had once been my lover, manager, coach and trusted mentor was doing this three months from the biggest moment of my life. I didn't understand. I was confused. Above all else, it made me so sad.

I tried to go about business as usual but I found it tough going in my next race in Lille, France, where I finished second to Pauline Davis in 22.90s. Luckily, the following week I raced in my favourite place in the world – Paris. There is something about Paris that gives me a good feeling every time I'm there. It's such a magical city, and the moment I arrived at the track I knew I could forget my troubles for one night. I warmed up with Tamsyn Lewis, who had joined our training group in London, and was watched every step of the way by one little boy. He was leaning over the fence yelling 'Cathy, Cathy!' which in his beautiful French accent sounded like 'Caaarrzzy'. It showed how big Pérec was in this country that her main competitor was not only recognised but also supported. The French people, especially the media, had always shown an interest in me and I felt a bond with the Parisians. I certainly fed off the positive vibe and it was a rare night because I was totally happy and relaxed before the race. There were no last-minute niggles or worries. I was buzzing, and that flowed on to the track where I turned the tables on Davis, winning in the slick time of 22.62s.

Five days later we travelled to Athens for the big test. After a botched 400m in Turin and two reasonable 200m races, tonight I would be running my first major 400m of the season. Fort and the others were on edge, as this race was going to tell us a lot about how our preparation was going. It was a quality line-up, too, Lorraine Graham and in-form American Michelle Collins the main dangers.

I started strongly and ran the first 150 metres aggressively before backing off into an easy rhythm along the back straight. Collins had slipped away on the turn and entered the straight a metre in front, but I had plenty left. With eighty metres to go I burst through and maintained a two-metre advantage to the line, winning in 50.04s from Collins in 50.41s.

I was excited about the race and was surprised to see a large media pack waiting for me in the mixed zone. They'd all come out to see if the legal action and the latest barb from Nick – that I would 'self-destruct' – had derailed my campaign. 'It plays on my mind,' I told the reporters. 'I really don't need this now.' I'd only heard about Nick's apparent verbal assault second-hand because I was deliberately not reading any newspapers, watching TV news or scouring the Internet. I just didn't want to know. As for Nick, I still had those words he'd said to Steve Miller – 'Freeman will not make it to the start line without me' – imprinted on my brain.

Although, off the track, things continued to get crazier by the day, on the track momentum was building. On 5 July I headed to Lausanne in Switzerland with a sub-fifty time in mind. The best way to describe the build-up is that it was chaotic, with school children all over the track during the warm-up because of a presentation that had been scheduled only minutes before the race. I kept thinking that Sydney was going to be all about chaos, so this was another good test. I felt strong from the gun and ran a controlled, aggressive race to win by over five metres in 49.56s. It was the fastest 400m of the year and knocked off Marion Jones's mark.

I was pretty pumped afterwards and all everyone wanted to know was when I would race against Pérec. John Smith thought I should get it over with now and 'kick her butt'. The Olympic champion had run a couple of 200m races and I thought it was inevitable that our paths would cross at some stage on the European circuit. However, Maurie was adamant that despite offers of huge money from promoters chasing the rematch we wouldn't be changing our schedule, which had been decided at the start of the year. Our game plan all along was aimed at peaking on one date, 25 September, and we weren't going to do anything to jeopardise that.

Three days later, back in London, I watched Pérec's first 400m of the season in Nice on TV. She looked as fit as ever and finished third in 50.32s, behind Britain's Katharine Merry. Afterwards her coach, Wolfgang Meier, the husband of world 400m record-holder Marita Koch, came out and declared that Pérec could run a second and a half faster. *Is that right?* I thought as I sat back on the couch and picked up another magazine. *Well, bring her on. I'm ready.*

CHAPTER 23
THE BIG CHILL

I had a three-week break until my next race at the end of July in Oslo, so I turned my attention to serious training and relaxing. I loved London because I could be anonymous there. I could go anywhere I liked without feeling that people were watching my every move. We had quickly settled into a training routine and, unlike Tom, Sean McLoughlan fitted in. He'd spent some time living in north Queensland, so that was a link between us straight away. Alexander and I had our own small but cosy apartment in Windsor, while the others shared just around the corner. It was a perfect little world with no distractions. We trained twice a day, usually at the Windsor track in the morning, and then we did weights/gym from four to five p.m. In between we ate, watched TV, read magazines and slept. Our rest day was usually Saturday, and Alexander and I made sure we did something different that day, like go to the movies or out to dinner. One weekend we took a trip to see the white cliffs of Dover.

I was so excited when British runner Donna Fraser joined us for this training block. I know most athletes would never train with one of their main rivals, but with Donna it was different. She was one of the nicest people you could ever meet and we loved hanging out. We both had the same attitude, that what we did on the track stayed on the track, and her presence brought a welcome relief from being surrounded by men every second of the day. She certainly brightened my spirits because there was some tension in our group, with Garry and Sean not seeing eye to eye.

I finally cracked one day and stormed into the room where Garry was sitting with Alexander and Maurie. 'Excuse me, Garry, can I have a word with you?' I said, and walked into the other room. I knew he had no faith in what I'd chosen to do, to break away from Nick and MTC. He still thought everything ought to be the same as it was before and he continually criticised Sean for any small mistake. It was so important to me that I had a training partner who was relaxed and wanted to be there; I was worried Garry's negativity would rub off on to Sean. The beauty about Garry and me is that we're both emotional and honest people who speak their minds. So after a spirited debate about Sean and the need for cohesion, we settled the issue and went back to normal, cracking gags and carrying on together.

Rab had come up with a novel idea to help alleviate the pressure that was beginning to build. As a group we were never to refer to the Sydney Games as the Olympics; instead we had to say 'just another school race' or 'the school sports'. It had to be just another race. Everyone made a conscious effort to go with the school thing and it got a lot of chuckles along the way.

What wasn't a laughing matter was my first sight of Nick since he had instigated the legal action. I'd just come back from Oslo where I'd won comfortably in 50.74s from Americans Suzianne Reid and Monique Hennagan. We were going through our regular warm-up at the Windsor track when Nick appeared with Sonia, their daughter Ciara and 1,500m runner Georgie Clarke. It really threw me off and I wasn't able to concentrate on the session. He made my skin crawl; I was so angry that he was there in my face, going on as if life was normal.

A week later I saw Nick again at Crystal Palace for the London grand prix. Not a word was spoken, but I was so mad that he was even in the same country as me. There had been a lot of talk about Pérec showing up for this race, but it didn't happen. As Sean and I began our warm-up I sensed something was wrong. My mind wasn't clear. The MTC drama was still clouding everything and I was struggling to get my head around the race. Then I felt it. As we were finishing the second sixty-metre run-through there was definitely a twinge in my right hamstring. I immediately went looking for Garry.

It was 5 August, and the Olympics were only six weeks away. If I tore my hamstring now my dream would be over. I was starting to really freak out when I found Garry. He calmed me down and went to work. After a couple of minutes of manipulation he told me to do another run-through. It certainly seemed better, but I still had this weird feeling. It was like I'd been spooked. 'I'm not running,' I told Maurie and Garry. 'I'm not risking it.' I could tell that both of them thought I should be out there, but all my life I'd relied on my instinct, and it was telling me to be cautious. Ana Guevara won the race in 50.12s just ahead of American Michelle Collins, with Katharine Merry third.

I'd started to become homesick. For three months we'd been away from my cats, family and beautiful home. With another month still to go, I came up with an idea to help alleviate the longing for Australia: I began a scrapbook of happy thoughts. Any photographs or images that I saw in magazines that made me happy – pictures of children, animals, beautiful landscapes or even old people – I'd cut out and stick in the book. In my dark moments I sought solace in that book.

The hamstring twinge didn't force me to miss any training and we put it down to a mental aberration. Fort, who had returned to Australia to oversee some other athletes' preparation in his role as the Victorian Institute of Sport coach, met us in Monaco for my next race on 18 August. Yet again the focus before the meet had been on Freeman v. Pérec, but as so often before it didn't happen, this time because Pérec's asking price was too high. Monaco always had a great feel about it. After missing the London grand prix I was very keen to re-establish myself and, as usual, conditions were perfect in Monaco. From the gun I ran with urgency and aggression and had the race in my control as we turned for home. I felt so strong all the way down the straight and won by nearly ten metres in my quickest time of the season, 49.48s. I played it cool afterwards, giving the press my standard line, 'I'm happy with how things are progressing.' If only they knew my real feelings. With a month to go I was ready for Sydney and I knew these girls couldn't beat me.

On the plane home to London my nose started running. No big deal, I thought; sometimes the air conditioning on planes can do this. The next morning I woke up in Windsor and my head felt like it had doubled in size. My throat was dry and my senses were all out of whack. My runny nose was now a full-blown cold. I had to be so careful while

I was racing because of the drug restrictions, and that meant I wasn't allowed to take any strong medication, which might have fixed the problem in a couple of days. Instead we had to try to control the symptoms with natural remedies, lots of honey and tea, plenty of herbal concoctions, Vicks VapoRub and throat drops. During training I carried around a bag full of tissues and cough lollies. I was getting really bad headaches and having trouble sleeping because of all the congestion. The problem was that my next race was in less than a week's time, in Brussels, and it was my last 400m before the Olympics.

As the race drew near, my condition if anything, worsened. I tried to have a sleep in the afternoon at the hotel in Brussels but the constant coughing and sneezing ensured I simply stared at the wall for an hour. And it wasn't just the ailment that was occupying my mind. I'd been given the Nike swift suit in London a couple of months earlier, and I'd brought it with me to Brussels because I was desperate to have a trial run before the Olympics. As I was putting it on, Alexander came back to find me pushing and prodding at the suit and obviously looking uncomfortable. He took one look at me and said, 'Honey, take it off.'

I checked myself out in the mirror again and adjusted the hood. 'Are you sure?'

He was adamant. 'Take it off.'

He was right. I was spending far too much time worrying about how I looked rather than thinking about the race, which was now only a couple of hours away.

By the time I got to the track I was verging on a state of panic. Fort asked how I was feeling and I shook my head. 'I don't know whether I can do this,' I said.

'Just do your warm-up and see how you are then,' my coach said.

I was really dragging behind Sean in the warm-up and he was trying to boost my spirits. My pockets were full of tissues but I was desperately trying to hide this from the other girls. I didn't want them to have any idea how I was feeling. After the final run-through, I walked over to Fort and said, 'OK, let's do it.' The stakes were too high to pull out of this one. I couldn't afford to miss this race, especially after pulling out of London. Anyway, whatever I did here I knew I would improve significantly in a month.

As we walked out on to the track I surveyed the field and realised it was probably the best line-up I'd faced all season. I kept saying over and over to myself on the blocks, 'C'mon, Freeman, you can do this.' Everything went to automatic at the sound of the gun and I was quickly into a good rhythm, striding purposefully along the back straight. Guevara was on my outside and was shading me at the top of the straight.

C'mon, Freeman!

From somewhere deep inside I pushed it and surged into the lead at the eighty-metre mark. I could hear my chest beginning to rattle, but luckily I had them covered again and slowed down on the line to win in 49.78s.

I doubled over, trying to catch my breath, as the other girls came and patted me on the back. I walked away from them because I thought they'd be able to hear my chest, which was making all sorts of funny noises. My heart felt like it was beating at twice its normal rate. I was hurting badly and quickly went in search of my clothes and tissues. Alexander rushed up to me with a big smile and hurriedly wrapped a jacket around me. Maurie and Fort had the same happy glow about them and I could sense their excitement about the performance. I knew they were thinking what I was thinking: if those girls couldn't beat me tonight they never would.

My final race in Europe was over 200m in Gateshead. My spirits had been boosted by the win in Brussels, and because I never took 200m races as seriously as the 400m, I decided this was the day to wear the full-body suit. It was now or never. When we arrived at Gateshead it was pouring with rain. *It couldn't have worked out better*, I thought as I adjusted the hood on the starting blocks. It was a tough field, with world champion Inger Miller alongside me. As usual I was slow out and at the top of the straight was three metres off Miller. Then I felt it. The sensation of cutting through the air that I'd experienced when training in the suit was happening again. I was lifting, and everything felt effortless as I gained on the leaders. I was going to do it, and a couple of strides before the line I pounced on Miller to win in 22.57s.

Not in my wildest dreams could I have thought of a better ending to my Olympic preparation. The suit was awesome and there was no doubt I felt lighter and faster in it. As I wiggled out of it in the changing rooms I knew exactly when I'd bring it out again, although I played it down to the others, including Alexander, as I didn't want anyone to know my plan. Five minutes after the race Alexander gave me a handful of pills. With the racing over until the Games I could now take something stronger to try to shake off the cold that was refusing to go away.

We immediately flew back to London to prepare for the flight home the following morning. I couldn't wait to go home, especially as we'd decided to return to Melbourne, not Sydney, in the lead-up to the Games. 'I just want to be in my own house, sleep in my own bed, relax and play with my cats,' I said to Alexander.

The excitement of finally being on the plane heading home was tempered by the realisation that the big day was drawing near. I'd started to have small panic attacks, although that wasn't unusual for me building up to major competitions. As I looked out at the disappearing skyline of Heathrow, I could sense one approaching. I shut my eyes and tried to fight the feeling of intense fear that gripped me. As quickly as it came it disappeared, and the voice of my inner confidence took over. I knew I could do this. I had won every one of my 400m races that season. I was the best; the other girls knew it and I knew it. I opened my eyes and breathed a sigh of relief. I was ready.

The biting wind was going straight through me. I adjusted my beanie and gloves but despite four layers of clothing I was still freezing. Melbourne was in the middle of a bitter cold spell and here I was trying to train for the Olympics looking like the Michelin Man. My little nephew George, who had come down from Brisbane with Mum and Bruce, was running alongside me chatting away. He was doing his best to put a smile on my face but I was worried about my cold in the 6°C weather. Both pockets of my tracksuit were filled with tissues that I was dropping along the track as I went. To top all this off the press had found out that we were training at Box Hill and were taking pictures of me and George through the fence, much to the disgust of Maurie and

Alexander, who were doing their best to get rid of them.

At home I'd already set up camp on the downstairs couch, which folded out into a bed. I sat there under a blanket in front of the television, drinking tea and rubbing Vicks VapoRub all over my throat and chest. George and I made it on to the front page of the Herald Sun and the paper contacted Alexander because Nelson Mandela was in town and apparently he'd asked to meet young George. We politely declined because the last thing we wanted at this point was more publicity.

I was still having trouble sleeping but managed to collapse again on the sofa bed after a hard two-hour training session. When I stirred I found my throat was really dry. I needed water and went to yell for Alexander, who was in the kitchen, but no sound came out of my mouth. I coughed and tried again. Nothing. I slumped down on to the couch and buried my head in the pillow. What was happening to me? I was falling apart. Alexander came over and asked if I was all right. I pointed to my mouth. 'I've lost my voice,' I mouthed to him. He quickly went and got me some water, then rang the doctor.

While I waited I turned on the TV. The first image that filled the screen was of me. It gave me such a fright. I sat up and realised it was a Channel 7 ad for the Olympics. The voiceover was saying, 'Catch all the Olympic action on Channel 7, starting next week.' Next week! *Shit. Shit. Shit.* I quickly switched the TV off and lay in the darkness. It felt like I was in my own private torture chamber. For the first time I seriously began to worry about whether I would be all right for the Games.

Dr Fuller explained that laryngitis was actually not as bad as it seemed because the rest of my body appeared to be slowly recovering from the fever. It was just my voice that was not following suit. Luckily it had returned by the time Sydney Olympics boss Michael Knight came to town later in the week to discuss the opening ceremony. He brought with him a video that creative director David Atkins had made to show me what I'd be doing. The footage was shot on a handy cam with David filling my role. He climbed three sets of stairs with a replica torch and then stepped into the middle of a pool of water. I was struck by the beautiful colour of the water. David placed the torch in it and a ring of fire erupted. Then the ring of fire started to rise above

David's head, water streaming down all around him like a waterfall. It was spectacular. All through the video David was giving me directions for each move. I had been so focused on my running that I hadn't really thought too much about the opening ceremony. Now, as I sat in my lounge room and watched what I had to do, I was hit by a panic attack. Not just about the opening ceremony, but everything. The whole Sydney package.

How was I going to do it?

CHAPTER 24
LIGHTING UP THE WORLD

The voice from the two-way radio in the front of the car blurted, 'Number four is finished.' It was after eleven p.m. and we were driving through the streets of Sydney on our way to the Olympic stadium for a midnight rehearsal of the opening ceremony. It was the only time deemed safe enough to ensure that my identity remained a secret. I didn't even know who else was part of the ceremony. They kept us apart for the rehearsal and we were each referred to only by number. I was number six.

Alexander and I had flown into town earlier in the day and had been whisked off the tarmac to a city hotel where we'd been booked under a different name. The security was intense and we'd been assigned two full-time bodyguards, Maree and David, who were to be with us throughout the Olympics. It felt like we were part of a spy operation with everyone speaking in codes and switching cars.

'Number five is ready,' the radio voice screeched as the car angled in to park outside another inner-city hotel. Out front was number five, Debbie Flintoff-King. She climbed in beside us and we chatted excitedly. One link of the puzzle was revealed. Debbie was the final runner of the torch relay and she was the one handing the torch over to me for the lighting of the cauldron.

We arrived at the stadium just before midnight but there was a delay. For about an hour we sat around while the coast was cleared. I was to wear a white lycra fireproof bodysuit for the ceremony but, thankfully, for the practice I was allowed to add a jumper and jacket. It was freezing, and I couldn't help but wonder what this was doing for the cold I was still treating with medication. Debbie and I practised a few changeovers. It was very eerie in the empty stadium and hard to picture what it would be like in less than 24 hours' time.

After an hour or so Debbie had to leave, so Alexander replaced her for the final practice run. He was beaming as he jogged down the middle of the stadium with the torch. We did a mock embrace at the changeover and then I saluted both sides of the empty stadium. I was wearing an earpiece through which David Atkins was giving instructions, and my next task was to jog up the five flights of stairs to the pond. I paused as I tried to make out the ten steps I had to follow through ankle-deep water to get to the middle. I kept thinking what a disaster it would be if I fell in. I cautiously took the first couple of steps and then suddenly I was gripped with fear. My foot had slipped slightly. I paused and got my nerve back before making it to the middle. How hard was this going to be tomorrow night?

For the lighting itself I had to bend forward to my left and lower the torch. It was only for show because the ring of fire was actually lit by remote control. The force of the flames took me by surprise and I quickly jumped back. I had to keep repeating the exercise until the flames were at a safe level. The next bit was the tricky part: the frame of the burning cauldron had to rise above me while I stood in the middle of a circular water-fall. It was going to look spectacular, but whether I'd make it out alive was the more pressing question. The heat from the cauldron was intense and I realised why my suit was fireproof. When the cauldron reached the top I had to pause for a moment before walking out. I'd already been hit by some of the spray from the waterfall, but as I left the pond I was drenched by more water and could feel it seeping down my back and chest. My hair was saturated. I started to panic.

I walked back down the stairs to the bottom where the next night I was to stand with Debbie and the others to watch the cauldron make its way up the seventy-metre track to the top. I was starting to shake when I got back to the control centre under the stand and Alexander took one look at me and began yelling instructions to the organisers. 'Excuse me, can we get some blankets here? A heater, a hot drink?' They'd been so engrossed in the technical side of things they hadn't noticed I was turning blue in the corner. Alexander was furious and suddenly had them running everywhere looking for hair dryers and dry clothes. It was nearly four a.m. by the time we were heading back to the hotel. I was exhausted and anxious about my cold. I was convinced the drenching I'd received would spark it off again.

The big day started with the Australian team induction at the University of Western Sydney campus. Swimming coach Laurie Lawrence was there to give us a rev-up along with racing car driver Peter Brock and former distance great John Landy. It was good to see everybody and to catch up with Tamsyn Lewis and Nova Peris-Kneebone but I felt uncomfortable with all the media there. I was determined to stay in the background and tried to hide up the back for the team photo. The debate about who was going to light the cauldron had been raging in the press and everyone was talking about it. Mona read out a betting market from one of the newspapers. 'I think we should be having some bets on you, Catherine,' he said. About a dozen people looked straight at me.

'I don't think you need to worry about that,' I said, laughing. I was quite enjoying my acting performance so far. My standard line to any opening ceremony query was, 'I wish.'

From there we went out to the athletes' village to check in. I was rooming with Tamsyn, but through John Coates and the AOC an apartment across the road from the archery was also organised for me and Alexander. It was perfect, because even in the village I'd be stopped by volunteers or athletes from other countries for my autograph; having the apartment was my escape. I'd decided to stay in the village while I was racing as being around the other athletes helped me relax.

Nova joined Sean and I for an afternoon training session at the warm-up track. It was the last thing I wanted to do: my lack of sleep was really starting to kick in. We were doing a set of 150-metre run-throughs and I was struggling to keep up. Sean gave me a couple of funny looks – I'm sure he was wondering what the hell was going on.

Soon you'll know all, partner. Soon the world will know all.

I got ready for the opening ceremony back at the hotel, where we were staying for one more night. I'd convinced the organisers that it would be best if I marched into the stadium with the rest of the Australian team. I loved being part of a team and thrived on the camaraderie occasions like this generated. It was also a perfect decoy: if I didn't show up with the team the secret would be out of the bag from the start. I was remarkably relaxed considering what was ahead of me, although one particular part of the lighting was playing on my mind: I was petrified about falling in the water. The steps were quite slippery and they didn't want me to be looking down as I moved into the middle of the pool.

We all assembled at the SuperDome where we sat around for what seemed like hours. When we finally got the call to start moving towards the stadium entrance I was next to Lee Naylor, Alison Inverarity and Melinda Gainsford-Taylor. 'I really thought it would be you lighting the cauldron,' Melinda said. I shrugged and smiled. The noise was building with every step, and the excitement throughout the group was infectious. I saw some Aboriginal dancers who had obviously been part of the ceremony on the car-park roof opposite and they were waving and yelling at us.

The place was going off, and the roar when we entered the stadium was overwhelming. I was filled with a sudden sense of pride. Everyone around me was screaming and hugging each other. Some were crying with happiness, like Alison, who had already passed Melinda and me some tissues. I felt like crying too, but I had to control my emotions for what was to come.

Slowly we made our way around the track, waving at the frenzied crowd. It was such a moving experience that for a few moments I actually forgot about lighting the flame. Then, as we got around to our position on the infield, I began to drift back through the group. I got caught again chatting with Nova and the hockey girls so I had to wait until their attention was diverted before I took off. The instructions had been to look out for a woman with headphones and a clipboard on the side of the track. I was standing behind the hundreds of Australian athletes when I felt someone touch me on the shoulder. It was my contact, and she had Maree beside her. As we darted to the exit I heard a man's voice behind me say, 'I told you, Cathy's lighting the flame.' I smiled and kept moving.

The woman was talking rapidly into her walkie-talkie and moving at such a furious pace that I was having trouble keeping up. Several other people with clipboards had joined my escort, and we were winding our way through a maze of corridors when we ran into Dawn Fraser. She gave me a quizzical look and I managed to get out a quick hello before being rushed away. I figured then that Dawn was one of the mystery numbers.

We arrived at the changing room and I discarded my red Australian jacket, yellow shirt, green skirt and bag. The body-suit was white with a splash of blue down the right-hand side and I had matching runners. Two make-up artists went to work on my face, freshening up my red lipstick and pushing my hair back. This whole process only took a few minutes because I had to get to my entrance point where a team of technicians were waiting for me. They put in my earpiece and each of them fired different questions at me, 'Is that working? How's the sound? Can you hear them?' This went on for what seemed like half an hour while I waited underneath the stadium.

I was getting a bit claustrophobic with the tech guys continually in my face when suddenly the earpiece went dead. All I could hear in my left ear was static. 'Guys, we've got a problem,' I said to one of the clipboard brigade. A frenzy of activity followed; the earpiece was ripped from my ear and the walkie-talkies were going berserk. After a couple of minutes of fiddling they gave me back the earpiece but still all I had was static. Through all the mayhem I remained calm, thinking, *OK, I'll just have to try to guess my way through this*. I knew my time was coming closer as the people around me were getting more frantic. Finally I heard a voice in my ear. 'Yeah, I've got it,' I said. Relief swept through the dozen people who now surrounded me. I moved closer to the exit to try to see what was going on but the stadium's main lights were out and the spotlight was travelling around the other side. 'OK, Cathy, here we go,' said the voice. It was David.

Good luck, Freeman.

A rush of adrenalin flooded through me when I moved out on to the track. The whole stadium was in darkness apart from the single spotlight that was following Debbie and the thousands of tiny flickering lights, like candles, in the stands. It was as if I was floating in space with stars all around me. The sound of my name being read out shook me from my dream. What the hell? The announcer had stuffed up. Debbie was still about fifty metres away from me. She was slowly jogging along the pathway that had been formed by officials linking arms through the middle of the athletes. As I waited at the bottom of the stairs all I could think about was not tripping and not falling in the water. The roar of the crowd was amazing when Debbie arrived, and we embraced. It was significant that I was receiving the torch from her. Ever since my Commonwealth Games success in 1994, I had publicly stated that my aim was to be like Debbie Flintoff-King, the last Australian to have won a track and field Olympic gold medal. I even went to the extent of going to the same yoga instructor Debbie had used. 'Enjoy it,' she whispered in my ear. 'It's great.'

I transferred the torch to my right hand and held it up to the sky. I started giggling and had to put my hand over my mouth. It was all too bizarre. I couldn't let myself get emotional because it wasn't what I was there for; the real job was in ten days' time. I turned and looked at the stairs and waited for the signal to start the climb. There were three flights up to the orchestra level and then two more to the pond. I started slowly, but quickly found rhythm and made it unscathed. I paused at the pond to catch my breath. This was it. If I could get through the next ten steps, I could get through anything.

The first step was a bit shaky but the next felt good, so I went for it. I virtually skipped over the others and couldn't help but smile as I turned around to salute the crowd from the middle of the pond. I was instantly blinded by light as the flashes from thousands of cameras around the stadium went off. I tried to look out at the whole stadium but I couldn't see much except for all the different lights. Even though I knew the cauldron was going to light I was still worried about making sure I got the flame down in the right spot. It worked perfectly, and I stepped back into the middle of the pond as the ring of flame ignited.

The cauldron, which looked like a giant saucepan, started to crank into action. As it rose higher and the water started to thin out I could see some Australian uniforms down at the very front. Everyone appeared to be in awe of what was happening around me. Once again I was getting hit by a lot of water spray. 'You can come out now, Cathy,' the voice in my ear said. I had to wipe the water off my face when I got to the edge of the stage.

I'd done it. All I had to do now was wait for a minute or so while the cauldron went up and then walk down the stairs. I was glancing down at the orchestra when suddenly the conductor turned towards me with a look of horror on his face. What was going on?

'We've got a slight technical hitch, Cathy,' the voice in my ear explained. 'Nothing that can't be fixed!'

Yeah, no worries, I'm fine out here. I'm just soaking wet, my legs are shaking violently and there are billions of people around the world staring at me right now.

Three seconds later I heard a series of men's voices in the earpiece all speaking over each other: 'Fuck. Fuck, fuck, fuck!' I tried not to laugh because there was a cameraman right next to me. I figured there must be something wrong with the cauldron. I wanted to turn around but thought I'd better not. The conductor had started waving his arms around madly to get the music going again. I couldn't help but giggle slightly. This poor guy had gone from being quite cool and relaxed to manic in a matter of seconds. I will never forget that look on his face.

I tried to see if there was any movement, any sparks flying, anything at all to indicate that they were working on the problem. The whole process was supposed to take around ninety seconds yet I was still standing there after what must have been three or maybe even four minutes. What the hell was I going to do if this continued? Normally in these situations you hear murmurings in the crowd as they start to realise something has gone amiss. Instead, it was deathly quiet.

'OK, Cathy, a last wave and then you can go down,' the voice of a much more relaxed David said in my ear. The roar of the crowd confirmed that the cauldron had started its ascent.

I was so relieved it was over. As I neared the bottom of the stairs I noticed six women there waiting for me. I had guessed correctly, because Dawn was there standing next to Debbie. Beside her was my former coach and good friend Raelene Boyle, who was standing behind the wheelchair of athletics great Betty Cuthbert. Shirley Strickland (also athletics) and Shane Gould (swimming), who I had never met before, were the others. I hugged and kissed them all, then stood and watched the cauldron make its way up the track over the rushing water. I was shivering. Dawn grabbed a jacket from one of the officials to wrap around me and kept rubbing my back.

As the cauldron reached the top I began to think about my race. I was so honoured and proud to have been chosen to light the Olympic cauldron. It was such a powerful statement for the Aboriginal people and for reconciliation in this country. But my mind, heart and soul were all focused on running. I was here to win a gold medal.

Once the lights came back on in the stadium and the crowd started to disperse I hurried back to the changing rooms to dry out. I made a mental note to see the team doctor the following day because I'd need more medication to keep another bout of flu at bay. I quickly got dressed. Someone came and took the torch from me and they must have taken the suit as well because it wasn't there when I went to leave. We weren't able to go for an hour or so, but once the crowd had thinned sufficiently we were escorted to a car. Unfortunately, we then had to wait again while they tracked down the announcer, who was also staying at our hotel.

It was after three a.m. when I got back and still Alexander wasn't there. I was so looking forward to sharing my magical night with him. I was so hyped up, and even though I knew I badly needed sleep I just wanted to talk to someone about the biggest night of my life. As I paced around the empty room I got more and more upset. I knew he had to help get Mum, Bruce and my brothers back to where they were staying, but this was ridiculous. Eventually I climbed into bed and turned out the light.

Ten more sleeps to go.

CHAPTER 25
IN THE ZONE WITH ELVIS

It was to be the big session, the final gut-buster before tapering down for the first race of the Olympics. Fort had given me a lazy Saturday to recover from the opening ceremony with notice that Sunday afternoon was the big one. As I arrived at the warm-up track with Sean and Nova I was beginning to feel good. I could sense the cold leaving my system, although the doctor we saw in the village wanted me to remain on medication leading into the first round. I was looking forward to a good workout because, understandably, the opening ceremony had been a major distraction. I needed to zone back in on the racing.

After our usual warm-up of walking, stretching and jogging, Fort wanted 2 x 300m run-throughs followed by 3 x 120m sprints. On the second three hundred metres I clicked into race mode and pushed Sean all the way. It felt good, and it had Fort nodding his head positively. The sprints were important for my confidence because I needed to feel that the speed was there. The first two 120m sprints flowed freely, but on the third I nailed it. I glided down the straight and wasn't surprised to find out later that it was the fastest flying 100m – around 10.30s – that I'd run in training. I was ready.

Already we had settled into a good routine. Having Maree and David around – my bitch and my bastard, as I jokingly referred to them – was brilliant. Both were from Sydney and David had done security for celebrities and politicians in the past. He had been working on the Olympics for the past six months. Maree worked as an undercover police officer and had only just been seconded to the Games. I don't like saying no to people who ask for autographs and photos, but Maree and David were able to control the hundreds of requests that came my way each day. It's not that I didn't want to do them, but if I stopped and did one I'd have to do them all. I was determined to have minimal distractions, and there would be plenty of time after 25 September to sign autographs. Both my bodyguards had all-area access passes and if we wanted to go anywhere they would arrive on our doorstep with the car. The other bonus was they were easy to get along with. We constantly chatted about things like fashion, surfing, policework, anything but running, and I felt comfortable having them around.

I had agreed to do one major press conference before I started racing and that was on the Tuesday morning, 19 September. I was on a panel alongside sprinter Matt Shirvington, former Test cricketer Peter Burge and javelin thrower Louise Currey, with John Coates controlling proceedings. I was shocked by how many people were there. I was expecting to see just the usual faces from the Australian media but instead the auditorium was packed. Most of the questions were coming from foreign journalists, and most of them were aimed at me. Some were about the opening ceremony and some about the Stolen Generation, which, with John's help, I managed to answer without causing a national controversy. I was also asked what I remembered about my experience in the Olympic final in Atlanta. A string of Pérec questions followed and I admitted to being concerned for her when I heard about what had happened on her arrival at Sydney airport. Apparently, she was dressed all in black and wearing a long black wig. She became very agitated and pushed a cameraman out of the way as she tried to run to a waiting car. 'I hope that you guys are treating her nicely and giving her all the respect she deserves,' I said to the journalists.

The only other official function I had to attend was the following night's Australian team dinner. I wanted Mum, Bruce and my brothers to come. They were staying with some Baha'i friends near Homebush and they met us at the apartment. After a late-afternoon training session David drove us all into town to the restaurant by the harbour. I really didn't like these functions, and my mood worsened when I was told about the seating arrangements: I was apparently expected to sit at Prime Minister John Howard's table. Normally I let these sorts of things go by and play along, but tonight I wasn't in the mood.

The government's continued refusal to apologise for the Stolen Generation fuelled my resentment. I was frustrated by how insensitive and untruthful the government had been about the whole issue. How could they continue to deny it had happened? My own grandmother was taken away from her mother. She didn't know her birthday, so we didn't even know how old she was when she died. The facts are that parts of people's lives were taken away. They were stolen. I'll never know who my grandfather was or who my great-grandmother was. That hurts, and the pain is very strong. It passes down through generations and leaves a sense of sadness and anger. A line commonly used by some Australians and many politicians around this time was, 'Why should we apologise? We weren't around.' But saying sorry isn't about the legal issues; it's not about money; it's not about ownership – it's about acknowledging that past governments were wrong. Forget about the colour issue, forget that it's an Australian Aboriginal issue, just think of it as a human issue. One day this country will be strong enough to admit to this crime against humanity.

In the lead-up to the Olympics there had been pressure placed on me from some sections of the Aboriginal community to boycott the Games; they believed the world's attention could then be diverted to their fight to improve living standards in Aboriginal communities. I eventually went public in my newspaper column to get the message across that there was more to gain from having Cathy Freeman on the world stage representing Aboriginal people. I wanted them to feel proud, and to show them that anything was possible. I'd spoken to Carl Lewis about this a couple of years before. He told me that he'd been through three Olympic boycotts in his career – the US boycott of the 1980 Moscow Games, the Eastern Bloc boycott of the 1984 Los Angeles Games, and the boycott by North Korea, Ethiopia and Cuba of the 1988 Games in Seoul – and that the only people it affected were those who didn't compete. The people who were there didn't think twice about who wasn't there, so it was a waste of time. His advice was: 'Go to the party with your best dress on and dance as well as you can. If you don't want to be noticed, don't go.' I was ready to dance.

The next morning I arranged to meet Fort at the village at eleven a.m. because I was going to have a massage. I passed a group of people talking at a table in the lounge and heard them mention Pérec's name. I wondered what they could possibly be talking about.

Fort was on his mobile phone when I approached and he quickly put it down. 'Have you heard?' he said.

'Heard what?' I replied.

'Pérec's gone. She flew out early this morning.'

'Arrrggghh,' was all that came out of my mouth at first.

Fort began to tell me what had happened, but I held up my hand. 'I don't want to know the details. I won't believe it until I see the empty lane out there tomorrow night.'

The truth was, it saddened me. I really liked Marie-José. She was the same age as Anne-Marie would have been. Although we'd never spent much time together socially, there was a bond between us. We'd gone through so many things side by side. Running is such a lonely sport that your opponents can become like a family or a sisterhood. We go through the nerves together, and because it's such a tension-packed environment we often lean on each other. I felt that now with Marie-José. I wished I could have helped her.

The funny thing was, her departure didn't surprise me. I think I'd just grown tired of waiting for our rematch to take place. For the past year all I'd heard was when Pérec was going to return, what she was going to run, how she was back better than ever. Each time I'd get really excited at the prospect of racing her, only to be let down. I'd become quite sick of it. There always seemed to be drama surrounding Marie-José; maybe she was one of those people who needed that sort of atmosphere to work in. I certainly didn't.

We only trained lightly in the afternoon, as my first race was now just over 24 hours away. The Olympic village was abuzz with the news of Pérec's midnight dash and the media was out in force at the warm-up track. I was now officially over it, as every person I ran into was bringing it up. I had reached the stage where I wanted to get moving. I was becoming more and more frustrated with all the waiting around. I had a job to do, Pérec or no Pérec, and I couldn't wait to start it.

I stayed the night in the village with Tamsyn, and the next morning Alexander came over for breakfast. I decided to kill some time by having my nails manicured before going for an afternoon nap. We headed for the warm-up track around five p.m. – all my races were scheduled between eight and half-past eight – and the first person I ran into was Marion Jones. We hugged and wished each other the best. I remembered the first time I'd encountered her, at the world juniors in Seoul in 1992. Everyone had been talking about this American girl who could run 22-something. I'd ended up getting the silver in the 200m behind a local Korean girl, and Marion had finished unplaced. After the race I saw her sitting down on the track alone and I went over and asked if she was all right. I'd thought she was going to run better and obviously so had she. She was so quiet then, and now in front of me was this happy, confident woman who was chasing an amazing five gold medals in the next week.

Fort's game plan for the Games revolved around winning every round. Normally the first couple of rounds are fairly relaxed because you know you only have to run in the first three or four to qualify. But given what had transpired at Athens in 1997 and at the 1999 Seville world championships, I understood Fort's urgency. His plan wasn't just about ensuring a good lane; he also wanted me to impose myself on the event early, as Pérec had done in Atlanta. I was the favourite, and I should show the other girls why from the start. Alexander also had his reasons for wanting me to win all four races. He was very superstitious, and when we had last stayed in Los Angeles our apartment number had been 1111. Alexander immediately interpreted that to mean I had to win four races to get what we wanted.

I was feeling the usual big-race nerves as we emerged from under the stands for the walk towards the start area. The crowd was big and loud. It felt like every step I took, someone was yelling, 'Go, Cathy!' I had to make sure I didn't get carried away. *Soak it up, but do your job*, I kept telling myself as I stood near the blocks waiting to be introduced. I was readjusting the pins in my hair when my name was read out and the crowd started roaring. I gave a quick wave then zoned in. My only real danger was American Monique Hennagan, who was on my outside in lane four.

This is it, Freeman.

I started brilliantly and went out so hard in the first hundred metres that as we straightened into the back straight I was already alongside Hennagan.

Wow! A wall of light hit me. I was blinded momentarily. I'd never seen so many flashes go off.

I must have Elvis Presley running alongside me.

By the 250-metre mark I had left Hennagan three metres in my wake and I extended that to more than five at the top of the straight.

I love this stadium. I love this place.

I switched off with sixty metres to go and started cruising. However, thirty metres later I had to get going again because Hennagan began to close. I crossed the line with a metre to spare in 51.64s.

One down, three to go.

I undid my spikes and walked past all the television interviewers. Maurie, who was working for the BBC again, had already told them I wouldn't be answering any questions until after the final. Some local journalists stopped me further along the mixed zone. I wanted to tell them about how Elvis Presley had risen from the dead and was running alongside me down the back straight, but I didn't think they'd understand.

'I wasn't sure how I was going to handle the excitement of the crowd, nor was I going to underestimate anyone,' I said. 'It was amazing. Everything went well and I'm looking forward to the second round.'

I headed off in search of Garry. I already knew that as long as my body stayed strong the gold medal was mine. This was my arrogance coming out. It is a side of me I never display in public. I have a Jekyll and Hyde personality: one minute I'm the shy girl from Mackay, the next I'm this arrogantly confident woman who is invincible. To be the best in the world you have to be arrogant. I know I've got it. On the track I feel it. What is it? Tiger Woods has it on the golf course. Michael Jordan had it on the basketball court. With Jordan, he wanted the ball so that he could take the game-winning shot because he knew he could make it; others only wish they could make it. The difference between the good ones and the greats is that the latter don't calculate the risks, they just take them. When I was fit I knew none of these girls could beat me. I'd always thought Pérec and I were at another level, and now that she was gone I knew I was going be the Olympic champion.

I returned to the village and again slept well, although Tamsyn provided some comic relief during the night. It was about two am. and she got up to go to the bathroom, tripped on a shoe on her way and fell flat on her face. I had already stirred so I cracked up laughing as I heard her hit the deck. We were still laughing about it over breakfast – cereal and fruit – the next morning. Then I went over to the apartment to catch up with Alexander and the family. They were all a bit quieter than usual. Bruce and the boys were really relaxed but Mum was uptight and nervous. She was walking about as if there was broken glass around the place and it was starting to get to me. My oldest brother, Gavin, was ribbing me because originally they'd been offered the chance to stay on a Channel 7 yacht on the harbour. I had pulled the plug on that idea because I didn't want the family constantly in the media where they could be manipulated.

Every time we got together one of us would bring up a story from our childhood in Mackay. 'You know, Dad is going to be somewhere in the stadium tonight,' Gavin said. 'He'll be watching over you.' Spirit is such an important part of Aboriginal culture and I knew Dad and Anne-Marie would be looking out for me. I wanted to keep the same routine as the first round so I tried to nap in the afternoon. Gavin's words about Dad stuck in my mind, and they came back to me again during the warm-up. Fort reiterated our goal to win every round, and then I was on my own.

There were a few more familiar faces in the call room for this round: my old sparring partner Falilat Ogunkoya, good friend Donna Fraser and the American girl everyone was talking about, La Tasha Colander-Richardson. She'd apparently run a sub-fifty time recently and I remember Maurie mentioning something about her. It was weird, but I was a lot more nervous than for the first round. I'd thought it would be the opposite, seeing as I'd already experienced the crowd and the stadium. I was again meticulous in following my pre-race routine, from the stepping out of the measurements for my blocks and the practice starts, to the adjustments of my hair and breathing exercises. It was all the same as on the previous night.

I was in lane four, with Colander-Richardson on my inside.

No mistakes, Freeman. We don't want a repeat of Seville.

I burst from the blocks like I had in round one and by the top of the back straight I knew I had already burnt off the American. By the bend I was well clear, and I entered the final hundred metres over five metres in front of Ogunkoya and Fraser. With eighty metres to go, I shut it down.

I wonder if Dad is watching. I hope he's proud of his little girl.

Luckily I snapped back out of my dream to ensure I held my advantage over the final fifty metres. I won in 50.31s from Ogunkoya (50.49s), with Fraser third in 50.77s. Colander-Richardson finished fifth.

As I took my spikes off I was angry that I'd let my focus be invaded by sentiment. I couldn't afford to have any weaknesses. What the hell was I doing thinking about my father during an Olympic quarter-final? That was it. I couldn't see my family again until after the final. They had become a distraction, and that was dangerous.

I told Alexander about my decision as I was having a massage. 'Hon, can you explain it to them?' I asked. 'It just freaked me out, and I can't have that happening right now.' He turned to walk away and I yelled after him, 'Tell them I love them so much.' It had to be done, because the semi-finals were when everything started to get serious. I'll never forget what Pérec did in the semi at Atlanta. She basically scared everyone off with a phenomenal run. I needed to do the same.

I don't know what it was, but when I woke up on semi-final morning I was feeling weird. I had slept well again but I was really sluggish. It was the same feeling that had stayed with me for nearly a month when I had the cold. I'd only stopped using the inhalant Dr Fuller had given me for the laryngitis a couple of days before. I thought having some food would spark me, but it didn't work. By the time I found Garry for my regular morning massage my head was throbbing and I was very drowsy. He quickly rang one of the team doctors who told him he was 'too busy' to come and see me and that I should call him. Garry was furious. He eventually tracked down another doctor who came and gave me something to perk me up. I then went over to the apartment with Alexander and tried to relax with some glossy magazines.

By the time I met Fort at the village to leave for the warm-up track I was feeling better. I think part of the reason for that was because I'd already started to focus on the race and refused to allow any negative thoughts in. Fort had been so good over the past few months. He had stepped up in Nick's absence and been a strong guiding force. I knew he was trying hard to portray a calm exterior when inside he was, naturally, a nervous wreck. I remembered our first big meet together, the 1992 nationals, and how I'd asked him to pin my numbers on. He was shaking so much that he couldn't do it. He worried about everything, and that had been one of the major issues in our split. While he wasn't exactly a different man, the Fort sitting next to me as we drove to the track gave the appearance of a happy and contented coach. I was just so happy he was there.

The weather had turned foul, with showers already starting to fall. Maurie met us at the warm-up track and quickly addressed the issue. 'You've won from lane one to eight in hot and cold conditions and you are very good at blocking these things out,' he said. I knew Maurie worried nearly as much as Fort – I called him 'Old Mother Hubbard' – but he was always good for advice and after he'd delivered that night's line he was gone. I would see him at the finish line. Sean was his usual no-hassles self as we warmed up. I appreciated that more than anything.

Jogging through the puddles reminded me of my old coach Mike Danila, back in Kooralbyn. He had taught me that being Aboriginal, being very casual, and being a Queenslander was a bad recipe, especially when it rained. When a storm hits in Queensland everything gets called off. He would always say to me, 'You've got to train whatever the weather is,' so I'd be out there running through slush while everyone else would be rugged up inside. I owed Danila a lot and wondered where he was.

I felt a niggle in my hamstring and went over to Garry a couple of times for some work. After a few run-throughs I was feeling ready and quickly said my goodbyes. The feeling of loneliness that comes over you once you walk into the call room is so strange. Suddenly there's no one. No coach, no masseur, no training partner to motivate you or look out for you. It's just you and your mind. Often what happens in the next thirty minutes can decide the outcome of a race. You have to be able to control the demons that come looking to infiltrate your mind as you're walking up and down a tiny warm-up area with the best runners in the world. If you lose it there, it's over. This is where my laid-back personality is such a benefit. I can't explain how I do it, but I have an unbelievable ability to shut everything out. So the rain that was pelting down on me as I took off my tracksuit barely registered in my mind. I was there to win the semi-final, and that was it.

I was again in lane three, with Sandie Richards on my inside in two; Ogunkoya and Guevara were in four and five, and Donna was in lane seven. Once I'd shed my top I kept jumping up and down on the spot to keep warm as the rain swept across the track. I had to wipe it away from my face as I was being introduced, once again to an almighty roar, which I acknowledged with a clap of hands above my head. As we were called up to the blocks I pulled out both eyelids, a little habit of mine to ensure I am zoned in.

Focus, Freeman.

Richards always went out hard in her races so I knew what to expect. I was slightly slow away, mainly as a result of being cautious in the conditions, but felt relaxed as we entered the back straight. At 150 metres I sensed Richards getting closer. Fifty metres later, I went for it. I really worked the last section of the bend and was alongside Richards as we straightened.

Time to go.

With sixty metres to go I edged a metre clear of Richards. I couldn't believe how good I was feeling. At twenty metres I sensed Guevara and Ogunkoya closing, but I had them covered.

Cruising, Freeman.

I had nearly a metre to spare on the line. 50.01s – yeah! I was happy with that, given the conditions. I gave myself a clap. There was a lot more left inside.

I sensed from Fort and Alexander afterwards that they were thinking along the same lines. Nothing was said, but Team Freeman was a happy lot. Alexander and I headed back to the village for dinner and then on to the apartment because I'd decided I would stay there that night. I needed privacy and no distractions. I wanted to hide away from the world until 8.10 the following night, when I would run my little black butt off.

CHAPTER 26
THE RACE

I slept peacefully, just as I had before the Atlanta final. I tried to stay in bed for as long as possible but by nine a.m. I was just staring at the wall. I was thinking about something Maurie had said to me the previous night, 'Don't run the race over and over again in your mind. It will leave you flat mentally.' I had to keep my mind occupied as much as possible.

Breakfast was the usual four Weet-Bix with honey, hot water, milk and a piece of fruit. Alexander and Maree then went in search of some board games to keep us amused as the clock ticked down. I contemplated turning on the TV, but I'd made a rule not to watch any TV or read any newspapers while I was in Sydney and I wasn't about to break that on the day of the final. Alexander returned with a bag full of goodies: three games, two videos and several glossy magazines. We settled on a game of Scrabble.

I was getting some more fruit ready for lunch when the phone rang. It was Maurie touching base. 'G'day. Today's sports day,' he said. I smiled. I could hear the nervousness in his voice but he was determined to stick to our school theme. Like Alexander, he knew not to wish me good luck because hearing that before a race was one of my pet hates. Winning a gold medal had nothing to do with luck.

One of my rituals, which helped keep my mind busy, was getting my bag and uniform ready. Each night Alexander would do the laundry and the following morning I would go through a process to get everything ready. We were given four sets of our racing number – mine was 1110 – which had to go on the bag and uniform. I was very particular about wearing the same number in each race from the first round through to the final; the number on the bag also had to be the same throughout. So after the washing was collected I'd methodically re-attach the numbers and then keep going back to double-check. For the final there was one major change to my ritual: I had to attach the number to the swift suit. This was the special occasion I had been thinking about after Gateshead. I loved how I'd felt that day, how I slipped through the air, weightlessly and effortlessly. I knew the suit would attract attention, which normally I'd hate, but in an Olympic final everyone was going to be looking at me anyway. Really, I couldn't have cared less what I was wearing. It could have been a pink tutu with black stilettos and a fluorescent orange wig, as long as it enhanced my running performance and ensured I fulfilled my childhood dream. I knew the suit was going to do just that.

At three p.m. we went over to the village, where I caught up with Fort and Garry. I was feeling something in my hamstring so Garry and his partner, Ross Smith, both stretched and massaged it. I went to my room for a quick nap but ended up tidying the place instead. My mind was calm, and for reassurance I kept thinking back to how I'd felt before the Gothenburg world championships in 1995. I was so relaxed now, in comparison to then. I spent several minutes getting the swift suit on, which I then hid under tracksuit pants and a windcheater.

Just after five p.m. I went down and met Fort and Alexander, who were waiting at the van with Maree and David. On the short trip to the warm-up track I didn't say a word. I was already in my own world and pushing myself to keep the outside one at bay. I didn't like having Alexander around at the warm-up track so we said a quick goodbye. I didn't want to get emotional. He just gave me a peck on the lips and said, 'See you after the race.' I nodded, then walked over to where Sean was sitting with Donna Fraser. She had drawn lane two in the final and we'd decided to do our warm-up together. We all walked a lap and they were chatting away but none of it was registering with me. I was in another place. We did stride-throughs along the straight and walked the bends for two laps. Stretching was next, so I laid out my favourite towel. It was the Australian team towel from the 1990 Commonwealth

Games, my first senior team. I'd been known to refuse to do a weights session if I didn't have this towel, which by now was starting to look a bit the worse for wear.

I made a quick visit to Garry to get some more work on my hamstring. Then I sat down with Fort to go over the race plan. I'd done it a thousand times but I still liked to hear it explained to me. 'OK, Fort, what do you want me to do?' I said. I could tell he was nervous. Compared to previous plans it was very simple and conservative. It was certainly geared solely towards winning the race, not running fast. Basically, Fort wanted to ensure that no one could come over the top of me in the final fifty metres.

There's no chance of that, Fort.

I was to run the first forty metres fast, like in a 200m race, and then relax along the back straight. That was the most important part of the race, relaxing down the back straight. At the two-hundred-metre mark, begin to pick it up, work the bend and then go hard from the water jump to the top of the straight. 'Then it's leg speed, hold on and control,' he said.

'Sounds good,' I said, and wandered off.

John Smith came over and gave me a big hug. 'You can do it, girl,' he said.

Three eighty-metre run-throughs in flats came next. Everything felt light and easy. I went back over to Fort because I was concerned about being in lane six. I thought I was going to get either three or four. 'There's enough pace outside you,' he said. 'It's not a factor.' Falilat Ogunkoya was in lane eight, but my main dangers were Katharine Merry in three, Lorraine Graham in four and Ana Guevara in five.

The clock had ticked into the final hour and it was time for the spikes to come on. As I sat on my towel I looked up at the main stadium in the distance and tried to take it all in. Since Olympic chief Juan Antonio Samaranch had read out 'Syd-e-ney' seven years earlier, the Games had been like this freight train in the distance. When I was young, living in the tiny railway town of Coppabella, I'd lie in bed at night and listen to the trains approaching. At first it'd be just a faint sound, then you could distinctly make out the rattling of the carriages, and before you realised it, it was suddenly on top of you. Whoosh! That's what the Olympics had been like. I knew it was coming, I'd been watching the train get closer and closer over the years. Now it was suddenly right in front of me, hurtling towards me at top speed, and there was no escape. Whoosh!

'OK, two more to go.'

Sean's voice snapped me back from the freight train. We had to do two eighty-metre sprints and I held back slightly because I didn't want to over-exert myself in the warm-up. Then, on the last run-through, I thought I felt something in my quad. At times of intense pressure I was often hypersensitive about my body and that's why Garry was so important. He gave it a quick rub and also said some calming words. I went back to him a couple more times, as I could feel the emotions starting to build up inside. I had to keep it in there.

The first call for the women's 400m final came over the loudspeaker. I went over to Fort and we sat down and went through the race plan again. He had written it out on a small piece of paper for me to take into the call room. I started to get my things together, keeping an eye on the other girls because I wanted to make sure I wasn't late for the last call.

At 7.30 p.m. the final call came. Garry gave me one last quick rub and said, 'Go out and enjoy it.' Sean told me to have a 'good one' before he took off, leaving just Fort at the gate. I could tell he didn't know what to say. Right at that moment something strange happened.

'Will you still love me if I lose?' I said to Fort. For that split second I had let a doubt creep in.

'Of course I will, but you won't,' he replied. He then opened his arms. 'Come and give us a bit of a hug.'

I'd hugged him in Atlanta, but this was different. I was scared then; here I needed to be in control. *No emotions, Freeman.* I gave him a quick embrace, then turned and walked into the call room to face my destiny.

Not a word was uttered in the room. As we started the long walk through the tunnel to the stadium I could feel the electricity running through my body. It was such an amazing sensation, one I'd only experienced a couple of times before in my life. I knew then that something special lay ahead. I was on. I was feeding off the spirit and energy that had gripped the stadium.

Running for me is always more than just physical and mental; it is also emotional and spiritual. You can draw energy from the universe, the stars and the sun, everything around you. You can draw energy from what has happened in your life; the tragedies and successes. When you combine it all at the right moment it moves you, propels you forward. It's like your blood is boiling, like there are ants in your blood. You're overwhelmed by this sense of confidence – it's like you're floating. I don't know where it comes from and you can't practice having it. All I know is that just minutes away from the gold medal race I had that feeling.

From the moment I entered the stadium it was there, a dull noise in the back of my head. It was weird. All I could focus on was my lane; I couldn't see or hear anything else. I started taking deep breaths to get as much oxygen into my lungs as possible. After a couple of run-throughs I discarded my tracksuit bottoms and long-sleeved T-shirt to reveal the swift suit. I pulled and prodded at the suit to get comfortable as I waited behind the blocks.

Just do what you know, Freeman.

My mouth was dry. I took a sip from my water bottle.

Breathe, Freeman. Breathe.

I arched my neck back to get another lungful of oxygen, licked my lips and waited for the introductions. I pulled the hood on, zipped it up and made sure that my hair felt comfortable.

Just do what you know.

From somewhere I heard my name read out so I clapped a couple of times above my head. The whistle sounded and we moved to the blocks. I got my legs into position and my fingers perfectly on the line. I stared down at the track and waited for the gun. The muffled beating in my head was gradually getting louder.

The sound of the gun blasted through me and I leapt from the blocks. I sprinted confidently around the bend and clicked into cruise control.

Relax, Freeman. Relax.

Graham and Merry had both started well on my inside. As the two-hundred-metre mark loomed I started to release the throttle.

Wait until the water jump, Freeman.

I held back on the bend and entered the straight a stride behind Graham and Merry. I couldn't believe how much I had left, and how conservative I had been in the biggest race of my life. With each stride the beating inside my head was getting louder.

Just keep moving, Freeman.

As I surged with eighty metres to go I sensed something was wrong. Not with me, with them. They weren't there. There was no pressure on my inside. I knew it. I knew from the start that none of these girls had the strength to go with me.

You've done it, Freeman.

Bang. It struck. The muffled noise was now a full-on roar and with fifty metres to go it vibrated through my whole body. The sound in my head had been the crowd. For the first time I heard them, I connected with them. I was floating. I felt like they were carrying me in their arms to the finish line.

The gap was five metres when I crossed the line. I looked at the clock and cringed: 49.11s. Slow!

Stop it, Freeman, you're now an Olympic gold medallist.

My body was numb. I removed the hood and bent over to take my spikes off. I had a sudden urge to sit down. I was overwhelmed with a sense of relief. It felt like I'd been trapped in a sauna and the door had suddenly been flung open. The fresh air was intoxicating. My God, I could actually relax. I felt like I wanted to cry but nothing happened. Ever since I was a little girl running around in Mackay I had dreamt of this moment, and each time I would burst into tears after crossing the line. My mind was whirling like a film reel locked on fast-forward. Images from my life were flashing by. Then, suddenly, they came to a stop. All I could see now was the beautiful smile of my sister Anne-Marie. She had been with me all the way.

Slowly, the enormity of what I'd just done started to sink in. *I'm just a little black girl who can run fast, and here I am sitting in the Olympic stadium, with one hundred and twelve thousand people screaming my name.*

How the hell did I get here?

I felt dizzy. I had to get the spikes off so I could feel the air between my toes. I could finally rest. The sense of expectation had nearly suffocated me. The pressure of knowing everyone was expecting me to win had been in my face every minute of my life for the past four years. Donna Fraser came over to me and I could see her big black lips moving but I couldn't hear anything. The pressure valve I had managed to keep closed was slowly releasing. I sensed the nervous energy of the crowd around me also releasing. I got up, took a couple of steps, and then it flooded over me again and I doubled over, closed my eyes and breathed heavily.

I did it! I goddamn did it!

I looked over to try to find Maurie. I needed to know someone was there for me during all this madness. I hadn't done a victory lap since the 1994 Commonwealth Games and I waved my finger around in a circle at Maurie to see if I should do it. He nodded and said, 'Go around.' I then let out my first big smile. I was going to enjoy this. I walked over to the crowd where I saw plenty of Aboriginal flags and Australian flags. I didn't know who the people were but I got them to throw the flags on the ground because I didn't want to get into trouble about which one I picked up first. I tied them together and put them around my neck. 'Yeeeeaaaaahhhh!' I yelled out to the crowd, which was going crazy. There were photographers all over me. 'I can't move, guys,' I said. I wanted to run around this great stadium again. One of the photographers tripped and did a somersault, landing flat on his bum. I stopped because I recognised him as a guy from Brisbane. 'Are you all right, man?' I asked.

The Vanessa Amorosi song 'Absolutely Everybody' was playing and I started to skip along the track waving both flags madly. I loved it. Loved every second of it. The emotion I could see on people's faces made me feel so good. Little ol' me had made all these people happy. Then, suddenly, something weird happened. It was almost like a trance came over me. I was at the top of the home straight and for some reason I was looking intently into the crowd on the lower level. My eyes were drawn to a certain spot, and then I saw why – it was my family.

I couldn't believe it. I'd had no idea where they were sitting. I hadn't even been looking for them because I was keen to finish the victory lap and get out of the spotlight so I could relax. It was amazing, as though they were magnified and completely still while everything around them was going crazy. I saw my oldest brother, Gavin, first because he is the tallest and has lots of black hair. Mum and Garth were against the railing. They were all going off. I started punching the air and yelling, 'Yes! Yes!' Garth was bawling his eyes out and I climbed up and reached over to his outstretched hand. Mum was straddling the fence, trying to touch me. Norman and my nephew Gavin were yelling, 'One! One! One!' Bruce's big blue eyes were sparkling, his face had turned bright pink and he had a massive smile on his face.

The crowd was still screaming at me as I made my way back down to the finish line, where Pat Welsh from Channel 7 grabbed me.

'I know I've made a lot of people happy,' I said. He asked about the reaction of my family. 'Biggest smiles I've ever seen, and they are not even drunk, my brothers.' I moved down the line of interviewers until I got to Maurie and the BBC.

'Slow time,' I said to him.

'I don't think we care about that,' he said, and gave me a big hug.

We were just about to start the interview when Maurie pointed to the infield. 'Tatiana Grigorieva is about to jump here. If she gets this, she's got a medal for sure,' he said.

I turned and watched. As she cleared the bar I jumped in the air. 'Wasn't that fantastic?' I screamed. I didn't want this night to end.

More interviews followed and I was about halfway down the line when I saw Alexander for the first time. He had tears in his eyes and I ran up and wrapped my arms around him. I was so happy to see him. Drugs couldn't produce the high I was on right now. Ernie Dingo came over to do an interview and I gave a special message to the indigenous kids out there, 'Don't ever underestimate what you can achieve.'

I told Alexander to find Mum and the rest of the family because I desperately wanted to see them after the medal ceremony, then I hurried down to the changing room to get ready. Again I had forgotten to bring a jacket, and team manager Peter Brukner went and chased down a yellow tracksuit top for me. I remember Fort had told me leading into the Games that when I had my hair down it made me look more Aboriginal; I'd decided to dye my hair back to its original colour – I'd had some blonde tips put in in Europe – for the same reason. I was feeling pretty calm as we waited to go out for the presentation and chatted happily with Lorraine Graham, who had won silver, and bronze medallist Katharine Merry. The crowd went berserk when we walked out. I looked over to Mum and the boys, who were still jumping up and down. I gave them another victory salute and pumped my fists. 'Yeah!' I yelled again.

Once we got behind the dais, Lorraine started making this high-pitched squeal that sounded like a seagull. She couldn't stop herself from doing it and I had trouble keeping a straight face as the ceremony began. When my name was read out I leapt up and started jumping up and down on the spot with my arms raised to the heavens. It felt like the sun was shining out of my chest and illuminating the stadium and the world. I turned around to the crowd in the back straight and saluted again. Kevan Gosper was laughing as he placed the gold medal around my neck. I did another circle of the dais holding up my gold medal, which was actually heavier than I'd imagined, for all to see. I couldn't stop giggling and instantly wanted to run over to my family in the stands. While the other girls were getting their medals I laughed at my brothers, who were sending me all sorts of hand signals. I congratulated Lorraine and Katharine with quick kisses and then turned to watch the Australian flag being raised as the national anthem started playing. I was very pleased with myself for remembering all the words. I gave one last victory salute before posing for photos with the other girls.

As we were led off the track I broke away to the side to give my flowers to Mum. I shaped to throw them, but she fought her way to the front and I handed them over. The crowd erupted and she started to cry. I so much wanted to hug her but it was impossible to climb up on the railing, so instead she blew kisses to me. As I walked back down to the exit I started to feel overwhelmed. Everyone was screaming my name and strangers in the crowd were in tears. And it was all because of me.

I was then whisked away by Alexander and David to a room underneath the stadium where my family was waiting. I just wanted to get to my mother. When I finally got my arms around her we stayed locked together. For a fleeting moment everything stopped and there was just the two of us. We'd been through so much together. Then I did the rounds, kissing and hugging Bruce and the boys. All of them looked exhausted, especially Garth, who had a bad headache. There wasn't a lot of talking as we all sat around and reflected for a moment. This period was really crazy. One minute you were all alone out on the track in your own little world, then, as soon as you finished, everyone was on top of you, invading your space.

Our family reunion only lasted a couple of minutes because I had to do a press conference. My family all came into the media room and stood at the back as questions were fired at me. I had reached the point where I didn't care about anything. I'd achieved my dream and done everything I'd set out to do. 'I'm blessed, what can I say? It was the greatest emotion I've ever felt,' I told the world's media. After a few minutes I was starting to get worried about my family because I could tell they were uncomfortable with all the attention. I just wanted to get them back to the apartment so we could spend some time together.

Before I could leave I still had to warm-down, have a massage and do a drug test. However, the interviews weren't finished yet, and I had to go upstairs to chat with Bruce McAvaney on Channel 7. We'd known each other for years and I was hanging it on him about his favourite saying of 'speeeeeecial'. He asked me how I had handled all the hometown pressures.

'I don't think about losing,' I said. 'I don't think about winning either. All I think about is what I have to do in the race.'

I still hadn't seen Fort or the rest of the gang. They were all waiting for me in the drug-testing area, and as soon as I saw my coach that wave of disappointment over the time hit again. I thought I could have run under my Atlanta time of 48.63s.

'The time, a bit slow,' I said as we hugged. 'Are you disappointed with the time?'

'Nah,' was all he could say.

As I was getting everything ready for the drug test I saw Nick walk into the room. Sonia O'Sullivan had won the silver medal in the 5,000m not long after my race. He was holding his baby girl, and suddenly he spun around and looked straight at me. Our eyes locked, and the moment seemed like it was frozen in time. I sensed he wanted to say something, and I knew I wanted to as well. He had been such an important part of this night. Yet, sadly, words now failed us. Ciara distracted him and he looked down at her. The moment was lost, and I quickly left the room.

I climbed on to the massage table for the most satisfying massage of my life. As Garry rubbed my legs, his smile was bigger than mine – if that was possible. He was explaining how I'd set a personal best in the number of times I'd come over to him with niggles in the thirty minutes leading up to the final. I'd thought it was only a couple. 'You were at your best,' he said. He then mentioned how Carl Lewis had come up to me just as I was walking through the gate to the call room. 'Was Carl there?' I asked. My God, I must have been so focused because I couldn't remember any of this. In fact, I couldn't remember much until the gun went off.

Chris Wardlaw came over and I was so happy to see him because he'd played such an integral role in my life over the past twelve months.

'I know you've just won a gold medal,' he said, 'but I have to ask you this: do you want to run the two hundred? Because we have to do entries in an hour.'

The second spot had been left open for me ahead of Nova. In Atlanta I had struggled to come up for the 200m, but I figured I'd be able to keep the adrenalin flowing in Sydney.

'Yeah, I'm keen to run it,' I said.

From somewhere, through all the euphoria, I remembered I had relay training the next day. I grabbed my mobile phone and dialled John Quinn's number. 'Hi, John, it's Freeman,' I said. 'I just wanted to check what time relay training is tomorrow.' I think he was shocked to hear from me. My mind was already sorting through all the madness that was surrounding me and starting to focus on getting back to normal.

After a brief jog and another massage we started to pack everything up. It was after one a.m., and the place was deserted. All that was left in the Olympic stadium was our little group and a bunch of cleaners. We had to walk back under the stands to get to the van. It was the first time I had been able to gather my thoughts since crossing the line nearly five hours earlier. I was just so relieved and happy it was finally over.

'Yeah!' I yelled at the top of my voice as we drove away from the track. 'I won, I won! This is the happiest moment of my life!' It was the first time I'd really let my emotions out because there were no cameras or microphones around, just my husband, Garry, Maree and David.

We got back to the apartment at two a.m. and ate some Indian take-away. Everyone was still very emotional. Garth was searching around for aspirins for his headache. Bruce, my first coach, was sitting back in his chair, taking it all in. 'It only took seventeen years,' he said. Norman couldn't stop shaking his head. He was the one who could most relate to what I'd done. He had been a great talent as a teenager and at one stage he'd moved down to Melbourne to live and train with me and Nick. He'd even caught the eye of Linford Christie, who invited Norman to go overseas and train with him. However, like his father, Norman's real passion was rugby league and he soon returned home. 'I can't believe it, I can't fucking believe it,' he kept saying.

The boys wanted to go out and party, and Gavin was adamant he wouldn't have to pay for a drink all night because he had a picture of me on his jumper. I didn't even want a drink. I was having a celebration of my own just sitting back watching my family feeling so happy.

There was a beautiful calmness about the apartment. It was nearly four a.m. by the time we climbed into bed. I couldn't sleep, but the darkness was my friend. I could feel my body totally relax, and I knew already that I was a different person. I was able to breathe again. I was free.

CHAPTER 27
Breathing Again

'C mon, hon, let's go.'

I was pestering Alexander to get ready because Maree was waiting downstairs to take us into town. I was still buzzing and had only slept for three hours. I was on a mission of a different kind now. After each major victory I liked to reward myself. I loved jewellery, especially watches, and months ago I had selected the Cartier watch I wanted in Sydney. Maree had done some investigations and arranged for us to visit Watches of Switzerland in George Street. As soon as I walked in I saw it behind the glass. It had a beautiful silver band, and when I tried it on I instantly fell in love with it. I knew it was expensive but I figured I'd earned a little extravagance. Next on my list was some beauty work – a manicure. It was all so relaxing, and then we found this beautiful little café right by the water. Finally Alexander and I had some time alone and we laughed about some of the things that had happened in the past twelve months. I still couldn't believe it was over. Just little things like not having to worry about what I ate felt so good, and I allowed myself some ice-cream for dessert. I still had the 200m to run, but the intense expectation that had haunted me for the 400m wouldn't be there.

I could have stayed staring out at Sydney Harbour all day but I had to do a press conference back at the media centre with Tatiana, who had won the silver medal in the pole vault, and the two Aussie beach volleyball girls, Kern Pottharst and Natalie Cook, who had also won gold the previous day. John Coates was again in charge, and again the auditorium was packed. I was asked about everything from reconciliation to the swift suit and sitting down on the track.

'I wanted to feel really comfortable and do something that would make me feel normal because life for a while has been anything but normal for me,' I said. 'So I just wanted to sit down and take my shoes and socks off and do what I would be doing in the company of friends.'

Then the inevitable 'What now?' question.

'Retirement? Sure, it has crossed my mind. Living in another country? Sure, it's crossed my mind. All sorts of things have crossed my mind, but what I love most about life is the mystery and question marks that lie ahead.'

The thing was, I'd never thought about my life post-September 2000. And I didn't want to do it now. I wanted to enjoy being an Olympic gold medallist.

I had to be at the warm-up track at eight a.m. the next day to get ready for the opening round of the 200m. I felt like I'd been drunk and was now in the middle of one almighty hangover because I'd lost all my orientation. My head was out of whack and my body seemed to be following suit. Luckily, instinct and the adrenalin which was still flowing through my body took over in the opening round. I managed to finish third, which meant I had to front up again that night for the next round. As I hadn't let myself experience it during the 400m, I made sure I soaked up the atmosphere of the crowd when I was introduced for the quarter-final. I was looking around at everyone, waving and smiling. It was good to wear the Australian colours again and to feel the buzz of the crowd in the stadium. I ran an improved race and closed late to finish third behind Jamaica's Beverley McDonald in 22.75s. My late burst hid the fact that I was tired and flat. I thought a good ten hours' sleep would help my cause, but when I hit the warm-up track the next day to prepare for the semi-final I'd had enough.

'I don't really want to do this,' I announced to Fort and Sean.

'You've got to do it,' Sean replied.

There's nothing that gets my back up more than someone telling me I have to do something. I looked at Fort, and I knew he was wishing Sean hadn't said that. 'I don't have to do anything,' I barked back at him, and walked off.

For the past decade I'd done exactly what I was expected to do because I knew it was all geared towards living out my dream. Now I didn't want to play that game any more. Fort came over and started talking about the race and got me thinking how it would be nice to break my personal best, which was still the 22.25s I'd run at the Commonwealth Games six years before. The vibe of the stadium again got to me, and by the time I was on the blocks I was ready to go. However, my start was terrible and after a hundred metres I was clearly at the tail. I had an in-built hatred of losing anything, even if my head wasn't right, so I dug deep down the straight and flew to just grab fourth in 22.71s. I had made the Olympic final and was pretty happy about it. Who knows, maybe I could do a Pérec?

A couple of hours later, as we were heading around to the blocks, I had a sneaking suspicion that wouldn't be the case. I'd decided not to wear the swift suit because I wanted it to be remembered for that one special occasion. It was great to see Australia with two representatives: Melinda Gainsford-Taylor had made it through to her first Olympic final. I was in lane two and decided to simply give it everything one last time. I again started slowly, and by the time I looked up it seemed Marion Jones was already fifty metres ahead. I made some late ground but was really never in the race, and I finished seventh in a season's best of 22.53s, a step behind Melinda. I lingered out on the track afterwards and watched Marion celebrate. As I stood there, memories of my own victory lap came flooding back. With all the madness that had followed my victory and the bunkered focus I'd had in the lead-up, my memory was fairly patchy about certain aspects of my greatest night. I hoped in time it would all surface.

The next day was a rest day because team management had decided I should sit out the qualifying round for the 4 x 400m relay. I went down to the track to warm up with the team – Tamsyn, Nova, Susan Andrews and Jana Pittman – but John Quinn told me not to bother. I've never been a very good spectator and it certainly felt weird to watch the girls as I sat in the stands with Alexander. I started to get sweaty palms as the relay team appeared on the track. Alexander was also a nervous spectator. From the very first race he'd seen me run he had developed a ritual of crossing two fingers on each hand from the time I appeared behind the blocks. It had brought good fortune in the past, so for the Olympic final he had crossed his fingers from the moment he arrived in the stand, ninety minutes before the race. I couldn't stop laughing when he told me about it. Thankfully, the relay girls didn't need any of his lucky charms: they set a new national record in finishing second to qualify for the next day's final.

We had a team meeting at ten a.m. where John ran through the order of running. Melinda Gainsford-Taylor and I had come in to replace Susan and Jana. John worked as fitness coach for the Essendon football club in the AFL and his motivational speech to us was given in his typically, low-key, relaxed fashion. Quinny had one of the best temperaments for a coach I've ever seen, and I couldn't help but think back twelve months to the last relay meeting I'd been involved in at Seville. Thank God this one was completely the opposite. For once there seemed genuine hope about a positive result for an Australian relay team.

From that meeting I went down the hall to another room where I spent two hours signing hundreds of posters, envelopes, letters and T-shirts for the Australian Olympic Committee. The final wasn't until 9.30 p.m. so I had an afternoon nap to pass the time. I was excited about the relay and my final race on the wonderful track. Nova was going to lead us off, Tamsyn was second, with Melinda running the third leg before linking up with me.

The atmosphere when we arrived on the track was electric. We got away to a good start and hovered between third and fifth behind the Americans, who had stolen a massive lead. I took the baton in fourth spot, but unfortunately the other girls were over ten metres ahead. Slowly but surely I began to make ground but my legs were feeling a bit heavy. I threw everything at it down the home straight but there was to be no fairytale ending. With ten metres to go I conceded. There would be no medal, with the gap to third still at five metres. I switched off and didn't realise that Ogunkoya was right behind me; she nabbed me on the line for fourth. I felt a little embarrassed about that, but we'd still managed to set another Australian record. My body was hurting. I paused to give one last wave goodbye to the crowd before disappearing to begin life after the Olympics.

It started in earnest thirty minutes later on Garry's massage table when I had my first drink – champagne out of a plastic cup. Alexander and I arranged to meet the family at the Nike headquarters just next to the village. I went back there first to collect all my gear and it turned out that the family had become separated. My brothers had been partying non-stop for three days and had gone missing again. Instead of any wild celebrations, I settled for a quiet dinner. I treated myself to an apple tart with custard, which I ate before the main meal.

The following morning in bed, after a glorious sleep-in, Alexander and I discussed the future for the first time. We agreed that we were each going to plan something in a three-week block, which we weren't allowed to tell the other person about. Already everyone was asking what was next for Cathy Freeman, including my mother, who thought I should take a year off and have a baby. All I knew was that it didn't feel like I'd run my last race. I decided not to go to the closing ceremony because the last thing I wanted was to be mixing with crowds. The family came over and we watched it on television with a few drinks and a lot of laughs. We could see the fireworks from the balcony. I went inside to get another drink and I looked back at my family out on the deck. I had never seen them so happy together. Right at that moment the penny dropped. It was over. I'd done it.

Ticker-tape parades in Sydney and Melbourne were part of the official celebrations, while back at home our personal celebration was an indulgent party. My training partner Evette Cordy and I had planned it back in May while we were in America. She made a sponge cake that was the length of the dining-room table and then coated it with a special chocolate sauce. The woman from the restaurant where we discovered the sauce had refused to give Evette the recipe so she had to keep going back and sampling to figure it out. The ingredients included chocolate topping and melted Mars Bars. It was so good. I had a few drinks, too, but I was still really drunk on happiness.

A few days later Alexander and I headed north to Darwin to party with Nova and her family and friends up there. I then made a special trip to Rockhampton to visit Anne-Marie's grave. Every time I went there I burst into tears. When everything had seemed to be falling apart earlier in the year, she had been the strength inside me that kept me sane. Whenever I thought I couldn't cope she would enter my thoughts. Anne-Marie had been my guardian angel. 'I did it for you,' I whispered as I placed flowers on her headstone. Tears began to stream down my face. I wished so much she could have been there. The next day we drove to Woorabinda to visit my father's grave.

On 23 October I made an emotional return to my home-town of Mackay. I had barely got off the plane when I heard a little girl yell, 'Aunty Catherine, Aunty Catherine!' It was my niece Astrid and she came running up to me and jumped into my lap. It was so good to see my extended family, all the nieces and nephews and friends who had helped create me. There were a thousand people lining the main street and balloons and streamers everywhere. I was really moved by it, and I told the crowd, 'I have never made any secret of the pride I have in myself. Part of being who I am is knowing where I came from, so it was not really just me who won the gold medal, it was you.'

However, the adulation was starting to take its toll. Everywhere I went I was getting mobbed, and the emotion I saw in people's eyes when they talked to me about the opening ceremony or the gold medal race was actually scary. I couldn't believe that I had touched so many people's lives. It was wonderful, but it was also overwhelming. After a month of constant public appearances I'd reached the point where I couldn't wait to get overseas and disappear from the spotlight.

I wanted to be a nobody again.

CHAPTER 28
BEING A NOBODY

The van stopped at the bottom of the hill. The door opened and six men piled out. I looked anxiously at Alexander. We were jogging down a dirt track in a national park in the mountains of Chile. The men signalled us to stop. My God, were we getting ambushed? I grabbed Alexander's arm as one of the men pulled out a camera. In broken English he asked if they could have their photo taken with me. I nearly died. How the hell did they know who I was?

One of the reasons we'd chosen Chile as our getaway was because we figured track and field wasn't a big sport in that part of South America. I had been shocked by the level of recognition I received overseas. We'd flown from Australia to the States, and it had started almost immediately. In Washington, a little girl in a lift knew who I was; in New York, some construction workers yelled out my name, and a Mormon family in Salt Lake City had asked for my autograph. It was a real spin-out.

We had to attend one official function, the International Amateur Athletic Federation awards in Monaco, where I was presented with the Inspirational Award. After that we went travelling, and it was great just doing simple things that everyone else takes for granted, like having some wine with dinner, or eating what I wanted, whenever I wanted. However, this all masked the problem that kept gnawing away at me as each week passed: what should I do now? I was lost. The Olympic gold medal had been this carrot on a stick that I'd chased for twenty years, and now I had the carrot. What came next? If I took a year off, would I be able to come back? Should I have a child? I was driving myself into depression worrying about the future.

Alexander and I talked about it for hours, but he knew it was something that had to come from my heart. There was still a month to go before I was due back at training in Melbourne. I had started to feel uncomfortable with my body because I was putting on heaps of weight. I was so used to feeling strong and in shape that it really freaked me out. And I was missing training. I never thought I'd say that. I kept thinking about that old saying, 'You're a long time retired.' Plus, I was only going to be able to compete at the elite level for a certain period of time. Maybe I should just make the most of it? Maybe. I was so confused.

That confusion deepened in the new year after a month back in Melbourne with Fort and the training group. I wasn't the same athlete. For some reason I was paranoid about injury and used that as an excuse for allowing myself to accept a much lower standard than usual. I wasn't blinking an eye if I forgot to do a circuit session, which had never happened before. I was happy to be late for training, and to eat a little more chocolate or dessert. And when I was at training I was just hanging in there, going through the motions. It was weird, because previously, even if I was sick or had a hangover, I'd bounce out of bed and go to training – it was second nature. Right now I was going to training simply because I didn't know any different.

I desperately needed a distraction, and it came early in February when I had to fly back to the States to attend the Espy Awards. The ceremony was at the magnificent MGM Grand Hotel in Las Vegas and I decided to bring Bruce and Mum along for the occasion. The awards, which were the creation of the ESPN television network, brought together the who's who of the sports and entertainment worlds, with famous people everywhere you looked. I felt so out of place, and that was multiplied by a thousand when my name was read out to receive the Arthur Ashe Courage and Humanitarian Award. I couldn't believe everyone in the room was standing and applauding as I made my way to the stage. Before I could accept the award from actor Samuel L. Jackson, a ten-minute tribute was played on the big screen. It featured words from actor Russell Crowe, author and historian Robert Hughes and even a couple of lines from my own family. By the time I got to the microphone I was in total shock. 'Wow,' I said. 'Now I'm supposed to say a speech and I'm going to cry.' Among the previous winners was Muhammad Ali.

I was slowly beginning to understand just what an impact my achievements at the Sydney Olympics had made in terms of raising awareness of the plight of Australia's indigenous people. It was a wonderful feeling.

But when I returned home I was snapped back to reality because the legal dispute with Nick was back on the agenda. I had been summoned to my accountant's office for a meeting with a bunch of lawyers and barristers. I hated having to do this. I hated Nick for putting me through this. That hatred was about to go to a whole new level.

'It could be possible that you will have to pay a million dollars in taxes.'

Alistair Hamblin's words hung in the air. Had I heard right?

'A million dollars,' I repeated slowly. 'You've got to be joking.'

I felt my spirits deflate instantly. I was in a state of shock as I drove home. There was no one around when I got there and suddenly I had a feeling I hadn't experienced for years. I felt like self-destructing. I found a packet of my nephew Gavin's cigarettes and lit one up. This was supposed to be the happiest time of my life. Less than five months ago I'd won an Olympic gold medal. But this legal dispute was like a big chain around my neck and it kept dragging me down. Today it had just been yanked really hard and I was on the ground. The disturbing thing was, I didn't want to get up.

The phone rang just as I was starting my second cigarette. It was my brother Norman. He was upset over an article he'd just read in the paper that questioned the validity of the Stolen Generation. The article mentioned my name and our nanna's plight in the story, which was about Aboriginal leader Dr Lowitja O'Donoghue. He quickly sensed that I wasn't really listening. 'What's wrong?' he asked. I told him about the tax bill and how I'd hit the wall and was currently enjoying a smoke. 'You'd better knock that off,' he said.

'Yes, Dad,' I said, but I didn't. I went in search of some Scotch.

I had always been a fighter, but for one of the few times in my life I was giving up. I went upstairs to bed and stayed there for two days.

This had never happened to me before, not even when I'd gone through the break-up with Nick in 1997. I don't know whether it was the Olympics finally catching up with me, or some sort of depression, but I was suddenly very tired. I couldn't even be bothered to change my clothes. Alexander was away for a few days and I didn't want to see anybody or talk to anyone.

I'd never felt like not running before. Running had been my life for so long and I'd never pictured myself not doing it – that's what frightened me the most. I was letting go of something and there was no guarantee I was ever going to get it back. Was it the right thing to do? Over and over I kept asking myself, and Alexander, this question. Every night I was ringing Mum in Brisbane. Eventually my feelings spilled over during a meeting with my new manager, Chris Giannopoulos, from IMG. We'd been discussing some future projects when he stopped and said, 'Look, Cath, what's wrong?'

I suddenly got embarrassed. 'What do you mean?' I said.

'I can sense it. Something's worrying you, so let's talk about it.'

I told him everything.

'This is not unusual for elite sports-people,' Chris said. 'I know several of our clients have experienced similar things.'

He suggested that I see psychologist Dr Noel Blundell, who had previously helped a number of tennis players and golfers. I went away and talked to Alexander about it, and he agreed that we didn't have anything to lose, so I made the trip out to Noel's house in Mt Waverley a couple of days later.

The moment I sat down in his office I wanted to cry. One of the reasons I'd chosen running over team sports twenty years before was because running allowed you to be in total control. You owned it and controlled it. Somehow it felt like I'd lost that control. Noel kept saying that what I was experiencing was to be expected. He had seen it with many Olympians after Atlanta in 1996 and Sydney. We talked about how traumatic the twelve months leading up to the Games had been, with all the expectation and the stress of the break-up with Nick. 'You've been through a lot,' he said. 'I'm surprised this hasn't happened sooner.' He kept giving me examples of elite athletes who had taken time off and come back to be the best again. I knew my body was telling me that, but my mind refused to give in. I was getting more and more upset.

'Why don't I want to do this?' I asked. 'This is what I do, this is what I'm good at, what I am best at, so why don't I want to do it?'

The psychologist paused for a moment. 'It's quite clear to me what you need to do, and I think it's quite clear to you as well. You just don't want to admit it.'

I knew I could try to run away from the truth, but it was always going to catch up with me. It was such a strange time. Running was the one sure thing in my life, the one thing that had always felt real. What the hell was I going to do without it? I had got to the point where I needed to be told what to do, and Noel had done just that. He showed me that there could be a life off the track.

A couple of days later I was at lunch with Lee Naylor and Melinda Gainsford-Taylor and I decided to ask their opinion. It felt like they were my big sisters because they reassured me that everything was going to be all right and that people could take time off and come back. Lee and Mel had both done it. Their support helped finalise my decision: I was going to take the year off. Fort was the first person I wanted to tell, but it wasn't him I was worried about – it was Maurie. The last time I'd suggested taking time off, in 1997, he'd got angry and talked me out of it. Also, he'd already put together a programme for me and was currently in negotiations about the Goodwill Games, which were being held in Brisbane later in the year.

I rang Maurie and asked him to come over for a chat. He seemed his usual jovial self when he arrived, and before we'd even sat down he said, 'You don't want to run, do you?'

I was stunned. 'How did you know?'

'It's been obvious,' he said. 'It's not what you want to do at the moment so it's better that you take a break now rather than force yourself.'

I jumped up and gave him a great big hug and a kiss on his forehead. It made me so happy that the people whose opinion I cherished the most were all 100 per cent behind me.

Next on my list were IMG, Royce Communications (my public relations firm) and Alistair Hamblin. I'd decided to do them all at once, later in the week. However, I was at IMG the day before the big meeting and Chris called me into his office. 'I just got an e-mail from the Goodwill Games people. Apparently you're not competing this year,' he said. I explained how I'd wanted to tell everybody together and he was also great about the whole thing. Now all that remained was to tell the world.

On 15 March 2001, six months after I had lit the Olympic cauldron, I held a press conference to announce I was taking a break. I had no regrets. Suddenly everything had become so clear in my mind. The irony was that a few hours earlier I'd had to do a photo shoot for one of my sponsors in my training gear at Olympic Park. As the questions started coming thick and fast, I was relieved at how comfortable and confident I was about my decision. 'It scares me,' I admitted, 'but there is no doubt in my mind that I will want to compete again. I can't imagine life without stepping on to the track and pushing myself to be the best in the world.'

I'll be back.

Alexander and I decided to leave immediately. Our first stop would be the family in Queensland, and then on to Portland. From there I'd sort out life as Mrs Alexander Bodecker, not Cathy Freeman. Before I left there was one last lunch with Fort and Rab at the Pavilion Café.

'You've got to train, don't get too unfit,' Rab said.

'Yeah, yeah. I'll do other things like play netball or something,' I said. Neither of them seemed too convinced.

'Don't get over sixty kilos. That's the cut-off weight,' Fort said.

'Yeah, yeah.' I giggled as the chorus from my favourite song came into my head: 'Cos I'm free, to do what I want, any old time'.

CHAPTER 29
JUST ANOTHER FACE
IN THE CROWD

'She's not going to recognise me,' I said sheepishly as I scanned the track for a hole I could hide in. It was July 2001, and I had been in Rome for the past three weeks staying with my friend Danni Perpoli, a former 400m runner in Australia. She had dragged me down to her local track. Unfortunately for me, the great Merlene Ottey was now walking our way. Even though she had retired and was in her forties, she still looked fantastic. The same couldn't be said of me. My first three months of freedom had involved lots of good wine, good food and long nights, and it was starting to show.

'You've been feasting, girl,' Ottey declared with a laugh. 'You've been feasting.'

'Yeah, you could say that,' I said.

Danni wanted me to do some laps with her, but after about ten metres I had to stop because I could feel a twinge in my hamstring. Fort had always marvelled at how quickly I could put on weight and then how quickly I could shed it. He'd die if he saw me now. I was already well over his sixty-kilo cut-off point.

I loved having a normal life. Eating what I wanted, when I wanted, sleeping for as long as I wanted and staying up as late as I wanted. This was all foreign territory for me. For my entire adult life I'd lived the life of a disciplined athlete. I was just beginning to realise how many sacrifices that had involved.

I spent the first month of my new life hanging out with my family in Brisbane and Mackay. I visited several schools while I was there and got the chance to speak to some young Aboriginal kids. I love children, and one of the great things about being who I am is that it gives me the chance to help them. As a child, I had the amazing support of my parents, coaches and teachers, but unfortunately not every child benefits from such nurturing. That's one of the reasons I got involved with an Australian foundation called Inspire, which reaches out through the Internet to young people in rural regions who are having a tough time coping with life. I'd try to explain that so-called 'sporting icons' like me have bad days of low self-esteem and little self-worth as well, that they weren't alone out there. I'd tell them, 'Please take good care of yourself. Work hard and never lose sight of your own dream, whatever your goals are.

'Stay strong and proud, and never give in to anything or anybody. Use your experiences, good and bad, to your advantage; let them be your strength to make you ruthless and determined.

'Respect and be kind to yourself, and stay true to who you are.

'You are one of tomorrow's leaders. And who knows, you may parent a future leader some day, so live and learn for your child as well.'

In May, Alexander and I headed for Portland. I needed to relax completely and there was no way I could do that in Australia. I needed to be just another face in the crowd, and Portland was the ideal place. It was a kind of daggy city, a little bit grungy and certainly not picturesque. To appreciate it you had to get out and meet the people. We initially stayed in a hotel room near the city centre; later on we had our own apartment on the river. The Nike complex was out in the suburbs, so while Alexander went to work I explored the city, often by bike, and enrolled in Italian lessons in preparation for a trip to Rome. It was such an odd feeling for me to be able to get up, walk out the door and go somewhere not because I had to, but because I could. There weren't any foregone conclusions or judgements about why I was supposed to be there. I could just be me. For three weeks that involved volunteering at the office of a local newspaper called *Street Roots*. The idea of the paper was to empower the homeless, who would sell *Street Roots* on the streets and keep fifty cents out of the one-dollar cover price.

Every now and then I was forced to revert to Cathy Freeman, Olympic gold medallist. We flew to Monte Carlo for the Laureus World Sports

Awards, an event known as the Sports Oscars, where I was fortunate enough to be presented with the Sportswoman of the Year Award. Our next stop was Lausanne in Switzerland, where I received the Olympic Order from the International Olympic Committee.

My visit to Rome allowed me to play tourist. I'd come to the realisation that I had to step back from the small but all-consuming world of international track and field. I was now opening my mind to lots of things. I was taking more interest in reading and photography, which had always been a hobby of mine. I had bought a great automatic camera and I took it everywhere with me. Our mode of transport in Rome was Danni's scooter, which was a bit hair-raising at times but a lot of fun. We explored the Vatican and the Colosseum, where I couldn't get Russell Crowe and the film *Gladiator* out of my head. There was one scene in particular where he entered the Colosseum and faced a giant mass of loud and demanding spectators expecting an entertaining fight to the death. I can actually liken that to what I experienced in Sydney. Often when you make your way to the start of a race, time seems to go slowly and it feels like you are marching to your death.

After three weeks of partying in Rome I had to put my official hat back on and head to Moscow for two important Olympic announcements: the 2008 Olympic host city and the new IOC president to replace Mr Samaranch. My name had been linked to Beijing's bid because it had come out that I had some Chinese blood somewhere in my family tree. Apparently one of the Sibley men had married a Chinese woman during the gold rush in Australia.

I caught up with Maurie Plant at a couple of the European grand prix meets and he told me I looked good, but I felt uncomfortable around other athletes. It was still a bit weird being a spectator, although I wasn't as spun out as I'd been at the Prefontaine Classic in Eugene, Oregon, not long after I had arrived in the States. I had been excited about catching up with Nova Peris and seeing a few of the other guys, but when I got to the warm-up area I freaked out. I felt like a fish out of water. I couldn't stand being on the other side of the fence and had to leave.

It soon became obvious that my weight was the talk of the circuit. It was certainly the topic of conversation when I caught up for dinner with John Smith and the HSI guys, Ato Boldon and Maurice Greene.

Ato was trying his hardest to be kind. 'I don't think you've put on that much weight,' he said.

'Oh, she has,' John kept repeating. 'Man, she certainly has.'

A part of me didn't care what they thought. I had lived my dream, I had won my gold medal and I was resting now. I wasn't training so I could do what I wanted. These thoughts often pushed me to rub it in to my colleagues and have that extra glass of red wine or a couple more Swiss chocolates.

After a full-on month of travelling, I returned to Portland in August knowing that it was time to make some big decisions. What did the future hold for Cathy Freeman?

I had only been back a couple of days when the answer hit me straight between the eyes. Alexander and I were having a lazy Sunday morning when I suddenly turned to him and said, 'Hon, I really want to have your child.'

I don't know where it came from, but it was so clear in my mind that I wanted to become a mother. Mum had been encouraging me to have a child and my best friend, Peta, had recently had a baby. I'd begun fantasising about it, seeing myself with this big belly. For two or three days I was obsessed by it and continually cornered Alexander on the subject. I could tell he wasn't quite as enthusiastic. My plan was that I'd retire from running and move to America. That was the answer. I could play Mum while Alexander pursued his career. I'd done everything I wanted-ed to in my own career so having a baby was the perfect get-out.

The idea of having a child affected everything I did that week. Alexander had bought a new car, a 1970 Chevy, and when we went to pick it up all I could think about was whether a baby seat would fit, or what a little girl or boy would look like buckled up in the back. It was very strange.

As quickly as the idea of falling pregnant had formed in my mind, it disappeared. By the end of the week I was beginning to have doubts. Once there was any hint of doubt, I knew I couldn't have a child. You can't have a child with doubts in your head. The price is too high. It's the one thing in your life you should be very, very clear about, whether it's the right thing for you and your relationship. Something was now telling me the timing wasn't right. What became even clearer was that I was scared. Actually, I was petrified about having a little life in my hands, a small being that would rely on me for everything. It was such a big challenge, responsibility and obligation. I knew I was being selfish thinking like that, but I had to be.

'Hon, I'm really mixed up,' I said to Alexander. 'I don't want to have a child because I'm scared.'

He seemed almost relieved. We'd been having some problems as it became more obvious that Alexander was frightened by the idea of me ditching my career and living in America. This was beginning to weigh heavily on my mind, and the more I thought about it the more disappointed I became. I was as close as I'd ever been to settling down and I was craving a normal lifestyle. A big part of me was ready for the house in the country with the white picket fence. Unfortunately, Alexander wasn't on the same page. Although he'd taken time off in the lead-up to the Olympics, he was very passionate about his work and it was a major priority in his life. He was constantly on the move, travelling around the world, and it meant we were regularly apart.

I had been asked to do some commentary work with the BBC and Channel 7 at the world championships in Edmonton, Canada. I knew that returning to the big stage of athletics was sure to stoke my desire to return to the track. I had got into a routine of going for a long jog in the afternoons in Portland. It had always been an aim of mine to be able to jog for an hour. I had grown up as a sprinter, but long-distance running had always intrigued me. I'm not saying I was contemplating a change of event, but I found the long jogs very relaxing and they helped to clear my mind. It also rammed home the fact that I felt so much better when I was out running.

It was certainly different attending the world championships and not being in my own little world, focused totally on my race. It was fun looking around and seeing how important athletics is to a lot of people. I wasn't quite prepared for how busy I was going to be. Maybe naively, I thought I could cruise in, say hello to a few people and watch some track and field. Instead, I was flat out. The commentary work was a bit of fun, working alongside Roger Black, Steve Cram, John Regis, Michael Johnson and Katharine Merry, who unfortunately was out of action because of injury. It seemed like every foreign journalist there wanted an interview so I spent a lot of my time fulfilling those engagements because I didn't want to be rude. I had recently been approached by London's *Daily Telegraph* to do a monthly column for the paper so that took up a bit of time, especially when my laptop computer kept jamming.

Before the women's 400m final I couldn't stay away from the warm-up area. I had to have a glimpse of how the girls were shaping up, and I found myself becoming nervous as I watched the race in the commentary box. I didn't feel like I wanted to be out there, but my competitive juices were certainly stirred. A big tall girl from Senegal, Amy Mbacke Thiam, was the surprise winner. An even bigger shock was the defeat of Marion Jones in the 100m. That is why I love sport – anything can happen.

I caught up with Fort while I was in Edmonton and he seemed to think I was starting training again in October. I had it in my head that it was November. At least we were both heading in the same direction. I'd come to the conclusion that I was ready to jump back into my old world. It was what I knew best, and at 28 I still had a good couple of years left in me. As long as there was still something inside pulling me towards running, I had to listen. Babies and a normal life could wait for now.

My time away from training had made me realise how much of a goal-orientated person I was. Training gave my life the structure I needed; it gave me direction, and I felt much stronger when I had that. Even the day-to-day performance goals in the gym or on the track were a source of strength. I realised how much I preferred being an athlete in the athletic arena to being an athlete in the political or corporate arenas. I'd got tired of everything about Cathy Freeman off the track. Having more time on my hands meant more time to do all the media things. When you're an athlete you enjoy the calm, peaceful time when you're jogging or stretching instead of having to be on the receiving end of directions all the time. You're working to your own agenda. That's what I craved again.

From Edmonton I flew to London and then on to Australia, once again without Alexander. I attended the Goodwill Games in Brisbane, where I had the honour of presenting Marion Jones with her gold medal after she reversed her shock world championship loss to Zhanna Pintusevich-Block. We caught up again the next week in Melbourne for the IAAF grand prix final. She didn't compete, but we hung out at a sponsor's function. It was really good to be home, despite the never-ending media questions about when I'd be training and racing again.

I was getting really excited about my trip up north for my brother Gavin's fortieth birthday party in Rockhampton, and Norman's appearance in the rugby league grand final in Mackay. I was looking forward to having a few beers with my family and a good old-fashioned laugh. Then my gaze was drawn to the television set at my brother's house in Mackay. The screen was filled with a picture of a building in flames. I thought it had to be a movie, but the newsreader looked distressed. I reached for the remote control and turned the volume up. It was New York. Oh, my God! A plane had just crashed into the World Trade Center. Terrorists were assaulting America. It took a while to fully register in my mind, and then I let out a scream. 'Alexander, Alexander! Where is my husband?' He was due to fly out to Australia in the next couple of days. I frantically dialled his number in Portland, praying that he was at home. He travels so much with his work that he could easily have been in New York. I never really kept track of exactly where he went because his schedule was so hectic.

C'mon, pick up!

After five rings I was really starting to get scared.

'Hello,' his voice boomed down the line.

'Thank God you're there,' I said. He was just getting ready to go to work and had no idea about the attack. 'Hon, turn on the TV.'

I stayed on the line as he digested the horror of what had happened. I told him not to come out to Australia because I didn't want him anywhere near a plane. It took him six days to sort out his flight, and by the time we caught up in Mackay he'd missed both the birthday party and the rugby match.

On 25 September, the anniversary of my gold-medal-winning

performance, there was a luncheon held in my honour in Sydney, where I was inducted into the Australian Institute of Sport Living Legends Hall of Fame. It was a great day, with tributes from my good friends Steve Moneghetti and Raelene Boyle, and a video message from Bruce McAvaney. I was asked all sorts of questions from the floor.

Where was my gold medal?

'I know it's somewhere in my bedroom, but I'm not exactly sure,' I said. 'I'm actually going to get a safe to put it in.'

Then there was the inevitable question about my new, rounder figure.

'I'm about eight kilos over my race weight,' I admitted.

The previous week I'd been in Brisbane, staying with Mum and Bruce. Each morning I'd dragged Mum out for a long walk, and after one particular workout we got home to find that someone had rung the local radio station saying they'd just seen Cathy Freeman down the street and she was clearly pregnant!

Despite the events of 11 September, I decided to go ahead with a planned trip back to the States. Like many others, I reasoned that if we let terrorists affect the way we lived our lives then they had won. We flew back to Portland with my nephew Gavin Leonard, who came over for a holiday. While Alexander went back to work, Gavin and I went up to LA and I took him to Disneyland, Hollywood, Venus Beach and all the other major tourist attractions. We then headed to Whistler in Canada, where we caught up with Jacqui Cooper, the Australian champion aerial skier with whom I'd recently become close friends. From there it was back to Portland, and then Alexander and I flew out to New York to attend the Women in Sport awards.

The flight into New York was eerie. Everyone on the plane had blank looks on their faces. When the city's skyline appeared I couldn't help but think what it must have been like for all those people on the hijacked planes. The security at the airport was intense. I had a hairpin taken from me because it was a sharp object. We caught a taxi to the hotel and there were military personnel lining the streets, checking under every van and bus. That afternoon I went for a jog around Central Park. There was a perimeter around the park where traffic couldn't go and I was surprised to find that life was going on as normal.

People were still happy, lying around laughing and playing with their dogs. It was hard to grasp that this place had recently been the target of a terrorist attack.

The following morning the award function organisers arranged for us to visit Ground Zero. It was one of the most moving experiences of my life. First we were taken to a restaurant about a five-minute drive from the actual attack site where all the police, firefighters and volunteers went to eat and take a breather from their horrific jobs. Everyone was pitching in to help. Gospel singers were performing, and famous faces mingled throughout, signing autographs or simply chatting. People from all walks of society were there to show they cared. Alexander went out to the kitchen to help and started cutting lettuces. Outside the restaurant there was a large board with photos of all the people still missing, and drawings and poems expressing sympathy and sadness. I spoke to several police and firemen and they were really happy to see us there. I was struck by how friendly and upbeat they were.

We were then taken to Ground Zero in a police car. We had to wear masks, and the closer we got the more horrible the damage to the surrounding buildings became. I didn't know what to say or think. I felt sick at the devastation in front of me. There were people everywhere with hard hats on, and bulldozers were crashing through the wreckage. People said you could smell the stench of human bones. It was sadder than I could ever have imagined. A month earlier I'd been with my family back in Mackay, on the other side of the planet, watching these buildings collapse on TV. Now, I was standing in the middle of it. What had happened to the world? What was safe now? Would there be peace?

All these questions remained with me at the awards dinner that night. The spirit there was amazing, and when the national anthem was played I sang it with gusto. I was so inspired by the spirit of the people in New York. What I saw there changed me for ever.

After the visit to New York I started to reassess every aspect of my life. I had returned to Melbourne without Alexander. Just before I'd left the States we'd had a serious argument. It had been happening quite a lot recently and I still had this sick feeling in my stomach when I got home. I wasn't happy with our marriage and I knew I had to do something about it. In the heat of the moment I had mentioned the word 'divorce', but Alexander had simply ignored it. It was as though he refused to accept that we were in trouble.

Thankfully, I was greeted with madness when I arrived home, which helped me forget about my marital problems. My personal assistant was going to live in Los Angeles so I had to start searching for a new one; I had the wedding of one of my business agents to attend; and my brother and his family were in town. It was great to have them staying in Kew with me. On the Sunday afternoon we fired up the barbecue, cranked up the stereo and enjoyed a few beers and some wonderful oil-soaked sausages. I knew they were bad for me but I wasn't starting back at training until Thursday so I was going to enjoy everything until then.

The next day I flew to Darwin to keep a promise I'd made more than a year before. I'd told the people of Gapuwiyak, a small Aboriginal community in the middle of the bush, that I would visit them. I relished getting back among my people and soaking up the rich Aboriginal culture that is very much alive in Gapuwiyak. Most of the school children are still learning English, as it isn't their first language. The people were extremely softly spoken and very shy; it was through dance, music and singing that they expressed themselves. It was an extraordinary experience to spend time with them, and I left feeling inspired and knowing that so much of my pride and self-esteem stems from my Aboriginality.

I arrived home on the Wednesday, and as it was my last night before training started I asked Gavin Leonard to get my favourite custard and apple pie while he was at the supermarket. I just needed one last indulgence. I ended up eating three-quarters of the pie, with cream smothered all over it, and washing it down with a sweet white wine. Magnificent!

That wasn't how I was feeling the next day when I arrived at Duncan MacKinnon Reserve in Murrumbeena to meet Fort for my first official training session. I dragged Jacqui Cooper along because I knew she'd be fun. I'd started to panic about my return, which had turned into a major event, with television crews, sponsors and my agents all on hand. It was a bit embarrassing as we jogged a couple of laps of the oval and did a few very slow run-throughs. I could feel the custard and apple pie all the way around. Suddenly it seemed as if the past year had just flown by. It was a distant memory now as I tried to get my head around the demands of training again, knowing the pain my body would have to endure to get back to its former self.

CHAPTER 30
CANCER

'It's not worth risking. I think you need to take at least three weeks off but it could be as many as six.'

Dr Peter Fuller's words had just dealt my comeback a severe blow. Everything had been going remarkably well, and after almost five months of solid training I'd managed to shed nearly all my excess weight. However, it all changed in a split second during a regular training exercise at Doncaster. We were doing some 200m run-throughs and I'd gone really hard around the bend and was cruising down the straight when suddenly, with sixty metres to go, I felt a sharp pain behind my right knee. I stopped straight away because it was similar to the feeling I'd experienced when I injured my foot in Oslo in 1998.

I immediately drove to my masseur Garry's house to see if he could work out what had happened. It felt fine to walk around on so we decided to test it again after a couple of days' rest. However, the moment I went to push off hard on it the pain shot through my knee again. Dr Fuller suggested we have an MRI scan done, and that was when he found the problem in my right femur, the big bone in the thigh. There was inflammation and bleeding behind the knee, and if I continued running it could become a major problem. My comeback had mainly concentrated on the 200m; I had only raced over 400m once, in Perth, where I'd won in 52.59s. I'd felt excited about being back and had hooked up with a new training partner, Andrew Krumins.

The injury was so deflating. I'd been on such a high after a whistle-stop appearance at the opening ceremony of the Winter Olympics at Salt Lake City. It was an amazing experience carrying the Olympic flag into the stadium next to some of the most famous people in the world: Bishop Desmond Tutu, filmmaker Steven Spielberg, ex-astronaut Senator John Glenn, former president of Poland Lech Walesa, Japanese ski jumper Kazuyoshi Funaki, French ski legend Jean-Claude Killy and French environmentalist Jean-Michel Cousteau. Wow! What a diverse and interesting group of people. I couldn't believe I was part of that. Unfortunately, the trip ended on a sad note because my good friend Jacqui Cooper badly injured her knee in training and was forced out of the Olympics.

My own injury break meant the national championships in Brisbane in April 2002, which would double as the selection trials for the Manchester Commonwealth Games, were now out of the equation. I tried to maintain my fitness working out in the pool, but it was obvious my body had broken down from the shock of losing ten kilos so quickly. My mind had shifted back into athlete mode, but my body had been unable to keep up.

I travelled to Brisbane for the nationals, but only as a spectator. I was still clinging to the hope that the knee would come good and I could do some races in Europe and be ready for the Commonwealth Games in July. My training was gradually improving and life was hectic as usual. Alexander and I were still having problems, and he had returned to work in the States. All my time seemed to be taken up with meeting after meeting.

One particular phone call changed everything.

I was on my way back from training when I got a call from Alexander. He wasn't in Portland, he was at our home in Kew, and I could sense there was something seriously wrong from the urgency in his voice.

'I need to talk to you,' he said.

When I got there he was sitting on the couch. I could tell he was upset.

'I think I have cancer,' he said slowly.

'What?' I said.

'I've got this lump in my throat and I'm scared it's cancer.'

I felt myself getting angry. Why? When? How? All these questions raced through my head before I realised I needed to take control. I rang

Dr Fuller and told him we were coming in to see him immediately. He quickly got us in to see a specialist who did a biopsy and told us we'd know the results within two days.

Alexander had known about the lump in his throat for a year. He'd thought it was just a throat infection at first but it had continued to grow. Now he was having trouble swallowing, he couldn't eat properly and his speech was affected. He had also begun to lose weight, and that's when he realised he couldn't live with it any more.

I prayed for him that night and the next, hoping he'd be wrong about the cancer. He was very physically fit and healthy for a 49-year-old and he was a non-smoker. However, he seemed adamant that he was in serious trouble. Instead of sitting around waiting for the phone call, we tried to keep a normal routine. I wasn't home when he got the call, but as soon as I walked through the front door I knew the news was bad.

'I've got cancer,' Alexander said. The blood drained from his face and he went a deathly shade of white.

I sat down next to him and hugged him. We were silent for a couple of minutes, then I felt myself getting angry again. I got up and started pacing the living room.

How can you live with that much fear and not talk to me about it? I'm your wife, and you didn't tell me anything for a whole year.

I could have picked up the TV cabinet and thrown it through the window. I was so angry – at him for not telling me, and at the cancer for invading our lives. I started to take a series of deep breaths to calm me down. Alexander didn't need me going crazy right now. He looked so helpless sitting there.

'What does it mean?' I asked. 'What can I do?'

There was really nothing I could do but stay by his side.

I knew at that moment there was no way I could leave him. There would be no more running and no more thoughts of breaking up. Alexander needed me like he'd never needed me before, and we were going to fight this evil disease together.

Over the next few days we were both very businesslike as we went about finding out where Alexander could get the best treatment and how we were going to attack the cancer. We were referred to Professor

Lester Peters and Professor Danny Rischin at the Peter MacCallum Cancer Institute in Melbourne. They did an examination. Alexander had started to deteriorate as the cancer spread to both sides of his mouth. His voice was getting more affected and he was even having trouble breathing.

The news from the doctors wasn't good, 'The tumour is inoperable and it is at an advanced stage.'

I felt my stomach drop. Alexander didn't flinch. He continued staring straight ahead. He had already started to prepare himself for the fight. His father had died of cancer and he'd told me before we came to the hospital that he was going to be different. 'We're going to win. I'm going to beat it,' he'd said.

The doctors went on to explain that cancer is rated on a scale of one to four, with four being the worst. Alexander's was a four. The only positive was that a clinical trial specific to this type of cancer was being conducted. It had been running for seven years and was available in three hospitals in Australia and one in New Zealand. The preliminary findings had been quite positive and Alexander could be, if not the last, then one of the last people to get into the trial. It involved a combination of radiation treatment and two types of chemotherapy. We were told the possible repercussions of the treatment long-term involved the loss of a certain range of hearing and some saliva glands; short-term, Alexander was likely to experience nausea, cramps, and the loss of hair, saliva glands and taste buds.

Our next task was to tell all the relevant people about what was happening. I found myself being very clinical in the process. I couldn't control how anyone else was going to react to the news and I couldn't afford to worry about them. It was hard, but I had to be a little bit cold because I had to focus my time and energy on Alexander. This was the way things were and we just had to do what we had to do. A lot of people got upset and everyone offered their help in any way they could, particularly Raelene Boyle, who had battled breast and ovarian cancer three times.

Word of Alexander's illness had leaked to the media, so I held a press conference to tell the world I wouldn't be running that season. The room was packed with cameras and reporters when I entered with Fort on one side and my PR manager, Richard Amos, on the other. 'My highest priority is to remain by my husband's side and to give him as much love and support as possible,' I said. I told them I wouldn't be racing in the individual 400m at Manchester but was leaving the door open for a relay spot, although the chances of me being there were remote. I made it quite clear that Alexander and I expected to win this battle. 'Anybody who becomes involved with Catherine Freeman has to be prepared to be really determined, and my husband's going to be just fine.'

Alexander and I had made a pact that we'd try to carry on as if everything was normal. We both knew it wasn't, but the power of the mind was so important. The major positive on our side of the equation was that Alexander was one of the strongest and most determined people I had ever met. You get a sense about people. You see it in their eyes if they have a strong spirit, and Alexander definitely had that inner strength. He would not go down without one hell of a fight.

I really struggled in the couple of weeks after the diagnosis. The only way I found I could deal with it all was by going out almost every night, drinking and partying with my friends. I knew I was running away from the situation and that it was a bizarre reaction, but I had to have an outlet. I hid my real feelings from Alexander. To him I was putting on an upbeat, brave face, but behind the façade I was a nervous wreck. I don't cry much, but there were several times when I had to run upstairs to our room and let the tears flow.

The seven-week treatment began on 17 June and we travelled to the hospital together. In keeping with his quest for normality, Alexander was determined to spend as little time in hospital as possible and he went home immediately after his first batch of chemotherapy. They had pumped two bags of the poison into his system through an IV drip in his arm.

I didn't really know what to expect. I'm not someone who likes to be overloaded with information, but there were four 'must do' things I had to know. For instance, if his temperature went past a certain point I had to ring the hospital. But nothing could have prepared me for how sick Alexander was on that first night. It was terrible watching him vomit uncontrollably and not being able to help him. It was this sense of help-lessness that I couldn't cope with. There were good and bad days with the treatment, and when Alexander was on a downer it was almost impossible to communicate. I felt lost. Was I helping him or not?

As the treatment progressed I moved into the spare room because Alexander was having sleepless nights. He'd break into sweats or be kept awake for hours by prolonged bouts of coughing. I also wasn't sleeping much, and I'd often sneak in and check on him to see if he was still breathing. I had this terrible fear that I'd walk in one day and he would be dead. I knew what it was like to lose someone close. I'd received phone calls before, 'Anne-Marie is dead', 'Nanna is dead', 'Dad is dead'. Just like that, your loved ones can be taken away from you.

There were moments when I was so frightened for Alexander. I'd be driving back to Kew and I'd think, *I hope my husband is alive when I get home*. I had this picture in my mind that I'd come up the driveway and everything would appear normal, but then I would walk upstairs and he'd be dead. This fear would grip me at the most unexpected moments, and I'd be paralysed. I think it was my own way of acknowl-edging that death was a possibility and that I had to prepare myself in case the worst happened.

To help keep my mind occupied I continued to train lightly. Fort wasn't around all the time because he was often away with other athletes, so I followed the programme by myself. I also kept active by becoming a per-sonal trainer for a friend of mine. Three mornings a week I'd go jogging with him, either around Albert Park Lake or up the Jolimont hills.

When the calendar clicked over into July, the inevitable questions about the Commonwealth Games started to come. My management company kept asking whether I was going. Fort was hinting at it and I could sense the momentum building. Little alarm bells were going off in my mind because I knew it would be a good idea for my long-term future if I had a fix of international athletics this year. But there was no way I was prepared to broach the subject with Alexander. No way! His health and welfare were priority number one.

I don't know whether he sensed something, but a couple of days later, as I was sitting in the hospital with him during another bout of chemotherapy, Alexander brought up the Games.

'So, hon, are you going to go to the Commonwealth Games?' he said.

I looked up from the magazine I was reading.

'You're going to have to make your decision soon as to whether you're going,' he continued.

'Mmm,' was all I said as I studied him closely. What was going on?

'Do you want to go?' he asked.

I paused for a couple of seconds and could hear the clock ticking above us. 'Yeah, I'd love to run, hon, but you know I'm not fussed.'

In the end I agreed to go to Manchester only if his best friends from the States, Don and Roger, came out to Australia to be with him.

'I don't want you to be alone,' I said. 'The only way I'm going to the Commonwealth Games is if you're not alone.'

He agreed, and that afternoon began arranging it.

On 23 July I arrived in Manchester to be greeted by a wall of cameras and reporters. It was Sydney all over again. It felt like I was walking out of the shadow of the last two years and into the glare again. I took my personal assistant, Nicole, and agent, Michelle, with me for moral support. I'd planned to stay at the athletes' village, but as soon as I got there I couldn't move a yard without being stopped for autographs and photos. I can never say no, but after about fifteen minutes I knew I couldn't stay there so I bunked down with the others in a house just outside the city.

The next day at the Australian team meeting I felt like I was back in Auckland as a sixteen-year-old. It was great to be in that environment again. Everyone had to stand up and say their name and where they were from. I was one of the last in the line.

'I'm Cathy Freeman, I'm running the 4 x 400m relay. I'm from Melbourne and I'm just happy to be here.'

It turned out that the head coach of the team, Keith Connor, wanted me to run a trial on Saturday, in two days' time, to see if I was in good enough shape for the relay the following week. The move shocked me and I really started to worry about it, but Fort was confident it wouldn't be a problem, despite the number of official duties on my agenda, including a luncheon with the Queen, which required getting dressed up in my full Australian team uniform. The organisers wanted me to present a bouquet to the Queen, but I declined. It felt like I'd already had my photo taken a thousand times and I was quickly running out of patience. I'd had enough.

The trial was at the warm-up track next to the main stadium. I couldn't believe how nervous I was. I was scared of discovering I'd been wasting my time, that I was going to let myself down, that I wasn't fit enough. Thankfully, after going twenty metres I knew everything was going to be fine. I could feel I was up on my toes. When I'm at my best, I'm on my toes and I seem to grow wings to replace my arms. It's like flying, floating, effortlessly moving along the track. While that wasn't quite the case this time, I could feel the energy surging through me from the tips of my toes. It was a great feeling, and I comfortably proved to everyone present that I was ready to race, although I was disappointed that they withheld from me the time I'd run.

Our semi-final was on the Tuesday, and I found myself very much on edge. I didn't train on the Monday because of some soreness from the trial. I began pacing the house and then went out in the car and wandered around the shops. I was restless. I just wanted to run because that's what I was born to do.

Race day arrived, and it wasn't until a few hours before the gun that I found out I wouldn't be running the last leg as expected. I was now running second. I loved being the anchor and I thought my previous performances might have been enough to warrant that, but 400m hurdler Jana Pittman was bringing us home. Lauren Hewitt was leading off, with Tamsyn Lewis running the third leg. Once again the communication from management about the relay was a joke. We ended up not having a practice of the baton changes until five minutes before we were called to race.

The race itself passed without incident. I felt in the zone, the crowd got me going and I took the team from fifth to second on my leg. We easily qualified for the final, which was on the following night. I really loved the theatre of the relay and I was so happy I'd made it around in one piece.

However, I was quickly brought back to reality the next afternoon when we were on our way to the track for the final. I called home to check how everything was going and Don answered the phone. As we had wooden floors all through the house, everything echoed, and I could clearly hear down the phone line Alexander throwing up in the background. The feeling of helplessness immediately swept over me again. I hung up and stayed silent for the rest of the trip to the stadium, consumed by thoughts of my sick husband.

Though nothing will ever compare with Sydney, obviously, there was definitely a sense of occasion about the Commonwealth Games final. I felt the pressure and the pride of running for Australia. When I got the baton I surged into the lead in the first two hundred metres and felt in control. Then the English girl came up on me as I entered the straight and managed to pass me just before the changeover. I was furious about letting her come over the top of me, but my anger didn't last long when I realised the favourites, Jamaica, were already out because they'd dropped their baton. Tamsyn made up the ground and changed to Jana in first place, who then ran brilliantly to win us the gold medal. Wow! We were all a bit in shock because no one had expected us to pull it off. We'd been thrown together at the last minute yet we'd won gold! I was really thrilled for the other three girls. I was excited, though probably not as much as the others. I realised that from now on I would compare everything I did to Sydney, and no matter what else I did in my career, nothing would ever come close.

The night turned into a mad rush. The victory lap, the dais, the anthem – it all seemed to happen very quickly. And then the interviews, where I sent a hello to Alexander and dedicated the win to him. 'I just want to send all my love to Alexander,' I said. 'Love you, hon.' The celebrations were a lot of fun. We all went dancing and I tried to unwind, but I found it difficult. My heart was elsewhere. I just wanted to go home.

CHAPTER 31
BEATING THE ODDS

The waiting was the hardest thing.

Once the seven-week chemotherapy and radiation treatment had finished it would be three months before we'd know whether Alexander had beaten the cancer. He was at his weakest in the last couple of weeks of the treatment. He couldn't eat because the radiation had fried his mouth; the only way he could consume food was by forcing a liquid supplement through his nose with a large syringe. Subsequently, he started to lose weight, and for the first time he began to look like a cancer patient. This was a real shock for Alexander. For someone who'd been physically active all of his life and who took pride in his appearance, it was a major reality check when his clothes began to hang off him. One morning I came downstairs and he was thinking about trying to go for a bike ride. He had put on a pair of cycling shorts and I did a double-take when I saw his legs – they were like toothpicks. While his strength of mind had pushed him through the nausea, vomiting and cramps, he found he couldn't cope with the physical deterioration or how he'd get dizzy from just walking up the stairs.

During my time at the Commonwealth Games I'd met up with Michael Johnson, who was there commentating for the BBC. I had always wanted to sit down and talk to him about how he coped with everything throughout his career. He was the greatest there had ever been – five Olympic gold medals and nine world titles – and I'd always been too shy to approach him. That was probably because he was such a guarded and private guy. However, he'd been really enthusiastic when we'd seen each other in Manchester – he'd greeted me with a big hug – so I decided a couple of weeks later to ring him and ask for some help.

I needed to be clear in my mind that I was doing the right thing by coming back. Basically, I just wanted to pick his brain, and we arranged a time in October when I could come and visit him in San Francisco.

Alexander desperately wanted to be healthy enough to travel with me on the trip and it became a goal he could work towards. Everything was going according to plan until a couple of weeks before we were due to leave. He'd had a good week and we'd been able to get out of the house a bit more, including a trip down to Lara, about forty minutes from Melbourne, where we had several horses stabled, including some beautiful Andalusians. Almost overnight, everything changed. Alexander contracted a viral infection that stopped him in his tracks. He was susceptible to it because his immune system was still recovering from the treatment. After a couple of days it was obvious that he couldn't go anywhere. He actually described his condition as the weakest he had felt in his whole life.

By the time we were scheduled to leave for the States, Alexander had improved significantly but still wasn't well enough to travel. Once again he was adamant that I should go on the trip. I took with me Fort, another 400m runner, Michael Hazel, as a training partner, and my personal assistant, Nicole.

It was the best thing I could have done. For ten days I was like a sponge, soaking up all that Michael could offer. We went to dinner together, he came down and watched a few training sessions, and we had some very intense, open and honest conversations. It was like we'd known each other for years. We talked about everything, from how to handle autograph hunters to the way my right hand protrudes as I run around the bend. He suggested that I look at shortening my stride. When I run the 400m, I run the first thirty to forty metres like a 200m; he thought I should try to run the first sixty to seventy metres like a 200m. In the gym Michael showed me a new technique that would help get extra strength into my legs. Most importantly, he agreed that my goals were realistic: I could come back and be the best again.

But there was one thing that Michael felt needed to change. 'You're too nice,' he stated out of the blue as we were finishing our last training session. 'You need to become more selfish.'

I had myself a mentor. He agreed to play a part in my future and be on hand for any advice. I felt inspired when we left San Francisco and headed for Portland to tie up some things at Nike. I was re-energised and comfortable that Cathy Freeman the athlete was back.

Catching up with some of Alexander's friends at Nike got me thinking about the amazing support everyone, friends and strangers, had shown towards him. Alexander had received letters and e-mails from people he hadn't seen for thirty years. He got a letter from his brother, who he hadn't heard from in years, giving him his unqualified support. Cyclist Lance Armstrong, who had recovered from cancer and gone on to win the Tour de France, sent an e-mail offering his best wishes. A work colleague made a bracelet with Alexander's name on it and wore it when he competed in the famous Hawaii Ironman triathlon. Another friend bought five hundred tulips, planted them in boxes for Alexander and told him they would be in full bloom in the spring when he returned to Oregon.

The outpouring from the community was amazing. Schoolchildren in Australia were sending Alexander notes, and people were always leaving messages about potential cures, such as special potions, in our letterbox. Daughters of friends were lighting candles in churches and praying for Alexander's health. The smallest thing could act as a pick-up for that day and help Alexander get through. Each week he sent out a newsletter to his closest friends via e-mail keeping them up to date with how everything was progressing.

The results of Alexander's final scan were due when I returned home. Alexander was determined that we find out together. All the early indicators had been positive: initial scans showed the tumour had shrunk. The doctors were also quietly confident that the treatment had been successful, but it all hinged on that final scan on 29 October.

On the day we were to fly home, I was at Nike's head office visiting Mark, one of Alexander's oldest friends, who had been at our wedding. We were chatting away when the phone rang. It was Alexander wanting to speak with me.

'Hon, Dr Peters called today,' he said.

I could feel myself stop breathing. *Please, please be good news.*

'He said the results of the scan were clean. I've got the all-clear.'

I let out a squeal. 'That's great, hon. Fantastic,' was all I could come up with. My mind was racing at a hundred miles an hour. He'd done it. He'd beaten cancer. Cancer makes your heart feel heavy with all the worry and uncertainty. Suddenly I felt this heaviness leave me. My heart now felt like a feather. It was like God had just taken this great big lead brick out of my heart. I started bouncing around the room. It felt so good to be able to smile again. This was the happiest I had ever felt. Winning Olympic gold at Sydney and getting married had both been amazing events, but this was an even higher level of happiness.

At the airport, Nicole and I had our own little celebration – a scotch and a glass of champagne. Professor Peters had apparently been as excited as we were and had told Alexander that a number of hospitals would have told him he had no chance. The average recovery rate for this particular type of cancer, at its advanced stage, was around 30 per cent. We'd beaten the odds. In his regular e-mail update, Alexander wrote: BODECKER 1, CANCER 0.

CHAPTER 32
GROWING APART

'This cancer will make us fall in love again.'

Alexander's words kept echoing over and over in my mind. That's exactly what he'd said to me six months before, just after he'd been diagnosed. I had also thought it was possible. If I was really in love with Alexander and we were meant to be together, then those feelings would be obvious during the cancer fight. But now that the dust had settled and life was beginning to get back to something like it was before, my concerns about our marriage came flooding back.

Alexander's ordeal had put enormous strain on the relationship. It had pulled us both to our knees. I kept asking myself if my feelings had changed. In a way I was hoping to convince myself that everything was good again. But it wasn't working. The sick feeling in my stomach was still there. Something would happen between us, and it would leave me feeling so unhappy. These were really extreme feelings of sadness, confusion, uncertainty and anger. Why was I feeling this way towards the man who was my husband? The first couple of times it happened I thought I was just being silly and complicated, but after the fourth or fifth time I knew you didn't get this type of feeling unless something was really wrong.

It had become obvious that we'd been growing apart for some time. Before his diagnosis, Alexander was in America for three weeks out of every month. Even when I was over there, he was always coming and going. I had been ready to try to settle down and live the life of a normal married couple, spending most of our time together, but Alexander didn't want that. He was scared about me giving up my running career and that pretty much quashed any thoughts I might've had about living overseas, having a child or being together properly. We talked about him working for Nike in Australia, but that would have meant he couldn't be with me when I went overseas to compete.

People are peculiar beasts. You get some who are willing to forego everything for their ambitions, whereas others are happy with the simple things in life, a quieter existence. Alexander liked to be in the fast lane, always pushing for more and more. That's how I lived my athletics life, but away from the track I was yearning for the slow lane. Because we'd lived apart so much during our three and a half years of marriage, I now found that my wings had grown too big and strong in his absence. I'd been forced to learn to deal with things by myself, and it had reached the point where the big question was, where did Alexander fit into my life?

I needed to head in a new direction. The legal battle with Nick had finally been resolved in an out-of-court settlement. It had dragged on for more than two years and caused a lot of unnecessary pain and heartache for all concerned. Now I had to fix my personal life, to be able to move forward.

While my head knew I had only one choice, my heart was getting torn apart. How could I do this to Alexander after what he'd been through? He'd just stared death in the face! I knew it was awful, I knew it was ruthless, but I also knew it was the best thing for both of us. I just couldn't continue this way, and I knew in the long run it would be better for Alexander to start rebuilding his life without me now, rather than having to do it in twelve months' or two years' time.

We went to Mackay for Christmas and I decided I'd tell him when we returned. Even though he wasn't totally out of the woods as far as the cancer was concerned, with another important scan in February 2003, I just couldn't let it drag on. At that moment it felt like a slow death, as if my soul was slowly being sucked out of me. I had to start thinking about myself again, about the goals I had to chase.

I wasn't myself at Christmas because I had to lie to my family about everything. When we got home I was snappy and irritable. I couldn't help it: I was sad, hurt and angry about what I knew I had to say to Alexander.

We'd only just got in our front door when I asked him, 'What are your travel plans?'

'I'm going over to Japan and then on to the States,' he said, before adding, 'It depends what you're doing.'

The conversation quickly degenerated and came back to how we'd spent so much time apart. He could tell I was very negative about us.

'Well, what do you want to do?' Alexander asked.

I just looked at him blankly. I wanted to say so much but nothing was coming out. 'You want a divorce,' he said. I went to open my mouth, but he interjected, 'I knew this was going to happen.'

We tried to talk about things again but ended up just covering the same old stuff. I was becoming more and more frustrated. He always maintained that he was in love with me and would never love anyone else. That was neither here nor there for me, because if I didn't feel the same way then how was the marriage going to work? He wanted us to go to counselling but I knew in my heart of hearts it was out of the question. We finally agreed to separate for a month.

Nothing changed while Alexander was overseas. That absolute feeling of love wasn't there. That feeling of not being able to be without each other, of wanting to run to that person when you have something happy to share, that absolute desperation you have for someone. It just wasn't there. And as the people around me know so well, when I make up my mind about something, that is it. I'd had doubts about our marriage for almost fourteen months.

Alexander flew back to Australia on the morning of my thirtieth birthday, Sunday, 16 February 2003. Nicole had organised a big party to celebrate at a bar in St Kilda with about 120 of my friends. I'd decided not to raise the issue of divorce with Alexander until after his important check-up on the Tuesday, when hopefully he'd get the all-clear. I wanted to know that his health was fine before we addressed our problem again. That was the plan, but during the twenty-minute trip home from the airport the situation got out of control.

'Where's your wedding ring?' Alexander asked.

Damn! I had totally forgotten that I didn't have it on. For the past couple of weeks I had stopped wearing it; I guess it was a mental thing as I was preparing for the split. I'd also forgotten how closely I was watched: the media had picked up on my missing ring. It turned out that Alexander had seen the stories this had sparked on the Internet. I began fumbling my way through an explanation, but then suddenly it all just came out.

'There is no hope,' I told him. 'I don't want counselling, I want a divorce. It's over.'

I felt awful, like I wanted to be sick. It was so brutal and torturous for him. But no matter how hard it felt I knew I had to be strong because this was the best thing for both of us. We tried talking again, but that made us more upset. I asked him to come to the party but he didn't want to be around me. That night Alexander stayed in a hotel and I spent my time at the party faking it to my friends, who naturally all wanted to know where he was. I felt so stupid because I was living a lie.

The next 48 hours were very strange. The man I had loved, the man I'd been married to for nearly four years, was sitting in a hotel room a few kilometres away, waiting to hear whether the cancer was out of his system. He might as well have been on the other side of the world, such was the feeling of distance that had suddenly come between us. A part of me desperately wanted to get into the car and drive over there, to be next to him in the doctor's office, to make sure he was all right. A bigger part of me knew that I couldn't.

Alexander flew out of Melbourne that Tuesday night. He didn't call before he left. Professor Peters rang me the next day with the good news that the scans were clear and the cancer had gone. I thanked him for everything he'd done, put the phone down and collapsed on the couch. I was so drained; I felt my body shut down. There were so many questions. Not only in my own head, but also the ones I knew would inevitably come my way. Had I rushed into the marriage? Had I been on the rebound from Nick? Was the age difference a problem? Was anyone else involved?

I knew there were things Alexander and I probably should have talked about more before we got married. I'm definitely the kind of person who can get drawn in by men who want me more than I want them. In a relationship it seems there's always one person who wants the other more. Certainly that's been the case in both my serious relationships. With Nick I was too young, and the reasons why that didn't work seem really obvious, but with Alexander I think maybe I should have spent more time on my own and slowed things between us right down. I had been under so much pressure for Sydney 2000. It's very hard to look back and think what I would change, what I would do differently. All I know is that, at the time, it just felt right.

A week later I spoke with Alexander on the phone. The media had found out about our break-up and my public relations company wanted to release a press statement.

'Catherine, this is your statement, not my statement,' was all he said.

CHAPTER 33
LOSING IT

'This is what you miss, isn't it?'

Maurie Plant pointed at the packed stands of the Olympic Stadium in Mexico City. There must have been fifty thousand people crammed in waiting for the race of the night, a special 300m event featuring their hometown hero, Ana Guevara, against Olympic champion Cathy Freeman. The cauldron-like atmosphere reminded me of Sydney. You could sense the anticipation and excitement among the crowd. Everyone was on a high. Everyone except me.

I had to bite my tongue when Maurie turned back and looked at me, waiting for my response. I just nodded.

Not really, Maurie. Something's wrong. It's not happening for me. I don't want to be here.

We had arrived in Mexico three days earlier to a welcome fit for a rock star or head of state. Maurie had warned me it was going to be big. During my two-year absence from the track Guevara had taken over as the world number one and the Mexicans worshipped their sporting heroes. But I wasn't prepared for the madness that greeted us when we got off the plane. As soon as Maurie, my training partner, Andrew, and I walked through customs, a mass of bodies converged on us. We had five policemen to shepherd us through the media pack. It felt like we were in the middle of a crowded nightclub and there seemed to be someone right there in my face with every step I took. Eventually we made it to the car that was waiting to take us to our hotel. We drove through the city accompanied by a police escort of four motorbikes. Madness! I was given the penthouse suite and felt a bit silly about the royal treatment, although I wasn't complaining. We were assigned a full-time bodyguard, Caesar, complete with gun, and it was made clear that whatever I wanted I could have.

The press conference the day before the meet was like the airport welcome. There were so many people crammed into one small room. Guevara looked very fit. She had made an impression on me early in 2000 when she raced in Australia. During the 400m at the Melbourne grand prix, my first encounter with her, I'd sensed she thought she could beat me with a hundred metres to go. If someone thinks they can beat the reigning world champion on their home turf it makes you watch your back. Guevara had finished fifth in the Olympic final at Sydney; since then I knew she had been very consistent. I'd watched a race from Zurich on TV the previous year when Guevara ran 49.16s. She just looked so comfortable.

I had come to Mexico expecting to lose. Although it was something I'd never done before, there was a good reason why I felt this way. My preparations back home in Australia had been far from ideal. The break-up with Alexander had affected my focus, training subsequently hadn't been great, and it had all caught up with me when I lined up against Jana Pittman at the Telstra A-series meet in Sydney on 22 March. I knew I was behind but I told Fort and Maurie to throw me to the wolves and not to be concerned about my winning streak of 25 400m races. In fact, my only loss since the Atlanta Games had been when I injured my foot in Oslo in 1998. I'd won 46 out of 47 races since then.

From the moment I saw Jana I sensed something special. She looked hungry. It was like seeing a vision of myself from the past. I could feel her confidence and self-belief in the way she was holding herself before the race. I saw the look on her face, the look in her eyes, and I knew what it was. I'd felt it so many times before. This girl was excited to be here.

The race was strange. Jana was on my outside, and for the first two hundred metres I was with her and it seemed to be quite slow. I was feeling comfortable, but I could again sense her aura of confidence. As we approached the home bend I sensed her making her move. It was time to go up a gear. But something was wrong. My body didn't react. I'd given up.

What are you doing, Freeman? Why don't you care about losing?

For that final hundred metres it was like I was in a trance. I just let Jana go. I didn't feel anything as I watched her surge ahead to win by ten metres in 50.43s.

What the hell just happened?

Usually when I'm in a big race, particularly early in the season, I exceed my own fitness levels. When your heart's in a race, when your spirit is alive, the competitiveness just kicks in. It's second nature. You don't have to think about it. So when you give it everything, especially when you're not fit, you are absolutely flattened after a race. This time, though, after congratulating Jana, I just walked off the track as if I was getting off a train at the station. I was so casual about everything. I wasn't angry about getting beaten.

I talked myself into not worrying about it because it was my first major race back and Jana was coming off a Commonwealth title and European season. She had also changed coaches and was now working with Phil King, who had guided his wife, Debbie Flintoff-King, to Olympic gold in Seoul in 1988. Jana had obviously been training hard during the off-season. She was twenty, and she was just starting out on her quest to be the best; I was ten years older and I had been the best. Now I was trying to remember how I did it.

Although I won my sixth national 400m title two weeks later in Brisbane, it didn't do much to boost my confidence. I had failed to run under the qualifying time for the world championships in Paris in August. That didn't bother Fort or me too much. We both figured that once we got overseas my training would improve and everything would click into place. But that wasn't how I felt as I paced behind the blocks in Mexico City. Being a 300m made the race slightly less stressful, but as I entered the home straight, already what seemed like miles behind Guevara, I again had that feeling of letting go.

What is happening to me?

Just as with the Pittman race, I felt like I hadn't given everything. In the end I didn't even get second: I was beaten by Romanian hurdler Ionela Tirlea. Guevara had blown us all away and finished almost ten metres ahead of me.

By the time I got to the drug-testing area, Maurie was waiting for me. He told me my time of 36.42s was a personal best, which surprised me and at least made me feel slightly better. I hadn't been totally embarrassing. Maurie was very positive about the race because, as he'd admitted to me earlier, he was excited about having Freeman back. He was really warm and happy about my comeback, and I felt like I'd been reunited with a long-lost friend. Maurie had been a constant throughout my career and he was confident we could go onwards and upwards again.

We were waiting around for about an hour for the drug testing so I began quizzing him about my situation. I was after reassurance. 'Where am I at? What do you think my potential is? Do I need a great big kick up the bum?' were some of the questions I fired at Maurie. He was very upbeat, but I was worried by the margins of my defeats. Pittman and Guevara had put daylight between themselves and me. It made me realise how much more work I needed to do in the next couple of months.

Our base in America was at the University of California, Berkeley, in Oakland, San Francisco. Garry Miritis joined us there and it was like the old team was getting back together, although there was one addition, the new man in my life, Joel Edgerton. We had been friends since meeting at the Logies, the Australian TV awards, the year before. Joel had starred in the high-rating TV series *The Secret Life of Us*, but I didn't have any idea who he was when we first met because I'd been living overseas when the series took off in Australia. The Logies was a wild night. Jacqui Cooper and Tiff Cherry had dragged me along, and Joel ended up hanging out with us. He was a gentleman from the start. He looked after my handbag without me even asking him to, and then took the drink out of my hand so I could have a dance. My first impression of him was just of a really nice, caring, kind person. He kept in contact, through Jacqui mainly, and recently we'd begun to see each other more.

My next race, the Prefontaine Classic in Eugene, Oregon, on 24 May, loomed large on my calendar for several reasons. It was my rematch with Guevara over 400m, and therefore D-day for my comeback. It was also Alexander's home turf. Nike was my major sponsor, and this was their big track and field event. They wanted me in Portland as part of the pre-meet publicity so it was inevitable that I'd cross paths with my former husband. In a way I was actually looking forward to it. I still cared for Alexander and wanted to know that everything was working out for him.

I thought I was on top of the whole situation until Garry, my training partner Andrew Krumins and I got to the airport. As we were waiting in the boarding lounge it just hit me all of a sudden. I was trying to anticipate what it was going to be like to see Alexander and how I would react. I kept asking Garry and Andrew about it, and it got to the point where I needed to have a Scotch to settle my nerves. I couldn't believe it. Just a couple of days out from an important race, and here I was sitting in an airport drinking alcohol. The Freeman of old would never have done that, and this lack of discipline and focus had become a worrying feature of my life over the past few weeks.

The flight into Portland did nothing to ease my nerves. It was hell. As we drove into the city, everywhere I looked I saw Alexander. Portland was the place where I'd first met Alexander, the place where I'd told him I wanted to have a baby, where I had met some of his dearest friends. We'd had some very happy times here.

The next morning we travelled out to the Nike complex where I had a media commitment alongside world 100m record holder Tim Montgomery. It was all about Nike's commitment to speed and the latest spikes they had developed. We had to do some starts from the blocks for the media. Tim was a really interesting guy and he put me on the phone to his partner, Marion Jones, who was expecting their first baby in July. She sounded so happy and told me everything about the pregnancy. Marion was planning to resume training in September, and she invited me to join her at her home base in North Carolina. It was a great opportunity, so I let her and Tim talk me into it.

After a series of interviews I couldn't take it any longer – I had to find Alexander. I knew his office was nearby, so with Garry and Andrew by my side I headed in that direction. As we approached I could hear the music pumping and I could see Alexander's silhouette through the glass windows. Garry and Andrew went in ahead of me because I was cornered by a couple of Nike people in the hallway. As soon as I got inside, out of nowhere I was overcome with a sense of happiness. Alexander looked great. He had really muscled up and was cut and buffed. He also had a little goatee, dyed blond like his hair. Alexander took one look at me and started to get emotional. That set me off, and the other guys quickly disappeared out of the office. We chatted for a while, and it was great just talking to him; he was still one of my closest friends despite what had happened. But after a while the conversation started to head in a direction I didn't want to deal with. There I was, naively thinking Alexander was going to be cool and that we'd be friends; instead, he was making it clear he wanted some form of reconciliation. He still loved me and wanted to try to make our marriage work.

'I've got to go now,' I said, looking out the door to see if Andrew and Garry were still there. 'I've got to train.'

I had to get out of there. As I left the office I could feel my heart turning to stone. I had this capacity to be so emotionless sometimes. But this time I felt I had no choice. I had to move on.

Andrew and Garry didn't say anything as we walked to the track at the Nike complex. We quickly got through the warm-up, but as we were about to start doing some 300s I felt a tightness in my throat. I knew exactly what that meant, and about five seconds later I started crying. It just came out of nowhere. I hardly ever cried. I didn't even cry when I won in Sydney, though I'd been sure I would, yet here I was standing under a tree beside an athletics track in Portland bawling my eyes out.

Andrew didn't know what to do. After a few seconds he said, 'Come here.' He put his arm around me, but I had to sit down as my body had started convulsing with the intensity of the sobs.

'Why me?' I kept asking Andrew. 'Why me? I'm such a simple girl. Why does this happen to me?'

After a few minutes it passed, and we sat there in silence.

'OK, we're going to do this,' I said.

But as I reached for my spikes I knew it wasn't going to happen so we packed up our gear and headed for the car. Garry had been over the other side and didn't know what had happened. He sensed something was wrong, and I was very embarrassed about it. Our driver, a guy called Dave, asked me if I was all right.

'I'm really sad,' was all I said.

I sat in the back with Andrew and turned my head to look out the window so he couldn't see that I was crying again. We decided to head off to Eugene immediately so we gathered our things at the hotel and checked out. Waves of sadness washed over me; I just couldn't stop crying. Alexander had always been able to pull at my heartstrings. I could feel his pain, and that made me so sad.

'You're only human, after all,' Garry said.

I was silent as we started the hour-long drive to Eugene, but Andrew and Garry wanted to cheer me up so they made Dave take a detour off the freeway to McDonald's and bought me some French fries. They also put on a CD of Maurie's featuring a really crass American comedian called Dice Clay. That worked. The jokes were so dirty and bad that everyone cracked up. By the time we got to Eugene, under the most beautiful sunset I'd ever seen in Oregon, my tears of sadness had been replaced with tears of laughter.

We still had one day to kill before the race, and this time we did train, albeit fairly lightly as it was a hot day. That night we went out to dinner, and then for a walk along the river where all three of us broke into song. 'When the moon hits your eyes like a big pizza pie, that's *amore*,' I bellowed out, much to the amusement of Andrew and Garry, who were surprised at how many old songs I knew. It was a beautiful night, and for a while I forgot about everything.

On race morning I decided to change my flight so that I could leave Oregon as soon as possible after the race. Joel was coming back to San Francisco from London and I desperately wanted to see him. While I was ringing the airline it struck me how odd this was: I was more worried about arranging to get out of the place than I was about running the actual race.

I knew the minute I entered the warm-up area that I was in trouble. My focus wasn't there. In the past, even if there was chaos all around me, I could always block it out and get the job done. This time I just couldn't focus.

Hey, Ana. I don't care about the result today. I don't need to. I have an

Olympic gold medal. I have two world championship gold medals. What do you have?

I couldn't believe what my mind was doing. I was losing it. Was I really scared? It was like nothing had any real meaning to me any more. The weird part was I'd always thrived on this scenario, racing against the best in the world.

A glimmer of hope appeared as we got on to the track. I felt more in control and was just doing my own thing, going through my regular routine before any race. On the blocks, the nervous energy was there, which was a good sign.

'On your marks,' the starter screamed. 'Set.'

What's happening? What's the delay? Why hasn't the gun gone off?

Then the gun blasted. I clearly missed the start, and after only a few metres I sensed something was wrong. At the fifty-metre mark there was still nothing happening. I was moving but I had no power. Once we were in the back straight several of the girls moved up and passed me.

Oh, well. Whatever.

Guevara was already miles ahead as we approached the bend, as were most of the other girls, some of whom I'd never seen before in my life. I was just letting them go past.

I'm the Olympic champion. What the hell am I doing?

With a hundred metres to go, finally something clicked. It was my conscience.

Oh, my God. I could come last.

Pride took over and I managed to find something in the straight. Guevara won in 49.34s; I finished fifth in 51.70s. I walked up and congratulated her, and was then grabbed by Carol Lewis, sister of Carl, who worked as a television presenter.

'Cathy, that was a good run for your first race back. How do you feel?' she asked, thrusting a microphone under my nose.

I feel like I never want to do that again. I hate this.

'I've got some more work to do,' I said with a smile.

I gathered my tracksuit and walked around to meet Andrew and Garry. The look on their faces told the story. I was still searching for answers in my own head as Garry began massaging my legs.

'I think I need to get away from running for a few days,' I said.

'Nah, you've got to get back on the horse,' Garry said.

Nothing annoyed me more than people trying to tell me what to do. Something very bizarre had just happened to me and I had to figure it out in my own time and in my own way.

'I know what I'm doing,' I snapped back.

No, you don't, Freeman. You have no idea what just happened.

I was still in a state of shock when we got back to San Francisco. My mind was a mess. All these emotions were whirling around inside me: I felt scared, confused, washed out. I almost didn't recognise myself. It felt like I'd lost the desire to win. Losing that was like losing a part of my soul or my heart. I told Joel that I needed to get away, so we got in the car almost immediately and took off, heading north to the coast. We didn't even tell the others what we were doing. Over the next couple of days I tried to come to terms with what had happened. Joel understood that I was struggling. He took me horse riding and hot-air ballooning, and did everything he could to help me forget about running for a while.

But as soon as I stepped out on to the track back in Oakland, I was miserable again. I didn't want to be there. I didn't want to train. It was as though I'd developed a phobia of the track. I found myself sitting on the ground staring at my spikes. I couldn't put them on. I just couldn't do it. After a couple of minutes Andrew and Fort realised something was seriously wrong.

'Let's go for a walk,' I said to Fort.

My heart wasn't in it any more. I suspected my coach knew as much, although he wasn't saying anything.

'You know what's going on, don't you, Fort?' I said.

He kept walking as though he didn't want to hear what I was about to say.

'I think it's over.'

CHAPTER 34
THE DECISION

'I want to give you another Olympic gold medal.' Michael Johnson was looking me straight in the eye from across the table. 'I think you can win next year. I want to give you another Olympic gold medal,' he repeated.

Johnson had appeared in Oakland, almost like a knight in shining armour. I wasn't sure if he was there off his own bat because he'd heard about the Eugene result or if he'd been asked to come and see me by Maurie, Athletics Australia or IMG. It didn't matter. He wanted to help. He wanted to be my saviour.

This was exactly what I'd hoped for since I first came back to San Francisco in October. I'd seriously considered ending my partnership with Fort and asking Michael to coach me. But he was now more than happy to work with Fort. He proposed that he be involved in a managerial role, overseeing every part of my life. He would work closely with my personal assistant, Nicole, and with IMG, because he understood exactly the kinds of demands I experienced.

Wow! I was blown away by what I was hearing. Michael Johnson, the greatest athlete I had ever known, was offering me the benefit of all his wisdom and experience. It was a once in a lifetime deal. He told me I was the only athlete he would do this for.

'This is great,' I said.

No, no. I think it's too late.

I sensed Michael was ready to start straight away and get everything back on track.

'First, we've got to get your head sorted out,' he said. 'But if your heart's not in it, then forget it.' Those were his parting words.

C'mon, Freeman. If anything is going to do it, this is it.

My brief flush of excitement was quickly overtaken by a sense of embarrassment and unease. This required total commitment. There was no way I was going to waste Michael's time, or anybody else's for that matter. I thought about what other people would do in my situation. They'd be crawling over broken glass to get Michael Johnson to help them. Yet, as I drove away, I didn't feel that same urge, and that's what scared me.

Over the next few days I thought constantly about Michael's offer, although it didn't get me any closer to the training track. I worked out in the gym a couple of times but that was it. I was still struggling to get my mind around what had happened in Eugene. I hadn't even tried to get second or third! Physically I knew I was in much better shape than 51.70s.

As more time went by it started to become clearer in my mind. It had now been almost two weeks since I'd spoken to Michael and I still didn't want to get back to him. I wasn't rushing to take up his magical offer.

It's another sign, Freeman.

Garry was convinced that leaving the States for London would turn things around. His theory was there were too many bad memories there and that I'd always enjoyed living and training in London.

'You've got to go and sort out your personal life with Alexander. That way your head will be clearer for training, and on the track too,' Garry said.

I knew where he was coming from but I still couldn't understand what was happening to me. All my life I'd been able to push my personal stuff to the side when I was on the track. What was different this time?

Read the signs, Freeman.

I realised I had to tell Alexander about Joel, though, because everyone knew except him. My mother knew, and so did Fort, Garry, Andrew, Nicole, Chris, Maurie and the others in the training group, like 800m runner Kris McCarthy and sprinter Lauren Hewitt, who had joined us in Oakland. I remembered how I'd felt when people were telling me about Sonia and Nick and the way I'd found out that she was pregnant. I was the last to know, and that had really hurt. I had no doubt that Nick and I would be on better terms now if he'd given me the respect of being upfront back then. Alexander was still one of my best friends and I didn't want to lose that. Joel was about to leave as he was due to start work on the film *King Arthur* in Ireland. I decided I had to go and see Alexander. I rang him on his mobile phone.

'Hi, hon, how are you doing?' he said.

It was exactly the same way he had spoken to me when we were together. He was in St Louis.

'When are you back in Portland?' I asked. 'I need to see you, I need to talk to you.'

Alexander suggested he could drop into Oakland on his way back up the west coast in a few days. I agreed, but rang him back a minute later because I needed to do this straight away. I knew that the waiting around would drive me nuts. We arranged to meet at the airport in Portland the following day.

Thirty seconds later, the phone rang. It was Alexander. 'What have you got to tell me?' he asked. 'Why do you have to see me? What's so urgent?' I could hear him getting more upset. 'Are you going to tell me to leave your family alone – or that you have a new boyfriend?'

I froze and nearly dropped the phone. 'I'm not going to talk about anything until I see you,' I said hurriedly, and hung up.

I had decided there were three things I had to tell Alexander. One – I was seeing Joel. Two – the divorce was definitely happening. Three – I still wanted to be in his life. His friendship was important to me.

Nicole had just arrived from Australia and I thought about taking her with me, but she was too jet-lagged so I decided to go it alone. Joel drove me to the airport and I got there a couple of hours before Alexander's flight was due in. I really wasn't myself. I felt lonely. To pass the time I wandered through the shops, and bought a pair of shoes in the Nike store. I was so lost in my own little world that I missed our scheduled meeting time of midday, and when I rushed back out to the arrivals hall I saw Alexander looking at me. He'd obviously seen me earlier. There were no hugs or kisses and our greeting was cold and sharp. For a few minutes we wandered around looking for somewhere to talk. The café was too busy. We considered a conference room on the next level but eventually decided to drive into the city. Alexander's new Porsche was in the car park, and on the way in I just let him talk while I stared out the window. We ended up down by the river, and we walked along there until we found a bench. It was a really hot day. Even though I was booked to fly out at four p.m., I was in no hurry to blurt out my news. I was happy to let the conversation flow naturally.

Alexander is incredibly articulate and he just took charge of the conversation, which covered all sorts of topics, including his career, my career and family. A couple of times I thought I might have an opportunity to break in, but it didn't happen. I'd never been under more pressure than I felt right then. Lighting the cauldron at the Sydney Games was a breeze compared with the anxiety that was pulsing through my veins as I sat listening to Alexander. I had to be so careful. I knew I was about to hurt him deeply, but I didn't want to say anything that would make it even worse.

The conversation moved on to my last race in Eugene. I'd started looking at my watch because I wanted to call Joel before he got on the plane to London. I knew he was really worried about me.

'I didn't see the race but I heard about the result,' Alexander said. 'I know you, Catherine, I know you. If you're up against the best you will fight tooth and nail.'

I told him what Garry had said about my personal baggage being a problem.

'It doesn't matter what's going on around you,' Alexander continued. 'You've always been able to lift against the best.' Then he paused and looked out over the water. 'You're just not into it. You've lost the passion. You don't have a passion.'

There it was. My opening.

'But I do have a passion,' I said cautiously. 'I'm seeing someone.'

Alexander turned and looked at me. 'Why would you do that to me? Why would you let me spill my heart and then tell me this?'

'I tried, but every time I saw an opportunity you just kept talking,' I said. 'It's Joel Edgerton.'

'Interesting,' was all Alexander said. He knew who Joel was. I'd told him when Jacqui and I had been hanging out with Joel the year before.

Alexander started nodding. 'It's funny: one high-profile person with another.' His mind was ticking over, and the moment stretched out. 'As long as you're happy,' he finally said. 'I just want you to be happy.'

I really wanted him to feel all right about it all. We talked for ages. Eventually I got up and told him I needed to go to the toilet. What I was really doing was going to call Joel. As Alexander walked away, back towards the car, I heard him scream out, 'Fuck!' I felt my stomach drop. He'd been so controlled on the bench.

Joel answered on the first ring. It was so reassuring to hear his voice. He always seemed to know how to make me feel better, and this was a time when I needed his understanding more than ever. We only talked briefly, as I was worried about what was happening with Alexander, but it was enough to keep me strong.

When I came back out, I walked back to the car park hoping Alexander would still be there. He was, and he seemed calm. On the way back to the airport he said, 'It's wonderful how we're talking now. But it's funny. We're talking about things now which, looking back over our marriage, we should have been talking about back then.'

That was so right, and it really hurt. What if we had communicated better? Would we still be together? I just felt so washed out and sad when it was time to say goodbye to Alexander. As we hugged I couldn't help but feel I was losing something very special.

I was exhausted when I got back to Oakland. The next day I still wasn't making any sense. I found myself laughing deliriously at stupid things, much to the amusement of Nicole and Andrew. I rang Mum in Australia, but she had her own personal crisis going on. She and Bruce had their own troubles, and one of her close friends was dying of cancer.

Everyone was excited about going to London. Rather than spurring me on, though, it actually gave me another reality check. I'd usually start training in November, and by January I'd be getting into reasonable shape for the domestic season. Then I'd go to America in April and really start hitting my straps so I'd be in peak shape when I got to London in June for the European circuit. Then it was all about maintaining that level. That's what I had to do to be a competitive athlete with a realistic chance of winning races. But I was so far behind my usual schedule it was almost laughable.

We set up base in Richmond. Nicole and I stayed in a nice private apartment with Fort, and Andrew and Kris shared another just around the corner. Garry had gone back to Australia. His theory, that dealing with the Alexander situation would result in improvement on the track, didn't translate into practice. Fort changed my whole training pro-gramme around in an attempt to get me going again. I was still running every day, but it was through parks and up hills, not on the track.

As my first scheduled race in Lille, France, got closer, my coach made one last attempt to get me on to the track. He convinced me to come down with the rest of the group as Kris and Lauren were having a track session. I went along with it, but when we got there I was overwhelmed by a wave of unhappiness. It was horrible, and I felt like crying. I was starting to get very frustrated with the whole situation. I knew Fort and the others were trying to help but I felt they were doing more harm than good by ignoring the obvious signs that I didn't want to run any more. It felt like nobody was listening to me. It was as if they just didn't want to believe that Cathy Freeman could retire.

My non-appearance in Lille obviously sounded the alarm bells back home and my manager, Chris Giannopoulos, decided to come to London to assess the situation. This gave me a chance to lay it all out on the table. I talked about Eugene, my phobia for the track and what had happened with Alexander. Chris had brought with him documents from my accountant to help me understand what my financial position would be, depending on whether or not I kept running to the Athens Olympics. For the first time I suddenly found myself worrying about finances. If this was the end I would obviously have to make significant changes in my life, and that was going to be hard. The hardest part was thinking I wouldn't be able to look after my family as much as I'd done in the past.

I sensed the same thing from Chris as I had from the others. Everyone was having a hard time realising that I might want to retire. This became even more obvious when Chris, Nicole and I had dinner with David Welch, the sports editor of the *Daily Telegraph*. I'd become good friends with him and another *Telegraph* journalist, Sue Mott, who helped me with my regular column.

'So are you going to Paris and then on to Athens next year?' David asked.

I'd been in regular contact with Sue, in particular, over the past few months so I was sure he had already worked out the answer.

'C'mon, David, what do you think?' I said. 'Listen to the tone of my voice, what do you think? I know you know me better than this.'

Chris was in the toilet during this conversation and Nicole nearly choked on her food as I spoke. My management wanted me to keep everything in-house, but the thing with me is that if you ask me a question I will always give a straight answer.

As soon as Chris came back, David excused himself, and I was sure he was going to ring Sue. Nicole, who floats between the roles of personal assistant, big sister, mother and friend, was ready to explode.

'That's it,' she blurted out. 'That is the final step.'

'What are you talking about?' Chris said.

'She's just gone and told them she's not running in Paris and that she's retiring.'

Then Chris started getting worked up, and between them they were going back and forth. It was like I wasn't there.

Hello, does anyone want to ask me about it?

I knew my retirement was going to be controversial, I knew people weren't going to like it, but, sadly, I also knew it was my only option.

Chris wanted me to take my time and think more about it as he didn't want me to have any regrets. He was keen to buy me more time, so on 20 June we released a statement saying I would no longer chase an individual 400m berth for the world championships in Paris but would instead focus only on the 4 x 400m relay. He also arranged for me to see a psychologist. I reluctantly went, but it did nothing for me. I had already explored every possible option in my head.

The following week I ran into Michael Johnson at Wimbledon. Although I hadn't got back to him since our meeting, I didn't have to explain myself or offer any excuses. He knew exactly what was happening. It was another chance meeting at the tennis that rattled me. The new International Olympic Committee president, Jacques Rogge, pleaded with me to keep running. 'We need you,' he said. He meant well, but that was the last thing I wanted to hear. I absolutely did not need that kind of pressure.

As the calendar clicked into July I could tell Fort was getting more and more on edge. Everyone was living in hope that I'd snap my fingers, return to the track and we could all live happily ever after.

'Keith Connor is wondering what's going on,' Fort said.

For some reason, I lost it. Connor, the Australian team coach, was the last person on my mind.

'Fort, you're my coach,' I said. 'You've seen the way I've been training, the way I sometimes haven't trained and the fact that I haven't been near a track in weeks. You know what's going on. How much more evidence do you need?'

I felt my relationship with my long-time coach had changed. We'd lost our chemistry. Although I was older and more experienced now, I still needed the same basic things as when we'd started together. We used to talk to each other so much, but we were spending a lot less time together, and that wasn't happening any more. I also felt an estrangement from athletes in general. For whatever reason, it seemed as though people wanted to keep their distance. In a way I was still craving some kind of acceptance. I had enjoyed sitting down with other athletes, coaches and administrators in the past, but I felt everybody looked at me differently now. Athletics had stopped being fun for me.

While these were factors in my mind, they weren't in themselves reasons to retire. I wasn't doing it for Joel either – an assumption I knew some people would make. 'She's got a new man in her life, it's fresh, it's exciting, so she doesn't want to run any more.' Yes, what Joel and I had was exciting. Although I'd given him every reason to walk away – and God knows I'd encouraged him to do that – our bond was stronger than I'd ever imagined it could be. We sparked off each other, we made each other laugh, we understood each other and we loved being together. But Joel knew that I wasn't retiring for him. The truth was that I didn't want to run any more because I'd lost one of the most precious things I had ever known – the heart to win.

A meeting with Keith Connor was arranged for 15 July at the Radisson Edwardian hotel at Heathrow airport. It was a really hot day and there were many better things I thought I could be doing than driving out to the airport with Fort to meet Keith.

'What am I going to say?' I asked my coach as we got out of the car.

Chris and Fort had talked about the meeting, and at this stage they thought all I'd have to do was tell Keith I was withdrawing from the relay in Paris.

We arrived first, and I had a look around a small jewellery shop inside the hotel until Keith arrived. He was a former triple jumper who'd won an Olympic bronze medal representing Great Britain. He was a big, tall black guy whose confidence at times bordered on arrogance, and his tough stance had put him offside with a lot of people. We parked ourselves on an antique couch and chairs in a corner of the hotel's large foyer. Businessmen were buzzing in and out.

'So, what training have you been doing?' Keith asked.

'Oh, not that much really,' I said, before Fort interjected and started to explain in more detail. Keith didn't like that and made it obvious that he wanted to talk to me alone, so Fort got up and left us. The conversation then skirted around other things for a few minutes before I dropped the bombshell.

'I'm not going to Paris,' I said.

Keith looked at me and nodded. 'And what about the future?' he asked.

'Well, essentially I'm retired,' I said.

It was almost a relief when the words came out. Keith seemed very enthusiastic about my decision. Then his mobile phone started ringing.

As he answered it, I looked around to see where Fort was. I thought he should know what I'd just done. I turned back and heard Keith say, 'Yes, I'm here with Cathy now. She's not running in Paris and she's retired.'

It was like being in a car crash when everything seems to happen in slow motion. I was watching him say the words but was helpless to stop him. The phone call was from a journalist in Australia. This was not the way it was supposed to happen.

Keith then thrust the phone at me. I managed to get a few words out. I was in shock. What about my family? What about my manager and my sponsors?

'I've got to ring Chris,' I said.

Back in Australia, Chris was out at dinner. He asked if he could call me back. 'Oh, not really, Chris. I've sort of retired,' I said.

There was silence at the end of the phone. When I told Chris what had happened he went nuts and demanded to talk to Keith. It seemed obvious that Keith had told the journalist to call him at a certain time because that was when he was meeting me. That was so wrong.

Fort seemed shocked when I called him over and told him what had happened. 'I thought we were just pulling out of Paris today,' he said.

For the next thirty minutes I was on the phone constantly to Chris, a couple of my friends and some other journalists as the news had obviously spread quickly. Keith tried to say that this was the best way, rather than doing a big press conference, and I was better off now that it was out. But that wasn't his decision to make: it should have been mine. This was not good business. I had an obligation to my sponsors, who had been so good to me. They deserved to be told before the news hit the front page of every newspaper in the country.

My head was still spinning when Keith left. Slowly, everything that had just happened started to sink in. I was becoming more and more furious with Keith. I knew my decision was right, but after thirteen years at the top level I deserved to go out when and how I chose. Before we left the hotel I bought a pair of earrings I'd spotted in the jewellery shop earlier. They would be a memento of this bizarre day. The day I retired.

In the car I was silent for a few minutes as I tried to take stock of the events of the past hour. Then it hit me.

'What the hell am I going to do now?'

CHAPTER 35
MAKING A DIFFERENCE

I could still be running right now. Who knows, one day I may run again. I still think about it. Throughout my life I've always been so in tune with my body. Now, for the first time, I feel like my body and my mind are two separate things. I look down at my legs and think I'm wasting something really good. I still get demons in my head about my sister, Anne-Marie.

Maybe if Athens had been in 2000 and the Sydney Olympics in 2004, I'd still be running.

The overriding feeling I have is that I've lived out my childhood dream. It was so amazing to achieve something that was seventeen years in the making. To find another dream is very hard. Some of the people I respect the most believe I could come back in the 400m hurdles or the 800m and do it all again. I just don't know. At the moment it feels as though there are so many more questions than answers.

What's it like being Cathy Freeman? That's a question I get asked over and over. There is no simple answer.

Overwhelming is one way to describe it. For example, I'll be in the supermarket and someone will call out my name, which is such a personal thing. I will look over, smile and say hi, and they will tell me that's all they wanted – a smile from Cathy Freeman. Wow! I get letters from people all around the world, and what they write just takes my breath away. I can't believe they feel this way about me, that I've touched them in such a special way. I often talk about another Cathy Freeman, who sits above it all and looks down on me conducting my life and just can't stop laughing.

Sometimes it feels like it's one big joke because what happens in my world is the total opposite to the sort of person I am. In fact, I'm constantly running away from being Cathy Freeman. Being on the TV news, in the newspapers or at fancy dinners – it's just not the real me. I understand it's part of what I have become, but inside I'm still very much the shy black girl from Mackay who can run fast.

I crave normality. I often want to shake people and tell them that they don't have to tread warily around me because I'm Cathy Freeman. I'm so much like you. I love my family – especially my three nieces and six nephews – and my cats. I love to laugh and sit around and have a few glasses of red wine with my friends. I have the same dreams as many of you reading this.

Maybe the best way to describe myself is as a cross between a little child and a wild desert cat. I love the innocence of children, and there's definitely a side of my personality that is playful, vague and giggly – 'on Planet C', some of my friends say – just like a child. But those who know me well often remark on how quickly that can change. I'll be my normal fluffy self until someone says something I don't like, then I get this look in my eyes that my friends tell me actually frightens them. That's the killer instinct of the wild desert cat coming out: they're always on guard, and they'll do anything to survive. Yet a wild cat will also play and roll around just like a domestic cat. That's me. Sometimes I long still to be a child, and not have to deal with the responsibilities of adult life.

I know I was born with a gift, an inner strength or passion to be the best. As a child I didn't think about why I did things; I didn't analyse it. But as I've got older I've started to understand what has been my driving force my whole life. The key to my whole being was the freedom I felt when I ran. That feeling used to beat anything else in the world. I experienced it the very first time I raced, way back in primary school, and when it was no longer there I knew it was the end.

I believe my mother, Cecelia, had a lot to do with me being able to harness my gift. She's a very tough woman. A single parent and a black woman of her generation had to be that way to survive. She's always had a great instinct, and I think she passed it on to me. Anne-Marie made me realise I had to make the most of the gift I'd been given. I know she's been with me all the way, the wind beneath my wings, guiding me through all the ups and downs.

People often ask me if the enormity of the Sydney Games has sunk in. This might sound strange, but the answer is that it hasn't, and I'm not sure if it ever will. Sydney was so big that it's almost traumatic to go back and think about what I dealt with. It's scary to think about all the emotions and energy my body absorbed. I now find myself pushing it away. Every day Sydney is with me, though. I'll meet someone on a plane, or at a function, and they'll tell me exactly what they were doing the night I won gold. It spins me out that it's a memory they will carry with them for the rest of their life.

I don't think I'll ever be able to properly describe what occurred on 25 September 2000. I'm intrigued by the fact that I didn't hear the crowd – didn't hear anything – in the lead-up to the race. One neurologist said I had simply trained myself to block out peripheral things so well that it had become an automatic reaction. I'd adjusted my awareness settings inside my mind to focus on only one thing – running the race.

And the future? Well, it is a bit scary. It's like I'm stepping away from a safe environment into the wilderness. Suddenly the support networks that have been a part of my life as an athlete are gone. There's a distinct sense of loss. I felt so empowered when I was training and racing. It is petrifying not to feel strong and indestructible any more. Out of everything I've been through, this is the most frightening.

In time I know I will find that sense of power again and I'm going to be dangerous. I'm not sure exactly what I'll be doing or where I will be. I'm considering living overseas for a few years just to take stock of my life and get away from being the public Cathy Freeman. I hope I eventually have the opportunity to challenge people, to affect their attitudes. I'm like an unofficial ambassador for Australia, and for the indigenous people of Australia.

I want to make a difference. That's why I have told my story. When people allow me into their hearts and minds, it is sacred and makes me feel special. If I can inspire people, if my journey helps a child, teenager or adult to find the courage to follow their dreams, then I'll know it has all been worth it.

INDEX